The Life and Times of Chinua Achebe

The Life and Times of Chinua Achebe introduces readers to the life, literary works, and times of arguably the most widely read African novelist of recent times, an icon, both in continental Africa and abroad.

The book weaves together the story of Chinua Achebe, a young Igboman whose novel *Things Fall Apart* opened the eyes of the world to a more realistic image of Africa that was warped by generations of European travelers, colonists, and writers. While continuing to write further influential novels and essays, Achebe also taught other African writers to use their skills to help their national leaders to fight for their freedoms in the postcolonial era, as internal warfare compounded the damage caused by European powers during the colonial era. In this book Kalu Ogbaa, an esteemed expert on Achebe and his works, draws on extensive research and personal interviews with the great man and his colleagues and friends, to tell the story of Achebe and his work.

This intimate and powerful new biography will be essential reading for students and scholars of Chinua Achebe, and to anyone with an interest in the literature and postcolonial politics of Africa.

Kalu Ogbaa is Professor of English and Faculty Scholar Award winner at Southern Connecticut State University, New Haven, where he teaches English, Africana Literary and Cultural Studies, as well as Commonwealth Literatures. He obtained his B.A. (Hons) degree in English from The University of Nigeria, Nsukka, MA in Black Studies from The Ohio State University, and PhD in English from The University of Texas at Austin.

Global Africa

Series Editors: Toyin Falola and Roy Doron

For more information about this series, please visit: https://www.routledge.com/
Global-Africa/book-series/GLOBAFR

The Life and Times of Chinua Achebe

Kalu Ogbaa

Routledge
Taylor & Francis Group

LONDON AND NEW YORK

First published 2022
by Routledge
2 Park Square, Milton Park, Abingdon, Oxon OX14 4RN

and by Routledge
605 Third Avenue, New York, NY 10158

Routledge is an imprint of the Taylor & Francis Group, an informa business

British Library Cataloguing-in-Publication Data
A catalogue record for this book is available from the British Library

Library of Congress Cataloging-in-Publication Data
Names: Ogbaa, Kalu, author.
Title: The life and times of Chinua Achebe / Kalu Ogbaa.
Description: Milton Park, Abingdon, Oxon ; New York, NY : Routledge,
    2021. | Series: Global Africa | Includes bibliographical references and
    index.
Subjects: LCSH: Achebe, Chinua. | Achebe, Chinua—Political and
    social views. | Authors, Nigerian—20th century—Biography.
Classification: LCC PR9387.9.A3 Z8464 2021 (print) | LCC
    PR9387.9.A3 (ebook) | DDC 823/.914 [B]—dc23
LC record available at https://lccn.loc.gov/2021009444
LC ebook record available at https://lccn.loc.gov/2021009445

ISBN: 978-1-032-02602-2 (hbk)
ISBN: 978-1-032-02380-9 (pbk)
ISBN: 978-1-003-18413-3 (ebk)

DOI: 10.4324/9781003184133

Typeset in Goudy
by Apex CoVantage, LLC

To the memory of my sister Mgbore Ogbaa
and
my brother Ikpo Ogbaa
For loving and taking care of me, their baby brother

Contents

Acknowledgments

The publication of this biography marks the culmination of over four decades of my concentrated study of Professor Chinua Achebe's literary works and sociopolitical and cultural activities that have had a lot of impact on many people all over the world, especially our Igbo people and their existential situation in our country Nigeria. The thought of writing the book crossed my mind in March 2013 during his funeral service in Providence, Rhode Island. As I heard people pouring out praises for the man and his works, I began to think of how to requite the deep love and kindness this world-renowned master storyteller bestowed on me, for he treated me as his *adoptive* son, literary disciple, and Igbo cultural inheritor all those years. While still wondering if I had the ability and capacity to tell his story – my story and those of others who knew him – as well as he deserved, I received a letter from his second son, Dr. Chidi Achebe, inviting me to write a biography of his father, which would update the information contained in two biographies of him published more than a decade earlier. I felt honored and inspired and immediately accepted to do it. Hence, I offer my profound gratitude first to Chidi and his mother, Professor Christie Achebe, for trusting my ability and competency to write the biography, and for all the useful assistance they gave me during my research. However, there are other people who contributed to the development and completion of the biography whose contributions I must acknowledge. Among those to whom I owe a debt of gratitude is Professor Bernth Lindfors. I wish to express my heartfelt thanks to him for making very important comments on the first draft of the manuscript and subsequently copyediting the final draft. Besides, I sincerely thank him for the overall support and guidance he has been giving me since my graduate years at the University of Texas at Austin, which deepened my research activities in Achebe studies. I also offer my gratitude to my fellow Igbo scholar, Professor Onwubiko Agozino of Virginia Tech University, for reading the manuscript and making beneficial comments on the cultural issues contained in it.

Furthermore, I am also indebted to some of my faculty colleagues and administrators at Southern Connecticut State University for their assistance and support: to Tony Rosso, Steve Larocco, Paul Petrie, Tim Parrish, Scott Ellis, Bob McEachern, Andrew Smith, Chuck Baraw, and Joel Dodson of our English Department, for reading and suggesting some improvement on some portions of the manuscript while I was working on it; to Dean Bruce Kalk, for granting me reassigned time for research; to Provost Bob Prezant and the University Research Committee, for granting me Senior-Level Faculty Fellowship that reduced my teaching load, thereby enabling me to finish the book project on time; and, to the Sabbatical Leave Committee and SCSU-AAUP Grants Committee, for awarding me sabbatical leave and research grants which allowed me some time and funds to work with. I hope that the book justifies the good judgment they made in giving me the awards.

I also would like to thank the family of the late Ezenwa-Ohaeto and his publishers as well as Phanuel Akubueze Egejuru and her publishers for their biographies on Achebe, out of which I excerpted some beneficial information in my work on the Eagle on Iroko.

Finally, I want to express my deepest gratitude and ever-abiding love to my family: my lovely wife Glory and our four awesome children Adanne, Ekeoma, Kalu, and Uchenna, for their patience and prayers while I worked on this book. May God continue to bless and protect them!

Illustrations

Introduction

Chinua Achebe, born on November 16, 1930 in Nigeria, was such a renowned author of numerous works of fiction, poetry, criticism, and political treatises that by the time he died in 2013 his life story had been retold numerous times in continental Africa and virtually all over the world where African literature, especially the modern African novel, is taught and studied. A young son of an evangelist father from a small Igbo village of Ikenga Ogidi in the then-Eastern Nigeria goes to a missionary school and church where he is introduced to an alien religion, education, culture, and civilization that take him beyond the village to Umuahia Town, also in the then-Eastern Nigeria, where he receives a secondary school education. Thereafter, he is admitted to study at the University College Ibadan in Western Nigeria, which was founded and run by white professors for the British Government in London. After graduation, he takes a teaching job at Merchants of Light Secondary School, Oba, as an English teacher before proceeding to Lagos, Nigeria's first capital city, where he is offered a job in the Talks Department by a white director of the Nigerian Broadcasting Service (NBS). While working there, he publishes his first novel, *Things Fall Apart* in 1958, at the young age of 28. On the surface, the author's life story appears simple; however, it is more complex than that because of the effects of the clash of cultures between Nigeria, which was then just 16 years old officially as a colony, and its colonial master Britain, when Achebe was born in 1930. Several important details of incidents and influences in the life of the young man who would grow up to become such an influential African writer are unknown to many of his international readers and his fellow citizens as well.

The aim of this book is to provide a description of Chinua Achebe's life and times. In order to do so, the book weaves together the straightforward story of Achebe as the young Igbo man who, by the virtue of publishing his novel *Things Fall Apart*, became famous and gave a more complicated account of the attitudes and ethos prevalent in colonial and postcolonial Nigeria and other West African countries. Moreover, what he wrote in that first novel and those he published after it made many scholars in the field to acknowledge him as the founder and promoter of the "modern African novel." For his fiction became an analytical tale of a concatenation of the sociocultural, religious, and political lives of Africans – indeed the Igbo and other Nigerian peoples – under British colonial rule and its aftermath during the postcolonial era. The end result is a book that demonstrates how deeply and uniquely involved Achebe was in the society he inhabited, and thus how important knowledge of his life and times is to the understanding of his fiction, poetry, and critical theory of African life and civilization at a time when the white world racially saw Africa as "the heart of darkness."

The documentary evidence of Achebe's life is enigmatic or controversial at best to those who never studied or understood him as a person or writer, especially in his native postwar Nigerian society where people's opinions on important issues are based not on their merits or basic facts but on ethnic sentiments. For instance, it was alarming to me personally as an Igbo scholar and to some other literary critics to find that something as basic and ordinary as an author choosing a befitting title like *There Was a Country: A Personal History of Biafra* for his final published book could spark so much venomous national uproar in 2012, to the extent that many feared Nigeria was gravitating toward another civil war. Nevertheless, as a lifelong student of his works, I could understand the situation clearer because only a few of those who commented on both sides of the debate about the contents of the book understood what Achebe's life and work had been before the publication of the so-called controversial book. Indeed, for those who have followed his literary works from the moment he started writing in his college journals and magazines at Ibadan, up to his maturity as the author of great novels and poetry after college, there was no doubt whatsoever that Achebe always courageously spoke truth to power. For in spite of the intimidating influence of his white college professors at Ibadan, and the overwhelming colonial powers that the British exerted over his native Nigeria, Achebe unflinchingly defied the odds as he attempted to carry out with commitment his goal of describing Africa in a more realistic way in his writings during the colonial and postcolonial periods in African literature.

Achebe's determination to write the way he did was like sowing a seed in his mind while he was still in college, which germinated and blossomed as a flower after his college years. Time and again, Achebe would grant professors, students, researchers, and journalists interviews in which he protested some erroneous European claim that because most African countries were illiterate before the coming of whites to the continent, they lacked culture and civilization. Also, some Europeans claimed that it was a misnomer to characterize African unwritten tradition or oral performance as a viable literature worthy of international attention and recognition. Such an erroneous position on traditional African literary culture was expressed in high places as a part of the white man's overall sociopolitical grand plan to devalue anything African and nonwhite the world over as justification and legitimacy for unethical and inhumane issues such as slavery, colonialism, and imperialism. This is the picture painted in "the novels of Africa" by such colonial writers as Joseph Conrad and Joyce Cary, whose novels were taught as compulsory texts to African students in British University Colleges in Africa – namely, Ibadan in Nigeria, Legon in Ghana, Fourah Bay in Sierra Leone, and Makerere in Uganda. The overall aim of the British was to create such students as people in "dark skins with white minds."

Obviously, Achebe and his colleagues knew that what they were compelled to read about Africa was neither true nor realistic of their native counties in which they lived, and that disturbed them greatly. And they also knew that slavery and colonialism were a rape of their continent. So, it had to be challenged, if not stopped, by well-informed African writers, critics, and teachers, who had to develop and teach their emerging written literatures from the existing oral tradition comprised of folktales, proverbs, rituals, and folk dances, so as to set the records straight, as it were. Fortunately, the way that Achebe deftly appropriated these indigenous African verbal elements in his narrative technique, which he interwove with classical European elements of fiction especially in his first novel, made the modern African novel a hybrid. In other words, Achebe appropriated the classical European elements as a foundation upon which he built African elements of fiction thereby creating unique qualities of Africanness in his novels. That way, the novels could tell more realistically the stories of Africa and its peoples. The end result was that Achebe's innovative effort made him a trail-blazer in the field of creative writing of modern African novels, most notably in his two rural novels, *Things Fall Apart* and *Arrow of God*. Achebe thus became known, and was revered, as the "Founder of Modern African Novel." And since then other African writers have been using the novels he wrote as templates for doing their own writings.

Much of what Achebe published from 1951 to 1966 – that is, before the Nigeria-Biafra War (1967–1970) – and from 1970 to 2012 – that is, after the war – are highly significant from a historical perspective in that all his novels serve as analytical reflections of the monumental historical and sociopolitical events that took place particularly in Nigeria and generally in other African countries during his times. That is why some literary critics feel comfortable dubbing the period as "The Age of Chinua Achebe" in African literature. While the four novels he published before the war can be seen as the most influential (for the reasons given above), the shorter pieces of literature – short stories, essays, and poems – he wrote during the war, and the longer pieces he wrote after the war – *The Trouble with Nigeria* (1983), *Anthills of the Savannah* (1987), and *There Was a Country: A Personal History of Biafra* (2012) – all serve as a window through which readers can get a glimpse of the mind of Chinua Achebe the novelist as a teacher, savvy political analyst, and highly esteemed literary guru. While playing these roles actively all through his life, Achebe inspires African readers, especially his fellow writers, to see themselves as proverbial travelers "who must first learn where the rain began to beat them before they can know their destination."

These early novels are tragedies. In *Things Fall Apart* he shows why Okonkwo, the strongman of Umuofia, fails to prevent the British colonial forces from finding a foothold in his clan, despite his strong fighting prowess; in *Arrow of God* he reveals why Ezeulu, the intellectual High Priest of Ulu, fails to stop the spread of British religious, educational, and administrative culture in Umuaro, despite his religious and political vision and strategies; in *No Longer at Ease* he explains why Obi Okonkwo, the London University graduate, fails to avoid taking bribes as a civil servant in Lagos, despite his initial enthusiasm to fight the endemic corruption in Nigerian civil service upon his return from London; and, in *A Man of the People* he exposes why Chief the Honorable M. A. Nanga and his fellow parliamentarians "started the country off down the slopes of inflation" (2), despite their firm promise to run their new independent country with an unquestionable spirit of patriotism.

One remarkable aspect of this period we can conveniently refer to as The Age of Achebe in African literature may be extended to cover the early part of the colonial period: 1900–1952. This was essentially a gestation period in Nigerian literature written in English and the coming together in print of ethnic vernacular oral literatures, for although the various peoples of Nigeria had been performing their literatures orally centuries before the advent of whites in the country, they did not have a printed national literature. As to be expected, the mission schools introduced literary works that embodied religious themes and were didactic in tone. Among the more popularly recommended books were John Bunyan's *The Pilgrim's Progress* and John Milton's *Paradise Lost* and *Paradise Regained*. However, the creative writings of Nigerians at this period can be described as "apprentice literature" in that their writers, especially the pioneer university students (1948–1952), were eager to imitate writers of foreign texts that their teachers brought from Europe and America. So they wrote songs like Chukude Osadebay's poem, "Young Africa's Thanks," in praise of British colonialism and missionary work in Nigeria:

> Thank you,
> Sons and daughters of Britannia.
> You gave me hospitals,
> You gave me schools,
> Easy communications too,
> Your western civilization.

While such sentiments expressed by a grateful colonial student in the poem on behalf of his nation may be gratifying to the British colonizers, the downside of the new dispensation is that the more the Nigerians embraced the British governmental, religious, and literary culture, the more they alienated themselves from their own indigenous ways of life.

As time went on, however, their alienation and general disenchantment with the white men's culture caused the Western-educated Nigerians to write "protest literature" lamenting the evil effects of colonialism and some aspects of Christianity on their people and themselves. To exemplify the point, we again cite another poem by Osadebay, "Young Africa's Lament":

> I am half starved;
> I asked for bread they gave me stone.
> I am thirsty;
> I asked for water they gave me slush.
> They tell the horse to wait a while,

Because green grasses would soon grow
And dry Sahara would yield great streams.

The biblical allusion contained in the poem is to Jesus Christ's admonitory charge to all God-fearing people to feed and give drinks to those who are hungry and thirsty. The failure of the whites to treat Nigerians (whom they were attempting to Christianize) with neighborly love characterizes the whites as hypocrites, which marks the beginning of the Africans' disillusionment with the white man's religious culture and general morality. Also, the whites may have been ironic in their response to the Africans' needs, especially in their reference to the arid Sahara Desert, yet during the second half of the colonial period – The Age of Chinua Achebe – "the green grasses" of creative writing began to sprout out of the "dry Sahara" of African countries, which gave birth to the development of more mature and world-class written literatures from the African continent.

What Achebe did as founder of the modern African novel can be likened to what Ralph Waldo Emerson did during the Transcendental Movement in American Literature when, in his seminal essay "The American Scholar," he asserted that "the sun that rises in Europe also rises here in America," which was a call for the development of an independent American national literature 100 years after their attainment of political independence from Great Britain. As a student of literature, history, and comparative literature in college, Achebe encountered the colonial history of Nigeria and other African countries, which began with the Partition of Africa by European countries meeting in Berlin, Germany, in December 1885. That gave the British the power and authority over the then West African territories named Northern and Southern Protectorates, which were later amalgamated as one British colonial country on January 1, 1914. Before then, British missionaries had come to the area around the 1840s to establish churches and mission schools in which Christianity was taught and used as a means of condemning anything African, including their traditional regions, culture, and civilization. Thus, the coming of the whites also attempted to deemphasize the use of oral traditions of the people as a viable literary practice.

More than the texts that Achebe studied, however, the actions of the British government in Nigeria shaped his world and times. The metaphoric war of independence, which began with the amalgamation of the two disparate British protectorates into one giant colonial country, was lost by the indigenous peoples from both protectorates. So one can say that the trouble with Nigeria began as the aftermath of the action that the British colonial government took when it allowed the precolonial Northern Protectorate to exist as one colonial region – Northern Nigeria – but divided the Southern Protectorate into two regions – Eastern Nigeria and Western Nigeria. In addition, they carved Lagos out of Western Nigeria, and proclaimed it a separate and independent territory, to serve as the first capital of Nigeria. Later on, the balkanization of the erstwhile Southern Protectorate gave unfair political advantages to Northern Nigerians in the sense that each time the federal government asked for a referendum on issues affecting the federation, the North always used its numerical strength as a weapon to cast overwhelming votes against the East or West. The situation got even worse when a third region – Midwest Nigeria – was created out of the Southern Region.

In spite of what the British did in favor of the North, Southern politicians were determined to change the overall Nigerian political situation through constitutional means. Hence, in August 1944, they formed the first political organization called the National Council of Nigeria and the Cameroons (NCNC), which, as a trailblazer, played a very important role in the political history of the country in that it inspired the formation of other nationalistic parties that led to the preparation of the Richard Constitution for the nation. Although this did not go into operation until 1947, it led to the writing of other constitutions and the formation of other political parties. Both political actions by the people eventuated in the British Government granting self-rule and political independence to Nigeria in 1957 and 1960, respectively. Chinua Achebe, who was then working in Lagos, witnessed all the political wrangling and bloody events, especially the bloody Fulani uprising in the Plateau region in the North and the bloody tussle between the Akintola and the Awolowo factions of the Action Group Party in the West. Those events took place between 1963, when Nigeria became a sovereign republic, and January 15, 1966, when the first of Nigeria's bloody coups took place. Those events were so uncontrollable through peaceful political means that Achebe suggested a solution: "[But] the Army obliged us by staging a coup at that point and locking up every member of the Government" as Achebe had predicted in *A Man of the People* (pp 147–48), which he wrote in 1964 but which was published officially in January 1966, the very month the first bloody coup in Nigeria took place. Unfortunately, heavily armed Northern Nigerian soldiers mistook the coincidence of the two events as a good reason to go after Achebe in his Lagos office, convinced that either he knew in advance of the plotting of the coup or that he actually took part in plotting it. That erroneous suspicion of Achebe the Igbo novelist, coupled with the fact that the leader of the coup plotters, Major Chukwuma Kaduna Nzogwu, was Igbo, influenced them to conclude that the coup was an Igbo affair – a conclusion that led to Northerners immediately engaging in acts of indiscriminate massacres of the Igbo people living then in Northern Nigeria.

The overall aftermath of the coup was that Northern Nigerian soldiers, assisted by their religious leaders and civilians, engaged in what they called reprisal countercoups on May 29, July 29, and September 29, 1966 against Eastern Nigerians (especially the Igbo) living in Northern Nigeria, which forced them to flee the North in droves to take refuge in their native Eastern Nigeria. Thereafter, because of the failure of the federal military government to protect them from the bloody Northern riots and violence, the returnee Easterners ironically became refugees in their own country. And among the refugees from other parts of Nigeria were Chinua Achebe and his family members. He lived through the war that ensued, and experienced the brutalities of three nations – Nigeria, Great Britain, and the USSR – as other Biafrans did. While serving as a Biafran Ambassador Extraordinaire, Achebe not only traveled around the world using his celebrity status to plead the cause of Biafra but also recorded and published some of the war incidents in shorter literary pieces, such as poetry, short stories, and essays, which included the poems "Dirge for Okigbo" and "Refugee Mother and Child," as well as other poems which appear in *Beware, Soul Brother* (1971); he also published short stories in *Girls at War and Other Stories* (1971).

After the Nigeria-Biafra War, Achebe's once revered Igbo ethnic group became marginalized collectively, both politically and economically. Hence, some individuals developed a degree of defeatist mentality that adversely affected their psyche. Ironically, however, the absence of the Igbo prewar mantle of leadership in postwar Nigeria (which other ethnic groups could not easily replace) adversely affected the overall political and economic wellbeing of the entire nation. Resultantly, and out of immediate necessity, the various Nigerian military regimes made frantic effort to recruit Igbo technocrats locally and from abroad to help them navigate the nation's metaphoric sinking ship out of the dangerous political and economic tsunami as it were. For example, Dr. Ngozi Okonjo-Iwuala, an Igbo woman who had worked at the International Monetary Fund (IMF) at its headquarters in New York, was recruited to serve as the Economic/Finance Minister in Abuja, Nigeria. Under her leadership, the Nigerian economy, which had been under water for a while, was saved from drowning. Instead, she brought it to a level where the outside world could do financial and economic business with the country once again. On the literary front, Chinua Achebe wrote a political analysis in his book, *The Trouble with Nigeria* (1983), in which he pointed out what caused Nigeria's failure as a divided country and suggested measures that could enable the nation to heal from its self-inflicted wounds. He followed the didactic theme of Nigeria's national introspection in his postwar and last novel, *Anthills of the Savannah* (1987).

In the end, for six decades (1952–2013) Chinua Achebe fought assiduously to create and maintain a form of literary independence for Africa through fiction, which he buttressed with the publications of poetry, literary criticism, and political treatises. During his notable career, Achebe witnessed major shifts in political power, beginning from the second phase of the colonial period, through the postcolonial period, to the war, and postwar periods in Nigeria. The phases of his writings mirror the major incidents in Nigerian sociopolitical history as follows:

> Phase I, 1952–1966: Achebe published essays, stories, and the groundbreaking novels, *Things Fall Apart, No Longer at Ease, Arrow of God,* and *A Man of the People,* which launched him into the limelight as a renowned author. Unfortunately, however, this first phase of his literary career came to an abrupt end because of the January 15, 1966 coup that served as a precursor to the civil war in 1967.
>
> Phase II, 1967–1970: Because of his wartime engagements, Achebe could only write shorter literary pieces, such as poems, essays, short stories, children's stories, and political speeches.
>
> Phase III, 1971–1999: This is a postwar period in which Achebe took up teaching positions in Nigerian and American universities that gave him time to do some brooding and introspection on the events of the war, while

publishing longer pieces on the war, as well as literary criticisms on African literature, including the novel, *Anthills of the Savannah* (1987).

Phase IV, 2000–2013: In spite of his physical disability, Chinua Achebe continued to teach and do some speeches and writing in two American universities, and he occasionally visited Nigeria to make inspirational speeches, especially to his ethnic Igbo people who seemed to have lost their bearing as a result of their loss of the war. Above all, he published his final work, *There Was a Country: A Personal History of Biafra*, in which he expressed his personal views on the war.

Finally, it was Chinua Achebe's great fortune to have lived when he did, and to have served humanity with character, courage, and great vision. As an Igboman who brought the Igbo ethos of hard work, rare personal talent, and sustained commitment to the realm of literary art, Achebe produced a corpus that millions of people all over the world have been fortunate and privileged to read. That is why it is imperative for readers of this book to understand the life lived by Achebe and the world he inhabited, which enabled him to make such great contributions to the development and celebration of African literature and culture during a period in African literary history that is dubbed as "The Age of Chinua Achebe" in memory of the founder of the modern African novel.

Timeline: Key Dates in the Life and Times of Chinua Achebe

1930   Born, November 16 in Ogidi Town, near Onitsha in Eastern
            Nigeria; fifth child of Isaiah Okafo Achebe, a catechist for the
            Church Missionary Society (CMS), and Janet N. Iloegbunam
            Achebe.

1936–1942   Attends Ogidi CMS Central School.

1943   Attends CMS Central School, Nekede, near Owerri Town.

1944–1948   Attends Government College, Umuahia.

1948–1953   Attends University College, Ibadan; earns B.A. (London) 1953.

1953–1954   Teaches for eight months at Merchant of Light School, Oba.

1954   Talks Producer, Nigerian Broadcasting Corporation (NBC), Lagos.

1955   Begins writing his first novel *Things Fall Apart*.

1956   Attends BBC Staff Training School, London.

1957   Head of Talks Department, NBC; completes writing *Things Fall
            Apart*.

1958   Controller, NBC, Eastern Region; *Things Fall Apart* is published.

1959   Wins Margaret Wrong Memorial Prize for African Literature.

1960   Nigeria attains political independence; Achebe wins Nigerian
            National Trophy; his second novel *No Longer at Ease* is published;
            travels in East and Central Africa on a Rockefeller Fellowship,
            1960–1961.

1961   Marries Christie Chinweifenu Okoli; Director of External
            Broadcasting, NBC; wins Nigerian National Trophy for Literature.

1962   Birth of daughter Chinelo; assumes Editorship of Heinemann
            African Writers Series; wins Langston Hughes Medallion.

1963   Travels in the United States, Brazil, and Britain on a UNESCO
            Fellowship.

1964   Birth of son Ikechukwu; third novel *Arrow of God* is published.

1965   Wins Jock Campbell/New Statesman Award.

1966   Fourth novel *A Man of the People* and a children's book *Chike
            and the River* are published; Nigeria experiences first military
            coup on January 15, and a countercoup on July 29; moves with
            family to Eastern Nigeria; *Arrow of God* wins Jock Campbell-New
            Statesman Award for Literature.

1967   Birth of son Chidi; Eastern Nigeria secedes as the Republic of
            Biafra from Nigeria, and a civil war – the Nigeria-Biafra War
            begins; appointed Senior Research Fellow, the University of
            Nigeria, Nsukka (1967–1972); establishes Citadel Press in Enugu
            with Christopher Okigbo; travels as Ambassador Extraordinaire to
            parts of Africa, Europe, and the United States on behalf of Biafra.
1969   Chairman of the National Guidance Council of Biafra.
1970   Birth of daughter Nwando Chioma; Biafra surrenders
            unconditionally to Nigeria on January 15.
1971   *Beware, Soul Brother* is published; *Okike: An African Journal of New
            Writing* is founded; edits *Nsukkascope*, a campus magazine; edits
            (with others) *The Insider: Stories of War and Peace from Nigeria*.
1972   *Girls at War and Other Stories* and *How the Leopard Got His
            Claws* (coauthored with John Iroaganachi) published; Founding
            Editor/Publisher of *Okike: An African Journal of New Writing*;
            joint-winner of first [British] Commonwealth Poetry Prize;
            accepts position as Visiting Professor of English at University of
            Massachusetts at Amherst, 1972–1975; resigns editorship (1962–
            1972 (first 100 titles)) of Heinemann African Writers Series;
            awarded honorary doctorate (D.Litt.) by Dartmouth College.
1972–75   Appointed Visiting Professor of English at University of
            Massachusetts, Amherst.
1974   Awarded honorary doctorate by Southampton University,
            England.
1975   *Morning Yet on Creation Day* is published; accepts appointment
            as University Professor of English at University of Connecticut,
            1975–1976; named honorary Fellow of Modern Language
            Association of America and Neil Gunn Fellow of the Scottish
            Arts Council; awarded honorary doctorate (D.Univ.) by Stirling
            University, Scotland; Lotus Award for Afro-Asian Writers.
1976   Resumes position at the University of Nigeria, Nsukka, as
            Professor of Literature (1976–1981); awarded honorary doctorate
            (LL.D.) by Prince Edward University, Canada.
1977   *The Drum: A Children's Story* is published.
1978   Edits (with Dubem Okafor) *Don't Let Him Die: An Anthology of
            Memorial Poems of Christopher Okigbo* (1932–1967).
1979   Accepts first Nigerian National Merit Award and appointment as
            Officer of the Federal Republic (OFR), another national honor;
            The Flute: A Children's Story is published; awarded honorary
            doctorates (D.H.L.) by University of Massachusetts at Amherst,
            and (D.Litt.) by University of Ife, Nigeria, respectively.
1981   Forms Association of Nigerian Authors and is elected its first
            President; takes early retirement from the University of Nigeria,
            Nsukka; made Fellow of the Royal Society of Literature (London);
            awarded honorary doctorates (D.Litt.) by University of Kent,

	England, and (D.Litt.) by the University of Nigeria, Nsukka, respectively.
1982	Edits (with Obiora Udechukwu) *Aka Weta: Egwu aguluagu Egwu edeluede*, a collection of poems in Igbo; Member, American Academy of Arts and Letters.
1983	*The Trouble with Nigeria, The Drum*, and *The Flute* are published; Appointed Deputy National Chairman of Peoples Redemption Party; Member Royal Society of Literature; Honorary Fellow, American Academy of Arts and Letters.
1984	Visiting Professor of English at University of Guelph, Ontario, Canada, and Regents Professor of English at University of California at Los Angeles; awarded honorary doctorates (D.Litt.) by University of Guelph and (D.Litt.) by Mount Allison University, Canada, respectively; founds *Uwa Ndi Igbo*, a bilingual journal of Igbo life and culture; receives Commonwealth Foundation Award.
1985	Awarded honorary doctorate (D.Litt.) by Franklin Pierce College, New Hampshire, USA; appointed Professor Emeritus at the University of Nigeria, Nsukka; edits (with C. L. Innes) *African Short Stories*, and *Contemporary African Short Stories*.
1986	Steps down as President of Association of Nigerian Authors; appointed Pro-Chancellor and Chair of the Council of Anambra State University of Technology at Awka, Nigeria; elected President-General of Ogidi Town Union.
1987	Fifth novel *Anthills of the Savannah* is published and shortlisted for Booker Prize Award; Fulbright Professor of African Studies at University of Massachusetts, Amherst, 1987–1988.
1988	*Hopes and Impediments* and *The University and the Leadership Factor in Nigerian Politics* are published; *The African Trilogy (Things Fall Apart, No Longer at Ease, and Arrow of God)* published in one volume by Picador in London; awarded honorary doctorate (D.Litt.) by Lagos State University, Nigeria.
1989	Visiting Distinguished Professor of English, City College of the City University of New York; May 25 proclaimed Chinua Achebe Day by the Borough of Manhattan; founds *African Commentary*, a magazine for people of African descent; elected first President of Nigerian chapter of PEN (poets, essayists and novelists); reelected President-General of Ogidi Town Union; appointed by Indian Government to an International Jury to award the annual Indira Gandhi Prize for Peace, Disarmament and Development (1989–1992); awarded honorary doctorates (D.H.L.) by Westfield College, Massachusetts, (D.Litt.) by Open University, Great Britain, and (D.Litt.) by University of Ibadan, Nigeria, respectively.
1990	Montgomery Fellow and Visiting Professor of English at Dartmouth College; symposium held at the University of

Nigeria, Nsukka, honoring him on his 60th birthday; receives citation from the USSR Academy of Sciences; receives Triple Eminence Award from the Association of Nigerian Authors; partially paralyzed in an automobile accident and convalesces in England; awarded honorary doctorate (LL.D.) by Georgetown University, USA; accepts Charles P. Stevenson, Jr., Chair of Literature at Bard College, New York, 1990–1998; major street in university town of Nsukka renamed "Chinua Achebe Road."

1991   Receives Langston Hughes Award from Lincoln University; awarded honorary doctorates (D.Litt.) by Skidmore College, USA, (D.Litt.) by The New School for Social Research, USA, (D.H.L.) by Hobart and William Smith Colleges, (D.H.L.) by Marymount Manhattan College, USA, and (LL.D.) by University of Port Harcourt, Nigeria, respectively; listed in *1000 Makers of the Twentieth Century by Sunday Times*, London.

1992   Edits (with C. L. Innes) *The Heinemann Book of Contemporary African Short Stories*; awarded honorary doctorates (D.Litt.) by City College, City University of New York, USA, and (D.Litt.) by Westfield State University, Massachusetts, USA.

1993   Appointed Visiting Fellow and Ashby Lecturer, Clare Hall, Cambridge University; awarded honorary doctorate (D.H.L.) by Colgate University, USA.

1994   Awarded honorary doctorate (D.Litt.) by Fitchburg State College, Massachusetts.

1996   Awarded honorary doctorates (D.Litt.) by State University of New York at Binghamton, (D.Litt.) Bates College, Lewiston, Massachusetts, and (D.Litt.) by Harvard University, Cambridge, USA, respectively; receives Campion Medal and Order of Kilimanjaro Award; awarded Campion Medal.

1997   Awarded honorary doctorates (D.Litt.) by Brown University, Providence, Rhode Island, USA, and (D.Litt.) by Syracuse University, Syracuse, New York, USA, awarded Honorary Citizenship of the City of Austin, Texas.

1998   Edits (with Robert Lyons) *Another Africa*. Awarded Honorary Vice President, Royal African Society, London.

1999   Awarded honorary doctorates (D.Litt.) by Ohio Wesleyan University, Delaware, Ohio, USA, and (D.Litt.) by Trinity College, Hartford, Connecticut, USA.

2000   Awarded honorary doctorate (D.Litt.) by University of Witwatersrand, South Africa, and *Home and Exile* is published; appointed Odenigbo Lecturer by the Catholic Archdiocese of Owerri, Nigeria.

2001   Awarded honorary doctorate (D.Litt.) by Haverford College, Pennsylvania, USA.

2002   Awarded honorary doctorates (D.Litt.) by Cape Town University, South Africa, and (D.H.L.) by Fairleigh Dickinson University, New Jersey, USA.

2004   Receives Phyllis Wheatley Award, Harlem Book Fair, New York, USA, Associate Member, Academy of American Poets.

2006   Awarded honorary doctorates (D.Litt.) by University of Massachusetts, Boston, USA, and (D.Litt.) by University of Toronto, Canada.

2007   Awarded honorary doctorate (D.Litt.) by University of Sokoto, Nigeria.

2009   Awarded honorary doctorate (D.Litt.) by Nnamdi Azikiwe University, Nigeria; and *The Education of a British-Protected Child* is published.

2010   Awarded honorary doctorate (D.Litt.) by Lesley University, Massachusetts, USA.

2012   *There Was a Country: A Personal History of Biafra* is published.

2013   March 21, Chinua Achebe dies, but as a storyteller, he made us what we are as his readers, for he created history and memory for us.

1 The Life and Education of Chinua Achebe

Chinua Achebe, the Nigerian novelist, poet, literary critic, and social activist, is considered by many to be the most influential African fiction writer of his times. He occupies a unique position in modern African literary development and celebration. Other novelists, such as Ngugi wa Thiong'o and Nadine Gordimer, dramatists such Wole Soyinka and Athol Fugard, and poets such as Christopher Okigbo and Dennis Brutus, have transcended national boundaries in continental Africa as well. Yet no African writer's living reputation can compare to that of Achebe, whose first four novels: *Things Fall Apart* (1958), *No Longer at Ease* (1960), *Arrow of God* (1964), and *A Man of the People* (1966)[1] appeared within the eight critical years when most African countries resumed their sovereignty after a century of European rule. Hence, the novels can be aptly interpreted as realizations in fiction of the same spirit that expressed itself politically in the struggle for independence. Like Léopold Sédar Senghor, Frantz Fanon, Okot p'Bitek, and Kofi Awoonor, Achebe often pictured contemporary Africans as cultural mestizos who must first find out the secret of their blood before they could come to their inheritance. Speaking at the conference on Commonwealth Literature held in Leeds University in September 1964, Achebe saw his initial achievements then in terms of the cultural reeducation of his contemporaries:

> I would be quite satisfied if my novels (especially the ones I set in the past) did no more than teach my readers that their past – with all its imperfections – was not one long night of savagery from which the first Europeans acting on God's behalf delivered them. Perhaps what I write is applied art as distinct from pure. But who cares? Art is important but so is education of the kind I have in mind. And I don't see that the two need be mutually exclusive.[2]

The pronouncement Achebe made in this quoted passage glimpses the overall agenda and task of Achebe the novelist as teacher. He went on to reemphasize the same idea in another but similar article, "The Role of the Writer in a New Nation," this time at home in Lagos, Nigeria:

> For me, at any rate there is a clear need to make a statement. This is my answer to those who say that a writer should be writing about contemporary

DOI: 10.4324/9781003184133-1

issues – about politics in 1964, about city life, about the last coup d'état. Of course, these are all legitimate themes for the writer but as far as I am concerned the fundamental theme must first be disposed of. The theme – put quite simply – is the African peoples did not hear of culture for the first time from Europeans; that their societies were not mindless but frequently had a philosophy of great depth and value and beauty, that they had poetry and, above all, they had dignity. It is this dignity that many African peoples all but lost during the colonial period and it is this that they must now regain.[3]

Achebe would go on to carry out his self-imposed writer-teacher role as a mantle of honor as well as a life of service to Africa particularly and humanity in general, right from the time he made the public declaration until his demise in 2013.

His Informal Christian and Igbo Cultural Education at Home

For Chinua Achebe to be able to carry out the burdensome role of the writer as teacher, he must have been thoroughly exposed to a life full of both influential formal and informal education before his writing career began. So as we explore his life in this chapter of the book, we must first go back to where it all began: his informal Christian and Igbo cultural educations, which he received first at home, when the Achebe family lived outside of his native town of Ogidi in Eastern Nigeria, followed by his formal education when they returned to the town.

Achebe's informal Christian and Igbo cultural educations began at home because both of his parents, from whom he acquired the two types of education which laid the foundation for his formal education, were devout Christians. According to him, in the 1800s, when the CMS came to the West African territory that the British later named Eastern Nigeria, they established their operational headquarters in Onitsha from whence they extended their area of influence to Ogidi Town. As was customary for the missionaries, they responded to the Igbo tradition that strangers must first pay their respects to prominent local personalities who included Chinua Achebe's great-grandfather, Udo Osinyi:

> The first missionaries who came to my village went to Udo Osinyi to pay their respects and seek support for their work. For a short while my great-grandfather allowed them to operate from his compound. He probably thought it was some kind of circus whose strange presence added luster to his household. But after a few days he sent them packing again. Not, as you might think, on account of the crazy theology they had begun to propound, but on the much more serious ground of musical aesthetics. Said the old man: "Your singing is too sad to come from a man's house. My neighbors might think it was my funeral dirge."

Achebe further describes how that missionary encounter with his great-grandfather specifically impacted his father:

My father had joined the new faith as a young man and risen rapidly in its ranks to become an evangelist and church leader. His maternal grandfather, who had brought him up (his own parents having died early), was a man of note in the village. He had taken the highest but one title that a man of wealth and honor might aspire to, and the feast he gave the town on his initiation became a byword for openhandedness bordering on prodigality. The grateful and approving community called him henceforth Udo Osinyi – Udo who cooks more than the whole people can eat.[4]

Achebe began the article containing both quoted passages by saying, "I was born in Ogidi in Eastern Nigeria of devout Christian parents. The line between Christian and non-Christian was much more defined in my village forty years ago." Achebe first made this speech in 1973. However, from what he later told his audience in a series of three lectures he gave at Harvard University in December 1998, he recollected that he and his parents did not live in Ogidi until he was five years old, when they returned to their homeland in Ogidi:

One of the earliest memories I can summon from the realm of childhood was a home-coming that was extraordinary even for such recollections. I was returning to my ancestral home for the first time. The paradox of returning for the first time need not detain us now because there are more engaging things at hand. I was five years old and riding in a motor vehicle also for the first time. I had looked forward very much to this experience, but it was not working right. Sitting in the back of the truck and facing what seemed the wrong way, I could not see where we were going, only where we were coming from. The dust and the smell and the speed and the roadside trees rushing forward as we rushed back finally overcame me with fear and dizziness. I was glad when it all finally came to a halt at my home and my town.[5]

Embodied in the last sentence of the quote is the feeling of being in exile and losing his ancestral home culture. That loss is further explained in the following sentences:

Of all our family, only my father had ever lived in Ogidi, to which he now brought us, and he had not lived there since he first began teaching for the Anglican Mission in 1904; it was now 1935. My mother, who had served beside him since their marriage five years into his career, had grown up in her own town, twenty-odd miles away.[6]

Although Achebe never lived in Ogidi before the family's return, his mother and his elder sister, Zinobia Uzoma, regularly narrated to him stories about Ogidi and Awka, his mother's hometown, coupled with stories from the Bible; for his father was a catechist and teacher, whose young family upbringing was based on Anglican Mission principles. At that point, both kinds of story served as preschool education for the young Chinua. According to Achebe's biographer Ezenwa-Ohaeto,

> When Chinua Achebe was a child, entertainment for children, especially if designed to quieten them or keep them busy, was conducted through games and narration of stories. Each mother or older child found it necessary to garner several stories for such purposes. Zinobia Uzoma, who had the responsibility for taking care of Chinua and Grace, was a very good mimic and would dramatize the characters in her stories. One of the tales she narrated was about a man known as Amanile who bought a "goat" not knowing it was a tortoise. Amanile would get up each day to procure grass for the "goat," but it would not eat. Whenever the man went out, however, tortoise ate his *alibo*, a local delicacy made of cassava flour. Other stories were narrated by Chinua's mother, whose experience of a different but related Igbo culture at Awka gave her access to myths, legends, folktales and stories centered on events and people. These storytelling sessions were part of Igbo tradition and fired the imaginations of gifted children. In later life Zinobia recollected that her younger brother Chinua had a retentive memory and would remind her of the stories he wanted to hear once more.[7]

Apart from this wellspring of his early education, Achebe told Ezenwa-Ohaeto about the walls of his father's house, which were filled with educational material, which aroused his curiosity and imagination to read and learn about other people and a variety of issues and places:

> My father filled our walls with a variety of educational material. There were Church Missionary Society yearly almanacs with pictures of bishops and other dignitaries. But the most interesting hangings were the large paste-ups which my father created himself. He had one of the village carpenters make him large but light wooden frames onto which he then gummed brown or black paper backing. On this paper he pasted colored and glossy pictures and illustrations of all kinds from an old magazine he had acquired somehow. I remember a most impressive picture of King George V in red and gold, wearing a sword. There was also a funny-looking man with an enormous stride. He was called Johnnie Walker. He was born in 1820 according to the picture and was still going strong. When I learned many years later that this extraordinary fellow was only an advertisement for whisky, I felt a great sense of personal loss.[8]

Upon his arrival in his ancestral home in the company of his family, Chinua was immediately thrust into another aspect of his Igbo childhood education and cultural experience: the effects of the clash of culture between the British missionaries, who were making a great effort to establish churches and schools in Igboland, and the Igbo elders, who were vehemently resisting the missionary effort in their communities, before Chinua was born. While the religious warfare was very acute in other parts of Igboland, it was less so initially in Ogidi because of the initial cordial relationship between the missionaries and Igbo leaders who were involved at the time.

On the part of the Igbo elders, for example, Achebe's great-grandfather was a powerful but tolerant man who initially welcomed the missionaries when they first came to Ogidi. With his approval, Achebe's father Okafor Achebe, described as "a young man [who] had acquired an enviable reputation as an excellent mas-querader, an accomplishment that was valued highly in the community," became one of the early converts of the CMS in Ogidi, and was baptized in 1904 by Rev. Sidney R. Smith and given the name Isaiah Achebe.

On the part of the missionaries, it should be noted as well that some of them, for example Rev. George T. Basden, learned to respect some Igbo institutions which made it possible for them to win the souls of some Igbo people as early converts. The CMS established Awka College for the training of teachers and catechists, which Achebe's father attended. There he came into contact with Basden, a missionary, amateur anthropologist, and teacher, who was so sensitive that he not only made some Igbo acquaintances but also accorded recognition to the culture of the people, which was why he attracted respect wherever he visited. The respect was mutual, for he confessed:

> A missionary has the unique opportunity of becoming acquainted with vil-lage life, for from the very nature of things the soundest policy is for him to live in the closest communion with the people whom he seeks to influence. So it comes about that he enters freely into the life of the natives, their huts are always open to him and he goes in and out more or less as one of them-selves. In like manner they expect the missionary's house to be free to them and to come and go as they please.[9]

That kind of friendly interaction between the missionaries and the Igbo people that Basden espoused made it possible for the missionaries to learn the Igbo lan-guage, which enabled them to preach directly to the people in their own lan-guage. According to Augustine S. O. Okwu,

> the Protestant white missionaries such as Thomas J. Dennis, George Bas-den, Sidney Smith, and the lay missionary workers E. A. Homby, R. Chol-let, Frances M. Dennis and Edith Warner visited the Igbo in their homes, preached and taught the people in the vernacular, and as a result were all given Igbo popular names.[10]

Ezenwa-Ohaeto emphasizes the same point as follows:

> Appreciation of Basden's political role was commemorated in the various titles he was awarded by Igbo communities. Onitsha conferred the title of *Omesilincha* which means "the one who accomplishes his duties or tasks com-pletely"; the Ogidi community gave him the title of *Onu nekwulu ora* – "the

mouth that speaks on behalf of the people"; and the Awka community called him *Omezuluoke*, "the one who fulfills his responsibility satisfactorily." The Nkwelle Ogidi community honored him with the gift of an elephant tusk and a staff, items expressing great respect. These titles and gifts emphasized Basden's roles as advocate, hard worker and responsible pioneer, clearly illustrating his personal dynamism and enterprise, and especially his willingness to use dialog rather than force or intimidation in his dealings with the people.[11]

That was the nature of interactions between some sensitive missionaries and the Igbo people in Ogidi before Isaiah Okafor Achebe and his young family came back to their ancestral home. However, once the missionaries found a foothold in various parts of Igboland, including Ogidi, they started to preach boldly against many aspects of Igbo customs and traditions, including their rituals and ceremonies, which partly constituted their traditional religion and worldview. That is why at most of their public ceremonies, there were dancing masquerades who represented symbolically the sprits of their dead-living ancestors. Unfortunately, however, some overzealous Igbo Christian converts began to destroy Igbo traditional religious icons and shrines, branding their people heathen. Such actions provoked a public clash of cultures that the young Chinua witnessed while acquiring both Igbo and Christian informal education at home until he went on to acquire formal education on many issues in the primary school at Ogidi from 1936 to 1943.

His Formal Education at the Primary School Level

In 1936, at the age of six, Chinua Achebe began his formal educational journey at St. Philip's Central School, Akpakaogwe Ogidi. Like in other CMS schools, the curricular offerings of the school were centered on basic literacy in the three R's (reading, writing, arithmetic), Christian Bible knowledge, and general studies comprising nature studies, history, music, physical education, and sports. Once he learned to read, Achebe appreciated more the contents of a variety of educational material on the walls of his father's home. At first, he only visually admired the photos, pictures, religious icons, and other images found in them; but as soon as he learned to read, he could analyze the literary meanings and purpose of the materials, as well as the stories they told. In addition, he was able to read on his own familiar stories from the Bible and the songs they sang from the hymn books during his family prayer meetings.

At school, teachers read and explained the Bible stories to all the pupils, who also were taught to sing songs from church hymn books. Furthermore, some of these school activities were repeated during Sunday school sessions. What became a special advantage for Chinua though was that the storytelling sessions of the oral tradition he experienced at home existed side by side with the book-reading sessions in school, which complemented the daily hymn-singing and Bible-reading activities by members of the catechist Achebe family. In addition,

Chinua was beginning to hear some of the folktales his mother and sister narrated to him at home were being narrated also in school by other pupils. He internalized some of the stories and later went on to write about them in both English and Igbo during his formal writing career.

Furthermore, during his primary school years, Chinua found himself at the crossroads of Igbo cultural education and worldview and Christian-cum-Western education and culture. While in the school premises, all the pupils were made to follow strictly the rules and regulations set by the board of education, which the headmaster of the school enforced religiously. Everything in that mission school was pro-Western and pro-Christian. But once the school was over each day, most of the pupils went back to their *heathen* homes. However, Chinua would return to his Christian home that was under the strict control of his catechist father. That meant that he was never afforded the opportunity then to experience life outside of the Christian environment unless he did so secretly and in disobedience to his father who was a strict disciplinarian. However, because of his inquisitive nature and frontier spirit, Chinua defied the odds to cross the boundary between the Christian and the non-Christian families in his town, to enable him to acquire as much Igbo culture as he could at such a tender age. But whenever he was caught doing so, his father punished him for getting involved with heathens, even though they all came from the same town and clan.

At the time, both Christians and non-Christians crossed boundaries during public Igbo ceremonies and Christian open-air evangelical activities. To each of the two groups, such public ceremonies looked like dramatic performances. For Chinua, the Igbo festivities featuring ancestral masquerades were more than mere public entertainment. Instead, they served as great educational opportunities for him to learn of his native Igbo traditional religious beliefs and worldview, and the verbal art of the elders and esoteric groups, which he later appropriated as raw material for writing his fiction.

Once he was enrolled in school, Chinua's world widened, for he began then to acquire more knowledge from his family home, the church, and the school. At home, visitors to his father came and went, after discussing the burning issues of the village and the church. He was available to help the mother do the home chores and to help pass around the kola nuts and wine his father served to the visitors. As the visiting elders and neighbors exchanged pleasantries and engaged in conversations with his father, they told stories of the land, while Chinua took notice of what was being said. Conversely, he listened attentively to the etiological animal tales and other folk stories that his mother and his sister narrated to him and other little children during storytelling sessions that constituted in the main the evening entertainment of the day. Fortunately, from those storytelling sessions, Achebe learned and internalized the Igbo storytelling habits that he later combined with formal Western narrative techniques to produce his first novel, *Things Fall Apart*, which was considered to be hybrid and the beginning of the modern African novel. The success he scored in the new creative writing experiment caused some scholars and critics of African literature to dub him "the founder of the modern African novel." He recreated some of those childhood folksongs and folktales, as well as the allegories in most of his novels, especially the rural ones, *Things Fall Apart* and *Arrow of God*.

Beginning from the time Chinua was born, his parents habitually took him to church and Sunday school as part of their daily life. Like most Christian converts, they developed a condescending attitude toward the Igbo traditional religious practitioners; but as Chinua attended primary school – especially at the upper classes – he became more aware of the activities of both religious institutions. He paid closer attention to the sermons preached in the church and the lessons taught during Sunday school sessions. Furthermore, as he continued to grow older while in both primary and secondary schools, he developed a critical eye with which he saw the merits and the demerits of each of the competing religions into which he had been thrust in his native land. That is why, during his writing career, he made the following statement about the religious conflicts:

> I was born in Ogidi in Eastern Nigeria of devout Christian parents. The line between Christian and non-Christian was much more definite in my village forty years ago than today. When I was growing up, I remember we tended to look down on the others. We were called in our language "the people of the church" or "the association of God." The others we called, with the conceit appropriate to followers of the religion, the heathen or even "the people of nothing."
>
> Thinking about it today I am not sure that it isn't they who should have been looking down on us for our apostasy. And perhaps they did. But the bounties of the Christian God were not to be taken lightly – education, paid jobs, and many other advantages that nobody in his right sense could underrate. And in fairness we should add that there was more than naked opportunism in the defection of many to the new religion. For in some ways and in certain circumstances, it stood firmly on the side of human behavior. It said, for instance, that twins were not evil and must no longer be abandoned in the forest to die. Think what they would have done for the unhappy woman whose heart, torn to shreds at every birth, could now hold on precariously to a new hope.[12]

The passage points to some bright spot in the encounter between European missionaries and native Africans during the era of missionary and colonial activities in Black Africa.

With regard to other school activities, Achebe was regarded as a hard-working and naturally intelligent boy by his fellow schoolmates and his teachers. His rapid mastery of the English language and hard work turned him into an avid reader; he used the strength of his reading skills to master other subjects, which included dictation, history, arithmetic, geography, nature study, and religious knowledge. Through the history lessons that his teachers taught them Chinua learned about countries such as Germany, Japan, Italy, and England, and personalities such as Hitler, Mussolini, Hirohito, and Churchill involved in the fighting of the World War II. The pupils were also taught lessons on the British Empire whose ruler was

Queen Victoria of England, and all the schools celebrated the Empire Day on May 24 each year, the Queen's birthday.

Achebe showed special interest early in the study of literature. In addition to reading English books like John Bunyan's *Pilgrim's Progress* and Shakespeare's *Midsummer Night's Dream*, he also read books written in Igbo like *Azu Ndu* and *Ije Onye Kraist*, both of which were his mother's favorite texts. The more he read the literary works that took him imaginatively to other places in Igboland and Europe, the more he wanted to learn about the entire universe and the human beings that dwell in it. At that point, learning world history ignited his interest in the pursuit of the "otherness" theory, which he would develop in future to challenge the Europeans' absolute claim that the whites were superior people and the non-whites were inferior as human beings. That is why he wrote about the religious struggle between the early Christian missionaries and the Igbo people when he said, "Nothing is absolute. *I am the truth, the way, and the life* would be called blasphemous or simply absurd, for is it not well known that a man may worship Ogwugwu to perfection and be killed by Udo?"[13]

Chinua Achebe continued to do well in all the subjects he took at the primary school in Ogidi up to late 1942, when he left to live with his elder brother, John Achebe, who was a teacher at the Central School in Nekede near Owerri. He continued to work as hard as he did at Ogidi in his new school. He had become a little mature so that he even helped to cook for his brother – a skill he learned from his mother. Once more, Chinua was blessed with a group of dedicated teachers, who not only instilled good discipline and work ethic in all their students, but also prepared them to take entrance examinations into secondary schools in Eastern Nigeria, especially the prestigious Government College, Umuahia, and Dennis Memorial Grammar School, Onitsha. While living in Nekede, Achebe read more books on literature and was also exposed to the famous Igbo artwork center known as *Mbari*, which contained representations of Igbo gods and goddesses, such as *Ala* and *Amadioha*, as well as the representations of white missionaries and British colonial officers in uniform. Excursions to *Mbari* and other Igbo cultural centers enriched his acquisition of Igbo social and cultural education (including their religion and oral history) that combined with his formal Western education (including Christianity) to make him a very intelligent and well-rounded student at that level. In the end, Achebe finished his primary school education in 1943 at Nekede, where he scored the highest mark in all the entrance examinations into secondary school that he took from that primary school. He was placed as number one on the list of students admitted into Government College, Umuahia, from all the primary schools in Eastern Nigeria.

His Secondary School Education at Government College, Umuahia

Chinua Achebe received his secondary school education from the then-prestigious Government College, Umuahia (GCU), from 1944 to 1947. He chose the college above another prestigious college, Dennis Memorial Grammar School (DMGS), Onitsha, the alma mater of his two elder brothers, which admitted him at the same time that GCU did. However, Achebe did not choose DMGS because fate and destiny drew him to GCU: whereas attending DMGS would have meant living his college life under missionary control, GCU offered him the freedom to experience life in a more secular academic and social milieu that satisfied his academic and social needs. I surmise that his elder brother John, who was sponsoring his education at the time, had everything to do with his choice; for as a teacher, John knew that the financial benefits Chinua would get from a government-sponsored GCU would be more than that from the mission-sponsored DMGS.

As soon as Chinua Achebe arrived on campus, his interest was immediately drawn to the physical environment, as well as the academic and disciplinary outlook of the college. Although he was known to his former schoolmates and teachers as a hard-working, naturally intelligent pupil at the primary school level, still his family, like any other family, was worried about his overall success in face of the reported strict discipline of the college. Temperamentally, however, he was mentally and psychologically poised to work hard so as to absorb the rigors the organized college life at Umuahia entailed. Nevertheless, before he left for GCU, the family prayed for his protection and success at the new place, and his brother John gave him useful academic advice, which was reinforced by the school orientation that prepared him to face college life with courage.

The first factor that would work for Achebe's hoped-for success was the staffing of the school. The first principal of the college, Mr. Robert Fisher, was an enterprising Englishman who set the foundational standard of discipline for the college. When he left, his successor, Mr. Hicks, a veteran of World War II who had served in Burma, continued running the college with the discipline model his predecessor had set. Hicks was the principal of the college when Achebe arrived in 1944. Later on, another teacher Mr. William Simpson, a Cambridge University graduate, succeeded Hicks as the principal in 1945. In addition, there were foreign teachers such as Adrian P. L. Slater and Charles Low, and Nigerian teachers such as Mr. J. C. Menakaya and Mr. G. J. Efon, who brought balanced expertise to teaching the students English, math, geography, history, physics, biology, chemistry, and other arts and science subjects at the college. In other words, the variety of courses, the pedagogy, and academic qualifications of the teachers (including degrees from Oxford and Cambridge Universities) at GCU were superior to those found in other secondary schools both in Nigeria and other West African countries.

Another important determining factor for students' success at GCU was the first-rate libraries and other academic facilities the school authorities built in support of the students' academic work and social life in the school. According to Ezenwa-Ohaeto, Chinua Achebe's world of stories widened at the college where he now read many literary texts such as *Treasure Island, Gulliver's Travels, The Prisoner of Zenda, Oliver Twist, David Copperfield, Tom Brown's Schooldays, She, Alan Quatermain,* and *Prester John.* Although some of the books contained white characters against the savages, Achebe could not distinguish them until later in his writing career. At the time, Achebe was still uncritical in his reading and he "often sided with the white characters against the savages." He explained the situation thus:

I did not see myself as an African to begin with. I took sides with the white men against the savages. In other words, I went through my first level of schooling thinking I was of the party of the white man in his hair-raising adventures and narrow escapades. The white man was good and reasonable and intelligent and courageous. The savages arrayed against him were sinister and stupid, or at the most, cunning. I hated their guts.[14]

Commenting on what Achebe said in this quoted passage, Ezenwa-Ohaeto wrote:

Achebe looks back on his encounter with literary works in this period of his schooling as innocent, although they "can be used to put you in the wrong crowd, in the party of the man who has come to dispossess you." But as he confesses, it all added up to a wonderful preparation for the day we would be old enough to read between the lines and ask questions.[15]

Judged by the nationalities of the principals and teaching staff of the school while Achebe was there, Government College, Umuahia, was an English school. They inspired the students to work hard even during their leisure hours, and that inspiration helped Achebe to develop the knack of reading and writing all the time. And what made the difference in his extraordinary literary success was attributed to a program in the college known as the Simpson Text-book Act. In an interview with Robert M. Wren, W. E. Alagoa, a graduate of the school, explained the Text-book Act thus:

It was enacted by Simpson, and was simply, "During game times, that is, from five to six, nobody may be under a roof; nobody may read a textbook. If you are not put down for games, go on a stroll with a friend, chat, discuss. Or make your companion a good book – a novel, a book of poems or essays. Sit under one of the many shrubs around and have a pleasant one hour." Disliked at first, it soon became quite popular. It helped to develop the reading habit. I would like to believe that it helped to create in the boys the urge to write. Most of the writers produced by Umuahia belong to the period when the Text-book Act was in force – the names of Achebe, Amadi, Aniebo, Okigbo, come readily to mind. They all belong to this period.[16]

To promote the students' interests in reading and writing outside of their official assigned class work, the staff created two magazines for them to express their creative interests: house magazines and a college magazine. Each house of the college published its own magazine, and collectively students from all the houses published one magazine for the college. Both magazines were edited by students under the guidance of one of their teachers Charles Low. Achebe was such a good and regular contributor to both magazines that Low appointed him editor of not only his house magazine but also the college magazine. In the end, Achebe's many submissions to, and editorial work on, both magazines became an invaluable practical experience he carried with him after graduation from secondary school at GCU to study at the University College, Ibadan.

Although we have so far emphasized how well Achebe acquitted himself in literary activities at GCU, reports from his classmates and school records show that he excelled in every subject that he ever took at the school. And the most persuasive evidence of that was that he completed the secondary school program in four years instead of the usual five it took others to finish. Even so, his performance at the school certificate examination, which Cambridge University conducted, was stellar and earned him the opportunity to apply for admission to a university college immediately:

> The final examination taken by Chinua Achebe's class at Government College became the apex of Chinua's brilliant secondary school career, fulfilling all the hopes of his teachers. Soon after, an examination was conducted for entry into the new University College, Ibadan which was expected to take off in late 1948. In that examination Chinua Achebe was said to have written as much as he believed was necessary and stopped well before time to hand in his paper. That decision caused some consternation, since the Ibadan University College was going to admit a limited number of students.
>
> In those days the fashionable courses at the university were engineering and medicine and John Achebe, his official guardian, took the decision that Chinua was to study medicine. He had been an all-round student and his choice did not seem outrageous. Chinua was not only one of the few students who passed the entrance examination to the University College and was selected, but he also earned a "Major" scholarship with its associated privileges. Achebe confirms that there were only two Major scholars in any year, and about eight "Minor" scholars, while the rest of the students paid fees.[17]

In the end, Achebe left Government College, Umuahia, physically grown and more mature, as well as well educated with a lot of pride for what he had achieved without being under the direct supervision of his parents, his elder brother John, or the CSM authorities. He looked forward to attending the University College, Ibadan with great expectations; for he had taken the entrance examination into the institution and passed with flying colors. Now he was ready as a young man to go to the next level of his formal academic journey.

His College Education at the University College, Ibadan

Chinua Achebe entered the University College, Ibadan (UCI) in 1948, the year in which the institution was established as one of the university colleges that the British established in four African countries to produce students who, upon graduation, would disseminate the so-called superior British culture and civilization throughout Africa, "the heart of darkness." Achebe and his fellow pioneer students had no senior students to look up to for guidance in living a well-structured and productive college life; neither did Professor Kenneth Mellanby, whom the British Labour government-established Eliot Commission had entrusted with the creation of UCI in 1947 without any handy faculty and staff, or a blueprint to guide him. As it were, he alone was UCI until he recruited faculty from such other British universities as Oxford and Cambridge and, of course, London University, which served as the administrative headquarters of the four British university colleges in Africa.

Based on his solid academic records at GCU, Umuahia, and his unbeatable performance at the extremely competitive entrance examination into UCI, Ibadan, Achebe became one of the first students to be admitted into the institution with full scholarship. In science and medicine, he attained "Major Scholar" status, thus becoming one of the crème de la crème in intellectual achievement. In any given year, there were only two selections for Major Scholar and about eight for Minor Scholar awards. Another measure of Major Scholar elitism that Achebe enjoyed was having a private room while other students shared.[18]

Achebe had originally qualified to study science at Ibadan, and when he started to take classes on science subjects, he thought he could do anything. Although he had a slight bent toward literature, he enjoyed chemistry, biology, as well as physics. But he did not enjoy mathematics the way he enjoyed other things. He said all that in an interview with Robert Wren to explain why he changed his major from medicine to English instead:

> I realized that the kind of interest you needed to pursue education was not the kind required in secondary school. It was clear to me early in the first year that I didn't want to do the grinding work in physics, or ultimately, in medicine. I didn't do well. I lost interest entirely. When I went to the dean and said I wanted to change, he said, "How do you know you can do English? and history? I mean, you came here on a scholarship because of your. . . ." He brought out the scores. He said, "Go and talk to the Dean of Arts, and if they will take you, we'll see." So I did, but I lost my scholarship.
>
> That year, my brother pitched in. My immediate older brother was a junior civil servant. He'd gone through secondary school, had not gone to a university, and was working. You were given money for transport and so on, by the government. He decided he would cancel his leave and give me money to help me with my fees. And my older brother, with whom I lived my last year in elementary school – he's now a priest – he had absolutely no doubt that I should go back, and then apply for a government bursary, which I got in the second year. Getting through the one year was quite traumatic. A large number of students were destroyed in the first year. I changed my course, but some people were thrown out of the university on the basis of the first year exams.[19]

Achebe's description of his first year experience at the University College, Ibadan echoes the experiences of many past and present Nigerian university students. This is because some parents and guardians of prospective university students want their children and wards to get into prestigious universities where they have to study such notable courses as medicine, law, and engineering, whether or not such students have the interest, the ability, and adequate funds to enable them to succeed in the chosen courses. The result is that many of them fail to pass their exams in the first year and, consequently, are thrown out of their institutions. This is unlike what usually happens in the United States where students can remain undecided in choosing their majors until academic advisors properly guided them to choose those that are right for them based on their interests and ability to succeed. Also, students can apply for federal loans and various scholarships and grants, or work part time to fund their programs until they graduate. In the case of Achebe specifically, changing his major from medicine to English at UCI led to losing his scholarship, but his family came to his immediate rescue; and thereafter the government gave him some bursary to continue his studies in his second year. At any rate, that change of major became a blessing in disguise for Achebe's worldwide followers and lovers of African literature today. For, if he had succeeded in pursuing medicine, his services to his patients after graduation might not have been as impactful on Africa and the outside world as his literary contributions have been before and after his death.

Culturally, Achebe's arrival at Ibadan created a huge opportunity for him to meet students from other Nigerian ethnic groups with their diverse cultures. The mixed student population at the college was unlike the population in the primary school he attended in Ogidi, which was comprised of only Igbo pupils from his native clan; nor was it like the one in the secondary school, Government College, Umuahia, where the student population was mainly Igbo students with just a few non-Igbo students from Eastern Nigeria. This meant that, apart from pursuing the Western education he was admitted to study at UCI, Achebe was informally introduced to other Nigerian ethnic cultures, especially those of the Yoruba and the Ijaw, all of which were in some ways similar. For instance, in their traditional religion and mythologies, the Igbo believed in the notion of *ogbanje* [a changeling; a child who repeatedly dies and returns to its mother to be reborn], which the Yoruba and the Ijaw called *abiku*. And all three ethnic groups also believed in the traditional art form Mbari, and in many gods and goddesses whose roles could be likened to those of angels and saints in Christian theology. Such Nigerian belief systems caused the students' white professors and Europeans outside the college to refer to the Nigerian ethnic cultures as part of the African cultures that they considered inferior to theirs. That might have been the reason why the African cultures, especially African literature, were not initially taught as part of the university curricular offerings at Ibadan.

Achebe and his coevals at the university began to see themselves not as a group of ethnic peoples but as one Nigerian people because the white professors saw themselves as "we," and the Nigerians as "they" – a dichotomized recognition of one group as white and the other as black; one as superior and the other as inferior; one as civilized and the other as savage; one as oppressors and the other as the oppressed. Consequently, the Nigerian students who used to see themselves through ethnic lenses began to see themselves from a nationalistic point of view; and in the course of their college education, they later saw things clearly from a pan-African perspective. That way the new sociopolitical consciousness the students developed in their minds helped them to embrace Nigerian patriotism as opposed to paying blind loyalty to their separate ethnic peoples. Furthermore, their professors compelled them to read some British "novels of Africa," such as *Mister Johnson* and *Heart of Darkness*, whose characters were mere caricatures of human beings, giving the impression that African peoples did not have understandable human languages, did not possess much intelligence, and lacked any viable culture at all; above all, that the African continent as a whole was the center of all evils in the world. And that image that the white world created of Africa gave them the excuse to create and legitimize such epochal issues as the slave trade of Africans, the partition of Africa into colonies of Western powers, with Great Britain adding its share of the colonies to the British Commonwealth. Consequently, all those measures not only enabled the colonialists to cart away the African natural and human resources to Europe and the Americas, but also, in so doing, they depopulated the African continent. Eventually, however, all these wrongs the whites did to Africans would cause Achebe and his fellow UCI students to protest by telling stories of ugly and deadly white/black encounters on the African continent.

Achebe became more sensitive to how the white people treated Africans and other non-whites all over the world during his second year at the university, when he became a student in the School of Arts, where he chose to study English, geography, and history as major subjects. In the Department of English, for example, he studied literary works by William Shakespeare, Joyce Cary, Joseph Conrad, William Butler Yeats, John Milton, Homer, Thomas Hardy, William Wordsworth, and a host of other notable European authors that increased his knowledge of the white people's educational systems, religion, culture, and civilization through their literatures as an extension of what he learned about them at GCU before coming to UCI for university education. The stories of the characters he read in novels and poems were stories about human beings albeit in foreign lands, and some of their circumstances reminded him of parallel conditions in Africa. As a future writer, he would go on to adopt some quoted lines from W. B. Yeats's poem, "The Second Coming" and T. S. Eliot's poem, "The Journey of the Magi" as epigraphs in his first African novel, *Things Fall Apart*, and his second novel, *No Longer at Ease*, respectively. Furthermore, Achebe created characters and episodes in *Things Fall Apart* that parallel those in Thomas Hardy's *The Mayor of Casterbridge*: we see that in the relationship between Okonkwo, the wealthy Igbo farmer, and his doting daughter being compared to that between the rich Welsh farmer who became a mayor and his doting daughter Elizabeth Jane. These parallel depictions proved that African peoples were not inferior to Europeans in a lot of ways, and that the cultures of the people from the two continents were sufficient to sustain their lives and beings until one group tried to destroy the culture of the other without total success.

With regard to religious matters, what was most intriguing to Achebe was how what the Christian missionaries condemned in Igbo traditional religion – namely, polytheism, or the worship of many gods and goddesses – was practiced by the

Greeks and Romans, which he read in such literary classics as Homer's *Iliad* and *Odyssey*. He also found some semblances of the so-called Igbo pagan worship in some Christian rites. For instance, the Igbo offer sacrifices to their dead-living ancestors in the spirit world with kola nut and palm wine, just as Christians offer sacrifices to their dead-living saints, especially on All Saints Day, in the form of Holy Communion that Jesus Christ performed with bread and wine during his Last Supper with his disciples. Readers of Achebe's novels, which he wrote after graduating from college, can find an example of the similarities in the two competing religions at Umuofia from the argument between a British missionary, Mr. Brown, and an Igbo religious leader, Akunna, in *Things Fall Apart* (179–181). Because of the similarities in the tenets of both religions, Mr. Brown was unable to win Akunna over to his side, despite his initial stance that Christianity was the only true and superior religion.

Achebe's choice to study geography and history alongside English his major interest enhanced his understanding of world affairs which he would need to function as a deeply knowledgeable and authentic writer after college. He was in primary and secondary schools at Ogidi and Umuahia during the years when World War II was being fought. While he was not conscious of World War I, certainly he was very much aware of what was going on during World War II: his principal at GCI was a veteran of the war, who created a military ambience at the college, and war effects were felt both in his town and schools where people were conscripted to fight for the British both in Burma and North Africa. Consequently, some Nigerian soldiers lost their lives in service to their "Motherland," Great Britain.

At the university Achebe was taught history that emphasized the roles Britain played during the World Wars, how it built the most formidable navy in the world at the time – "Rule Britannia, Britannia rules the waves!" they would sing – a feat enabling Britain to rename itself Great Britain. Besides, it had colonized before then a big nation like India and numerous other big and small countries in Africa, Asia, and the Americas that became the British Commonwealth; thus, all the citizens of those erstwhile colonial countries were dubbed British subjects. The history and geography of those places, which were implanted in Achebe's brain, became great lessons on how the British colonial and imperial systems victimized Africans and other non-whites all over the world. Initially at GCU, Achebe was impressed by the stories of bravery and civilization of Great Britain as opposed to the alleged savagery of his own African peoples. But while he studied at UCI, viewing the details of those stories about British heroism and superior culture with a more mature and critical eye, he became empowered to analyze the brutality of the American and European nations during the two World Wars. So, he had second thoughts about the vaunted superior culture and civilization of the whites, and his change of perspective on world affairs would become the great catalyst for Achebe engaging in protest writing when he became a professional author.

In the main, one of the British objectives in building the four university colleges in Africa was to produce educated African leaders who would spread *Pax*

Britannica in the continent. So, at the University College, Ibadan, students were trained to become future Nigerian sociopolitical and academic leaders. Achebe recollected how Professor Welch, the Vice Principal of the college, exhorted them to achieve that goal:

> I am an Englishman, you see. You are African, you know. Very soon you will run your own independence. We cannot teach you how to manage your affairs. We are not experts in African religion or anything. We may not be able to teach you what you want or even what you need. We can only teach you what we know. After that you can do what you like with it.[20]

Achebe took the professor's candid exhortation to heart and worked assiduously to succeed as a student. Thereafter, he did what he liked most with his college degree, which was working first as a senior broadcaster in NBS, and later as a professional writer and university professor. He even had a brief stint with party politicking after the civil war.

In summary, Chinua Achebe's educational journey began with an informal education at home when his family was living outside of their hometown of Ogidi. And upon returning when Chinua was five years old, they gave him one more year of informal education. Thereafter, at the age of six, he was formally enrolled for a Western education in one of the town's primary schools. From there his elder brother John took him to live with him in Nekede, near Owerri, where he finished his primary school education. Because of his persistent hard work, and the help of John who was a teacher then, as well as the dedication and guidance of his teachers, Chinua took entrance examinations for admission into two prestigious mission and government secondary schools – DMGS, Onitsha, and GCU – and passed them with distinction. However, he decided to attend GCU because of the financial advantage it had over DMGS. Upon graduating from secondary school, Chinua Achebe was immediately admitted into the UCI, which was newly established by the British in late 1948. It was there at Ibadan that his formal training as a writer took place. But before discussing his training, and the publications that made Achebe a world-class writer, we wish to highlight the lessons he learned during his educational journey.

Notes

1   All four novels were originally published by Heinemann Educational Books Ltd., London.
2   Chinua Achebe, "The Novelist as Teacher," in *Morning Yet on Creation Day*. New York: Anchor Press/Doubleday, 1976: 58.
3   Chinua Achebe, "The Role of the Writer in a New Nation," *Nigeria Magazine*, No. 81 (Lagos, Nigeria: Federal Ministry of Culture, 1964): 157–8.
4   Chinua Achebe, "Named for Victoria, Queen of England," in *Morning Yet on Creation Day*. Garden City, NY: Anchor Books Paperback Edition, 1976: 95–103.
5   Chinua Achebe, "My Home under Imperial Fire," in *Home and Exile*. New York: Oxford University Press, 2000: 1–2.
6   *Ibid.*, pp. 2–3.

7 Ezenwa-Ohaeto, *Chinua Achebe: A Biography*. Oxford, UK/Bloomington, IN: James Currey/Indiana University Press, 1997: 8.

8 *Ibid.*

9 G. T. Basden, *Among the Ibos of Nigeria*. New York: Barnes and Noble, 1966: 45.

10 Augustine S. O. Okwu, *Igbo Culture and the Christian Missions 1857–1957: Conversion in Theory and Practice*. Lanham, MD: The University Press of America, 2010: 238.

11 Ezenwa-Ohaeto, *Chinua Achebe*, p. 5.

12 Achebe, *Morning Yet on Creation Day*, p. 95.

13 *Ibid.*, p. 133.

14 Chinua Achebe, "African Literature as Restoration of Celebration," in Kirsten Holst Petersen and Anna Rutherford, eds. *Chinua Achebe: A Celebration*. Oxford: Heinemann Educational Books, 1991: 7.

15 Ezenwa-Ohaeto, *Chinua Achebe*, p. 27.

16 Robert M. Wren, *Those Magical Years: The Making of Nigerian Literature at Ibadan: 1948–1966*. Boulder, CO: Lynne Rienner Publishers, 1990: 79.

17 *Ibid.*, p. 58.

18 Tijan M. Sallah and Ngozi Okonjo-Iweala, *Chinua Achebe: Teacher of Light*. Trenton, NJ: Africa World Press, 2003: 52.

19 Wren, *Those Magical Years*, pp. 58–9.

20 *Ibid.*, p. 66.

2 Chinua Achebe's Education as Template

One of the reasons why biographies of great men and women in world affairs are written is to enable their readers to learn something from the life stories of such people. The story about Chinua Achebe's educational journey is told in this book to serve as a template for parents, guardians, and teachers who want their children, wards, and students to succeed as Achebe did at the end of his educational journey. That success is measured by how well prepared the students are in pursuing their career goals in life after their educational journeys. Just like the old saying, "Charity begins at home," Achebe's impactful educational journey began at his home in Ogidi in the form of informal Igbo education that laid a strong foundation for his formal Western education at the primary, secondary, and college levels. He showed interest in telling stories very early in life as he sat through storytelling sessions at home, where he acquired Igbo storytelling practices from his mother and elder sister. He internalized some of the folktales and folk stories he heard and later appropriated them as raw material for developing his fiction. The process of acquiring the art of fiction writing that he began in Government College, Umuahia, was perfected at the University College, Ibadan.

As we stated earlier in our discussion, Chinua Achebe did not live in his hometown in Ogidi until he and his family returned to it from other parts of Igboland, where his father was serving as CMS catechist and teacher. He was five years old then. However, throughout the time they were away from home, his mother and his sister narrated to him stories about Ogidi and Awka, the birthplaces of his father and mother respectively. The stories were so alluring to the young Chinua that he became very much aware of his culture and history while still abroad. In other words, although his parents moved from their hometown because of his father's job, the family was psychically connected to their hometown all the time. His mother and sister narrated hometown stories to him to ensure that when they visited or returned home finally following his father's retirement, Chinua would be ready to embrace the customs and culture of his people. In addition, his father taught him the biblical stories he needed to learn as a Christian child. Both kinds of stories were narrated to him in the Ogidi dialect of the Igbo language, even while the family was away from their hometown until he was admitted into the primary school, where his Western education began both in Igbo and in English. Because his overall education was a huge success, there are some important lessons to learn from it.

DOI: 10.4324/9781003184133-2

A Lesson in Cultural Education

The lesson that present-day Igbo and African parents and guardians should learn from what Chinua's parents and siblings did is how to educate their own children on the culture and history of their people, through the use of folktales, folk stories, and oral history. Unfortunately, like Chinua's parents, many parents and guardians of children do not live and work in their native Igboland, where their children would learn about their roots directly from their people. Instead, they live and work in non-Igbo states in Nigeria or in foreign countries, such as America and England, where the Igbo language, culture, and history are not included in the curriculum offered to their children. For instance, some Igbo parents who live in other Nigerian cities like Lagos would prefer to teach their children English and Yoruba and very little, if any, Igbo, ostensibly to help their children to fit well in their new communities. But the Yoruba, for example, whether at home in Nigeria or in the United States, always strive to teach their children Yoruba language and culture at home first before anything else. And that is what gives such parents and their children the enviable Yoruba ethno-cultural identity above those of other Nigerian ethnic groups.

To exemplify how some Igbo parents teach their children about culture, if an Igbo man or woman asked Igbo children a basic question when they are exchanging pleasantries in Igbo: "*Kedu ka idi, nwa m?*" – "How are you, my child?" they usually would answer in English, "Fine, Uncle or Auntie." The children's answer is also in English even if the exchange takes place in an Igbo village. They are taught wrongly to address every man as "Uncle" and every woman "Auntie" as proof of their respect for elders and Western education. Yet, the words may not convey accurately their relationship to the people so addressed. Culturally, the Yoruba children are taught always to answer in Yoruba any questions posed to them in Yoruba.

By chance, Chinua Achebe indirectly emphasized to me the importance of teaching cultural education to our Igbo people in 1972, when I went to interview him in his office at the University of Nigeria, Nsukka, where he was serving as Director of the Institute of African Studies. In our English Department, one of the offered courses was titled "The African Novel," and the recommended textbooks for the course included some of Achebe's novels. As President of the English Association, I wondered why, in the first place, Achebe was not appointed professor of English to teach in the department, or at least was not asked to teach his novels as a guest lecturer. None of my lecturers was prepared to answer the questions I asked them on the issue. So, I made an appointment to interview him directly to get some answers. As soon as his assistant ushered me into his office, I said to him, "Good afternoon, Sir!" He looked up from his work on the table, and answered in Igbo, "Kalu, *kedu; biko, nodu ana!*" Which means "How are you, Kalu; please, sit down," pointing to a chair for me to sit. When the interview began, he answered the question about his appointment at the university. Thereafter, we discussed a number of other issues, including the effect of the war that just ended on Igbo people, especially on us students.

Although I went to talk to him in English, knowing that he was owner of the language, I came out of his office humbled and educated in what mattered in our cherished Igbo culture. After that humbling experience, each time I met him we communicated in our Igbo language, a means that was both natural and easier for both of us. And because of that incident, which took place in my junior year at the University of Nigeria, Nsukka, I decided there and then that if I ever had the opportunity to pursue a higher degree in English, I would have to specialize in the study of his writings. Fortunately, when I attended the graduate schools at the Ohio State University at Columbus and the University of Texas at Austin, respectively, I kept in touch with Achebe and interviewed him numerous times, especially on Igbo culture and civilization in his published works. The lessons I learned from studying his writings and the personal relationship I had developed with him enabled me to write my doctoral dissertation on his novels that became an award winner at Austin, Texas. Eventually, I became one of the experts on Achebe and Igbo Studies, and readers and critics of my published works have since acknowledged them as significant contributions to the field of Africana literary and cultural studies.

A Lesson in Duality and Otherness

Chinua Achebe's educational journey teaches us that, with proper parental and teachers' guidance, one can combine the pursuit of Western education and the folkways of his people and still achieve great success. His father, Isaiah Okafor Achebe, was the first Christian convert in his non-Christian agnate family. He later went on to train as a catechist and teacher in the CMS. Despite his high status in the new religious dispensation, he did not totally condemn all aspects of the Igbo culture and customs he was raised in before his conversion to the white man's religion. Chinua must have noticed that his father did not show any dogmatic attitude about the differences between the Christian and non-Christian religious practices in his community, even though he favored the Christian ways he was teaching to the Christian converts. So, in utter disobedience of his father's orders, Chinua snuck out of his Christian home from time to time to learn what was happening in the non-Christian homes. When his father found out what Chinua did, he spanked but also forgave his son. Ironically, however, the forgiveness of the loving father emboldened the ever-curious son to go out more often to learn whatever he could about Igbo religious practices. That is why in his adulthood, Chinua Achebe could discuss the comparable tenets of the two religions in his rural novels, *Things Fall Apart* and *Arrow of God*. His knowledge of both conflicting religious cultures he acquired from childhood to adulthood empowered him to express the Igbo notion of duality, even as he boldly condemned what he perceived as an arrogant Christian boast that Christ is the only way for humanity to obtain salvation:

> It is important to stress what I said earlier: the central place in Igbo thought of the notion of duality. Wherever Something stands, Something Else will

stand beside it. Nothing is absolute. *I am the truth, the way and the life* would be called blasphemous or simply absurd, for is it not well known that a man may worship Ogwugwu to perfection and be killed by Udo? The world in which we live has its double and counterpart in the realm of spirits.[1]

The white people, who consider their cultures superior to all other world cultures, are usually reluctant to recognize or else completely fail to appreciate the cultures of non-whites. That is what creates most of the culture conflicts we see afflicting humanity all over the world. In contrast, however, the CMS missionaries in Achebe's town, Basden and Smith, recognized early in their missionary work the Igbo notion of duality as part of their culture, which other whites wanted to condemn *ab initio*. Hence, their recognition helped them to change their tactics in converting the Igbo with some success. In like manner, the Igbo elders, who received the missionaries when they first came to Igboland, were guided by the same notion of duality. They would not have been able to learn about the alien white culture if they did not accommodate the missionaries as their new neighbors. In his committed effort to let outsiders to know about the culture and civilization of the Igbo during his tenure as Director of African Studies Department at Nsukka, Achebe founded an Igbo journal, titled *Uwa Ndi Igbo*, which he coedited with Chukwuma Azuonye, as a means to disseminate information on all aspects of Igbo life, culture, and civilization to the outside world.

A glimpse of a lesson in duality and otherness that Achebe taught through his fiction can be found in his first novel *Things Fall Apart* where a British missionary and an Igbo religious leader, Brown and Akunna, had a debate on their respective religious beliefs in which there was neither a victor nor a vanquished. Instead, they ended up learning from, and respecting, each other:

> Whenever Mr. Brown went to the village he spent long hours with Akunna in his *obi* talking through an interpreter about religion. Neither of them succeeded in converting the other but they learned more about their different beliefs.
>
> "You say that there is one supreme God who made heaven and earth," said Akunna on one of Mr. Brown's visits. "We also believe in Him and call Him Chukwu. He made all the world and the other gods."
>
> "There are no other gods," said Mr. Brown. "Chukwu is the only God and all others are false. You carve a piece of wood – like that one" (he pointed at the rafters from which Akunna's carved *Ikenga* hung), and you call it a god. But it is still a piece of wood."
>
> "Yes," said Akunna. "It is indeed a piece of wood. The tree from which it came was made by Chukwu, as indeed all minor gods were. But He made them for His messengers so that we could approach Him through them. It is like yourself. You are the head of your church."
>
> "No," protested Mr. Brown. "The head of my church is God Himself."

"I know," said Akunna, "but there must be a head in this world among men. Somebody like yourself must be the head here."

"The head of my church in that sense is in England."

"That is exactly what I am saying. The head of your church is in your country. He has sent you here as his messenger. And you have also appointed your own messengers and servants. Or let me take another example, the District Commissioner. He is sent by your king."

"They have a queen," said the interpreter on his own account.

"Your queen sends her messenger, the District Commissioner. He finds that he cannot do the work alone and so he appoints *kotma* to help him. It is the same with God, or Chukwu. He appoints the smaller Gods to help Him because His work is too great for one person."

"You should not think of Him as a person," said Mr. Brown. "It is because you do so that you imagine He must need helpers. And the worst thing about it is that you give all the worship to the false gods you have created."

"That is not so. We make sacrifices to the little gods, but when they fail and there is no one else to turn to we go to Chukwu. It is right to do so. We approach a great man through his servants. But when his servants fail to help us, then we go to the last source of hope. We worry them more because we are afraid to worry their Master. Our fathers knew that Chukwu was the Overlord and that is why many of them gave their children the name Chukwuka – "Chukwu is Supreme."

"You said one interesting thing," said Mr. Brown. "You are afraid of Chukwu. In my religion Chukwu is a loving Father and need not be feared by those who do His will."

"But we must fear Him when we are not doing His will," said Akunna. "And who is to tell His will? It is too great to be known."

In this way Mr. Brown learned a good deal about the religion of the clan, and he came to the conclusion that a frontal attack on it would not succeed.

(*TFA*, pp. 179–81)

As one can see clearly from the passage, both religious leaders initially felt that each of their beliefs was superior to those of the other, but being open-minded and ready to learn of the other's beliefs enabled them to understand, but not necessarily accept, the other's beliefs. It is the kind of attitude that could create good neighborliness and peace in the world. What a great lesson to learn from Achebe's fiction!

A Lesson in Teachers' Dedicated Services

Another important lesson to learn from Achebe's educational success is about how his primary, secondary, and university teachers worked hard to make it happen. At every level of his education, Achebe was fortunate to have been taught and guided by teachers who were committed to seeing him succeed through his own hard work and discipline. At the primary school level, for example, Mr.

S. N. C. Okonkwo, who served in Chinua's school, was so young that the big boys and girls he taught would playfully give him knocks on the head, complaining that such a young man should not teach them. Thus, it was easy for Mr. Okonkwo to relate to little Chinua Achebe as they worked under the influence of Mr. Okongwu, a strict headmaster who came to Ogidi on transfer from St. Peter's School, Enugu. The strict nature of Okongwu and his adherence to discipline was immediately established when he addressed the teachers and pupils, enumerating a list of prohibitions which he stressed with the refrain, "A *raa eme ya eme!*" – "It is never done!" He was a man who wanted his students to perform better than all others in both academic and other school activities. Headmaster Okongwu also set high standards in the school, awarding prizes for punctuality, cleanliness, and class performances.[2] In the same manner, when Chinua transferred from Ogidi to Nekede to finish his primary school education, he was lucky to have dedicated teachers who not only taught him well in the classrooms, but also took him on excursions to Owerri Town where he saw the famous Mbari Art House, and visited some cultural centers that ultimately inspired his exploration of Igbo cultural elements in his college and after-college writing projects.

The dedication, guidance, discipline, and care of teachers who taught Chinua in the two primary schools he attended were similar to those he found in many of his teachers at his secondary school, Government College, Umuahia. As was discussed earlier in Chapter 1, Achebe received good discipline in the school because his principal, Mr. Hicks, a British World War II veteran, who served in Burma, had continued running the school with the discipline model established by the school's founding principal, Mr. Robert Fisher. In an interview he granted to Robert Wren more than 40 years after graduating from the school, Achebe recollected with fondness the individual contributions each of his other foreign teachers, such as William Simpson, Adrian Slater, and Charles Low, as well as the indigenous ones, such as J. C. Menakaya, and G. J. Efon, made to his overall success in that school. He remembered them especially for the work ethic they inculcated in him, and for teaching him the skill of reading and appreciation of literary texts critically. That in part is what inspired him to change his major from medicine to English at Ibadan.

Chinua Achebe was one of the pioneer students of the newly established University College, Ibadan. Which means that he and his colleagues did not have any upperclassmen to look up to for guidance. So, while they relied on their teachers' guidance in most areas of their university life, they had to rely on their own strengths in other areas. For Achebe, this is where the discipline and training in self-reliance, emanating from the Simpson Text-book Act he received at Government College, Umuahia, paid off. Once again, Achebe encountered a British principal and teachers of the University College, Ibadan who took their job of giving the pioneer students high quality education seriously. The institution's first principal, Professor Kenneth Mellanby, saw his job like a military mission that did not tolerate any margin of errors in its execution. He was given free rein by London to recruit professors and other personnel, develop the college facilities, and manage its budget any way he saw fit, as long as he and the professors strictly adhered to teaching the course syllabi approved for the college in England. The professors who needed to make any amendments to the syllabi had to seek permission first from London before doing so. The students struggled very hard to study and pass their courses, whether or not they liked or enjoyed what was being taught to them. Those who failed to pass their exams were summarily dismissed from the college, and the ratio of student failures during the first year was too high.

One may be tempted to ask, "What is wrong with dismissing students from college when they flunk their exams? Is it not what happens in every institution of higher learning?" Well, the difference in the Nigerian situation then is that the courses were designed in London to propagate a "colonizer/colonized" relationship in which the interest of Britain the colonizer was emphasized at the expense of Nigeria and her students as the colonized. Despite the disadvantage though, Chinua Achebe had British professors who taught him what he enjoyed in the English Department. Professor Alex Rodger, for example, was one of those professors who taught novels like Thomas Hardy's *The Mayor of Casterbridge* and *Far from the Madding Crowd* of which Achebe said:

> But I took to Hardy immediately. What appealed to me was his sense of reality, which is tragic; it's very close to mine. I think for the same reason I took to A. E. Houseman. There are a lot of funny things, a lot of comic things that happen in the world, and they're important. But I think that the things that really make the world, the human world, are the serious, the tragic. And this is, roughly, what Hardy says to me; this is what Houseman says to me. It is, you know, the man who fails who has a more interesting story than the successful person. If you ask me why, I don't know.[3]

Inspired by the novels Professor Rodger taught him, Achebe developed his own tragic heroes like Okonkwo in *Things Fall Apart* and Ezeulu in *Arrow of God*, using Hardy's model. Also, Achebe created the tragic hero Obi Okonkwo in *No Longer at Ease* to reflect the pessimism of some of the tragic characters he found in Houseman's poetry.

Achebe remembered Professor Joyce (Green) Garnier, who taught him Victorian literature, including Tennyson's works. She encouraged Achebe to write some short stories as class assignments. But when he wrote one for a prize, the professor remarked that Achebe's short story was an "interesting effort" without really telling him what was wrong with it. She merely said that the problem was that it lacked the form of a short story. Achebe continued to press for explanation of that remark on his short story to enable him to improve on his writing skill until at the end of the semester, when she finally said, "I read your short story again, and I don't think there's anything wrong with the form."[4] The answer that Garnier gave Achebe further inspired him to write more short stories after he graduated from college.

One more professor whose teaching influenced Achebe greatly at UCI was Dr. Geoffrey Parrinder, who had spent about 12 years as a Methodist missionary in

French-speaking West Africa, in Dahomey, and had written a book called *West African Religion*. After hearing a lot of good things from other students about Parrinder's teaching, Achebe enrolled in his comparative religion class. Forty years later, Achebe remarked that Parrinder was a very enthusiastic and knowledgeable teacher who enlightened him to renew his interest in African gods and religious systems. The outcome of that interest and awareness in African traditional religions inspired Achebe's exploration of Igbo gods, oracles, and divination as important Igbo folkways in his novels, which I wrote about in my award-winning doctoral dissertation at the University of Texas at Austin in May 1981, which I later published as a book in 1992.[5]

Looking at what goes on in current Nigerian primary and secondary schools, as well as in the universities, can anyone believe that students are receiving the kind of dedicated and committed teaching and care from their teachers as Achebe did during his time as a student? If so, what evidence do we have to prove that they do? If not, why shouldn't the teachers work the way that Achebe's teachers did to make them successful?

It is quite obvious to anyone who is familiar with the Nigerian system that the conditions in Nigerian educational institutions at all three levels are worse than they were during the colonial period, when Achebe received his education. First of all, teachers themselves lack professional discipline in their places of work. Many of them complain that they are underpaid for the work they do, and even their paltry salaries are not regularly paid when they are due. For that reason, some of them go moonlighting in all kinds of jobs, thereby neglecting the students they were assigned to teach. The principals of primary and secondary schools, and even the vice chancellors (presidents) of universities, are not immune to that kind of misbehavior. In some cases, these school executives would prefer to work privately with politicians and political parties to make extra money. Nobody dares to query or punish them for their illegal, constitutionally forbidden acts because the politicians and political parties they work for are "the law" in Nigeria.

Moreover, when the teachers fail to do their job, the students cannot learn anything from them; and yet the students insist on being promoted from one class to another even though they haven't done any work to deserve promotion. The few dedicated, committed, and caring teachers who insist on students working hard to earn their promotion are killed for not passing or giving them mass promotions. In addition, other corrupt teachers resort to forcing students to buy their prepared course handouts. Once the students purchase them, they are assured that they would pass their courses automatically. Which means that they don't have to study even the handouts in order to pass the tests based on them. The teachers spend their time preparing handouts that fetch them money. That is why they would argue, "What's the point working hard as dedicated, committed, and caring teachers when they can easily make money that way?"

Furthermore, the school authorities in most cases lack the resources to provide their schools with needed facilities, such as well-equipped libraries, science labs, and classrooms. Sometimes, the contractors that the government hired to provide those school resources would take the money but would not deliver. If they are taken to court, corrupt judges would delay presenting the cases for trial, which frustrates the school administrators from working promptly with due diligence.

But the most appalling case of the teachers' failure to teach with commitment, dedication, and care occurs at the university level. They constantly cancel classes and walk off their jobs and go on endless strikes that could last as long as six months to one whole academic year. Usually, the strikes are against the federal government whom they claim had not honored the service agreements they entered into with the university.

There is no gainsaying that the way that teachers and the federal government have been handling the problems of managing schools, colleges, and universities has created a drastic fall in the general standard of education in Nigeria. Both parties lack the British missionary zeal and colonial government officials' dedicated service to students during Chinua Achebe's times. That is why the former governor of the old Imo State, Chief Sam Mbakwe, was so frustrated that he cried out for the British, who left Nigeria on its attainment of political independence, to come back and manage the affairs of independent Nigeria, including its educational systems. Despite his wishful thinking, he went on to establish the first state university in Nigeria, the Imo State University, in order to demonstrate how to run universities efficiently for the benefit of students and their parents. In the end, that university became a template that later guided other state governments to build and run their own universities.

A Lesson in the Funding of Students' Education

The funding of education at all levels is the greatest challenge that children of poor parents and guardians face in every country. The problem is very dire in Nigeria where students pay tuition and fees from preschool through the university, despite the fact that about 70 percent of the population (especially the rural villagers) live in poverty. For that reason, funding poor children's education is difficult for their parents and guardians. In contrast, in an advanced country like the United States, the federal government offers free education to students in public schools up to the high school level, regardless of the economic status of their parents and guardians. Still, even in this advanced country, there are students from poor minority communities whose parents cannot provide them with adequate school supplies, clothes, and even food and shelter. Consequently, some of them live in government-funded shelters and low-cost housing projects and eat free meals that the public schools serve to them during weekdays.

Here, as in other educational matters, we examine the funding of Chinua Achebe's education during the colonial period to serve as an example of how students' education should be funded in this postcolonial era in Nigeria.

The advent of the whites in Nigeria taught people the importance of Western education. Chinua Achebe's father, who embraced it early in twentieth century Igboland, was among the first educated Igbo people to work and earn salaries beyond their villages and clans. Through the father, the children learned the importance of Western education firsthand, for it was through it that he was able to fund his children's education as far as they could go, while he was still in active service. He funded Chinua's primary school education halfway, and his elder brother took over the responsibility until he finished secondary school. Thereafter, he went to study at the University College, Ibadan, on full scholarship. This implies that the funding of students' education is the responsibility of parents, guardians, and siblings, if they can afford it. Chinua's father was exclusively responsible for educating his brothers, which enabled them to take over Chinua's funding from where their father stopped. Apart from Achebe's family, there have been cases in which parents did not allow their older children to go to school so they could work with the parents on their farms and marketplaces to raise money for the funding of their younger siblings' education. In turn, when such younger siblings finish their education and get good jobs, they assume the responsibility of taking care of their ailing and aged parents. That is why such children do not put away their parents and grandparents in nursing homes and hospices where they die in loneliness. In addition, the educated and working younger siblings are expected to take over the responsibility of funding the education of the children of their older siblings who forfeited their own education to maintain their younger siblings in school – an act that underscores the importance of the famous Igbo extended family system.

Furthermore, parents, guardians, and siblings make indirect investment in the funding of children's education by instilling in them the work ethic and discipline that enable them to work hard and excel in all their classwork and exams so they can qualify for all kinds of scholarships for their education. That is what the Achebe family did to make Chinua very successful in all levels of his education. As we said before, when Chinua was a toddler, his mother and sister taught him folktales and stories, and his two older brothers helped him with homework when he attended primary school. In addition, his parents found him caring teachers who further instilled in him the knack of reading, writing, and self-discipline as a groundwork of academic success in all his academic institutions. Achebe's brother John helped to prepare him for the highly competitive entrance exams he took and gained admission into two prestigious secondary schools. Again, all the help he got from parents and siblings led to his attending Government College, Umuahia, which was well-funded by the Eastern Nigerian government, and thereafter to enter the University College, Ibadan, on full scholarship. And when he changed his major, which made him lose his scholarship, one of his brothers was there to take over the payment of his tuition until he, once again, worked hard and earned a government bursary in his second year. In essence, without the help of his loving brother while he struggled to earn the bursary award, who knows if Achebe could have survived financially to go on to his second academic year at the university.

It is also important to know that where the immediate family members of students cannot afford to fund their education, the village community has to come to their aid by way of offering them free or loan scholarships, which students can repay upon graduation. After all, was it not the Igbo who said that it takes a village to raise a child? The educated ones in the community, who cannot help the students financially, can at least organize tutorial services to help prepare them for admission and scholarship tests, which can lessen the burden of funding their education. Achebe romanticized the idea of a community loan scholarship for one of the Igbo characters, Obi Okonkwo, in his second novel, *No Longer at Ease*.

Finally, during the colonial period, the fact that the active roles the church and government played in funding the schools that Achebe attended made him successful both in school and life should remind present-day voluntary agencies and the three branches of government to fund all three levels of education in Nigeria adequately. For, without the funding from government, community, and altruistic individuals, many bright but poor students may not be able to attain the highest levels of education that they are capable of attaining if they had the funding. When that happens, the individuals and their communities lose a great deal. But when all three agencies give the necessary assistance to poor students in our midst, good and great things usually happen.

In short, learning about Chinua Achebe's educational successes should remind Africans of the importance of acquiring their traditional and cultural education alongside Western education, which has been dominating other cultures and civilizations over many centuries. His parents and siblings taught him right from his infancy to embrace his Igbo culture. As he learned the culture at home, he simultaneously acquired Western education in school to the extent that he became a well-educated man and world-renowned author. But it was the thorough knowledge of English he acquired in the various schools he attended that enabled him to articulate in writing to his readers, especially the Western world, his Igbo notion of duality and otherness as a worldview that should enable them to recognize the beauty, the essence, and the adequacy of cultures for the people who own and practice them. Considering how succinctly Achebe romanticized his people's culture in his fiction, it is hoped that if the peoples of color around the world were inspired to embrace that notion, they would realize that their respective cultures cannot, and should not, plead inferior to the Western cultures that colonial and imperial powers were selling to them during the colonial eras. All told, Achebe was able to publish some of these ideas in fiction because of the dedicated services of his teachers who, in various ways, taught him to work hard to become successful in whatever he did in life. Nevertheless, no matter how hard he worked, and how well his teachers taught, guided, and encouraged him, he could not have excelled in his schools if his education was not well funded. Fortunately for him, all the factors that could enable a student to succeed came together to produce Achebe as not just a good student but also a remarkable writer whose published works revealed the beauty of his continent Africa, his fatherland Nigeria, and his ethnic Igbo people to readers all over the world. How he learned to write in such a profound way is the topic of the next segment of this chapter.

How Chinua Achebe Learned to Write Professionally

We understand from oral history that what is now known as African literature began as an unwritten oral performance of many aspects of African peoples' cultures, customs, and traditions. Until European missionaries and colonial officers came to the continent and introduced basic literacy education (except in Egypt and other parts of North Africa, which already had their own writing system), African peoples used vernacular verbal traditions to express their folklore, consisting of folksongs, folktales, proverbs, riddles, and other oral forms. An example of the songs and tales that fall into the category of oral literature is the famous Sundiata Epic, an epic poem of the Malinke people, which tells the story of the hero Sundiata Keita, founder of Mali Empire. As oral history, it goes back to the fourteenth century narrated or recited by generations of professional storytellers or griot poets. But in modern African societies, people narrate or recite less sophisticated folktales and folksongs, especially animal stories, to explain natural phenomena to young children. The stories are also intended to teach them lessons in human morality and good behavior. This is where Chinua Achebe began learning how to tell stories orally and, eventually, on the page when he became a professional writer.

The folklorist Alan Dundes argues that, "the identity of folklore and literature is an obvious fact. The Old Testament can be called a book of transitions, and it can be called literature of the ancient Hebrews."[6] One can see the transition of folklore into literature taking place in many African cultures like the Igbo, where folklore is indistinguishable from literature; for literature contains elements borrowed from folklore, and literary writers have imitated folklore in their writings. In that sense, folklore and literature are to be understood as complementary rather than exclusive and opposed modes in the people's expression of culture. As a child, Chinua Achebe began acquiring the Igbo storytelling skills informally as he sat through the nightly storytelling sessions at home and observed his mother, sister, and other adults telling groups of children some stories that contain folkloric elements and characteristic qualities of oral literary forms like the ones Dundes touched on in his argument.

Writing on the subject of orality in African literature, Ruth Finnegan argues:

> Many oral recitations arise in response to various social obligations which, in turn, are exploited by poet and narrator for his own purposes. The performer of oral pieces could thus be said to be more involved in actual social situations than the writer in more familiar literate traditions.
>
> These characteristic qualities of oral literary forms have several implications for the study of oral literature. It is always essential to raise points which would seem only secondary in the case of written literature – questions about the details of performance, audience, and occasion. To ignore these in an oral work is to risk missing much of the subtlety, flexibility, and individual originality of its creator, and, furthermore, to fail to give consideration to the aesthetic canons of those intimately concerned in the production and the reception of this form in literature.[7]

For the Igbo people, the social obligations that evoke responses from storytellers include the reciting of oral history of how the people's villages and clans were founded, the roles of gods and goddesses in human affairs, and the legendary roles of wrestlers and warriors who fought and defeated their rivals and enemies. Such recitations are done to inspire unity and solidarity among the people, and courage and bravery in clansmen who are committed to protecting their fatherland.

Through his careful observations of such recitation sessions, Chinua Achebe learned how to tell stories about the Igbo people. He used different language levels and imagery to inform his audiences on the Igbo culture, custom, and tradition. When the story is about ordinary people and children, he uses ordinary everyday language. Conversely, he uses esoteric and sententious expressions like proverbs and peculiar idiomatic expressions to describe the lives and exploits of titled elders and rulers of their societies. He applies the same discerning principle in his description of the genders, ages, statuses, and roles of characters, as well as the contexts and milieus under which they function in each story. For example, we see how the narrator uses the first type of language level in the two opening paragraphs of chapter one of *Things Fall Apart* to introduce Okonkwo's character and story:

> Okonkwo was well known throughout the nine villages and even beyond. His fame rested on solid personal achievements. As a young man of eighteen he had brought honor to his village by throwing Amalinze the Cat. Amalinze was the great wrestler who for seven years was unbeaten, from Umuofia to Mbaino. He was called the Cat because his back would never touch the earth. It was this man that Okonkwo threw in a fight which the old men agreed was one of the fiercest since the founder of their town engaged a spirit of the wild for seven days and seven nights.
>
> The drums beat and the flutes sang and spectators held their breath. Amalinze was a wily craftsman, but Okonkwo was as slippery as fish in water. Every nerve and every muscle stood out on their arms, on their backs and their thighs, and one almost heard them stretching to breaking point. In the end Okonkwo threw the Cat.
>
> (p. 1)

The level of language the narrator uses to introduce Okonkwo as the strongman of Umuofia, the occasion of the incident, and the implied thesis of the novel appears simple and easy for an audience of experienced and inexperienced readers to understand. But as simple as the narration may sound, the undergirding Igbo numerology, oral history, metaphors, and their stylized way of telling stories (all of which Achebe learned while growing up in his hometown) need some cultural exegesis for the audience to understand fully Achebe's message and intent in the novel.

On the other hand, the narrator uses a higher language level to describe the climactic incident that forced Okonkwo and his family out of his clan to take refuge in exile in his mother's homeland. The highly cadenced language is used to match the tempo, rhythm, metaphors, and tone of Okonkwo's unfortunate situation, which ultimately changes his life as a legendary hero:

> [But] before this quiet and final rite, the tumult increased tenfold. Drums beat violently and men leaped up and down in frenzy. Guns were fired on all

sides and sparks flew out as machetes clanged together in warriors' salutes. The air was full of dust and the smell of gunpowder. It was then that the one-handed spirit came, carrying a basket full of water. People made way for him on all sides and the noise subsided. Even the smell of gunpowder was swallowed in the sickly smell that now filled the air. He danced a few steps to the funeral drums and then went to see the corpse.

"Ezeudu!" he called in his guttural voice. "If you had been poor in your last life I would have asked you to be rich when you come again. But you were rich. If you had been a coward, I would have asked you to bring cour-age. But you were a fearless warrior. If you died young, I would have asked you to get life. But you lived long. So I shall ask you to come again the way you came before. If your death was the death of nature, go in peace. But if a man caused it, do allow him a moment's rest." He danced a few more steps and went away.

The drums and the dancing began again and reached fever-heat. Darkness was around the corner, and the burial was near. Guns fired the last salute and the cannon rent the sky. And then from the center of the delirious fury came a cry of agony and shouts of horror. It was as if a spell had been cast. All was silent. In the center of the crowd a boy lay in a pool of blood. It was the dead man's sixteen-year-old-son, who with his brothers and half-brothers had been dancing the traditional farewell to their father. Okonkwo's gun had exploded and a piece of iron had pierced the boy's heart.

The confusion that followed was without parallel in the tradition of Umuo-fia. Violent deaths were frequent, but nothing like this had ever happened.

(pp. 123–4)

The entire passage is a vivid description of a fatal accident that took place during the burial of a revered old man who had taken three of the highest titles of his Umuofia clan. For that reason, "Ezeudu was to be buried after dark with only a glowing brand to light the sacred ceremony" (p. 123). Achebe was enabled to describe the funeral oration accorded to the man whose burial was comparable to that of a four-star general in the Western world by his prior sound education in his people's folkways. And as a young curious spectator, Achebe observed the public celebrations of his town's seasonal and annual rituals and ceremonies, which included wrestling matches, new yam festivals, naming of age grades, traditional weddings, and the outings of masked spirits known as *egwugwu* who represent their dead-living ancestors. He had internalized some of these native cultural observances as a young man and went on as a writer to recreate them in his fiction.

So, as can be seen, before becoming a novelist, Chinua Achebe was already aware, to a certain degree, of questions about the details of performance, audience, and occasion, which he began learning at home and in his primary schools, where children are told folktales and other stories by their parents and siblings, as well as other adults and teachers. After thus acquiring basic Igbo storytelling skills informally, he began to acquire European storytelling skills in writing at Government College, Umuahia, where he was taught English by Charles Low, an avid reader of literary classics in Latin and Greek, who inspired him to take the study of literature seriously. Occasionally, Low would write some poems about ordinary incidents that occurred in their school that served as inspiration for Achebe to write his own stories. As we said earlier in this book, Low edited the college magazine and supervised the editorial work done on the students' house magazines. He so liked the quality of Achebe's submissions to both magazines that he made him his editorial assistant. Achebe and some of his fellow students, such as Chike Momah, Christopher Okigbo, Vincent Chukwuemeka Ike, Elechi Amadi, and Ralph Opara, wrote some short literary pieces that somehow became the literary foundation at Government College, Umuahia, on which the emerging Nigerian literature would be built at the University College, Ibadan, from 1948 to 1966. By the time the Umuahia students graduated from the secondary school, they had already mastered the use of both oral and written English to the extent that some of them aspired to study English as a major at the university, which enabled them to continue writing short stories, poetry, essays, and plays with some high measure of confidence.

In the English Department at Ibadan, Achebe met dedicated professors who taught him critical appreciation of literature and creative writing. Besides, as in GCU, there were magazines in UCI that served as platforms from which students practiced their writing skills. For example, *The Horn*, established by Martin Banham and J. P. Clark, provided a platform for students to publish their short plays; *Nigerian Student Verse* for poetry; *Black Orpheus*, founded by Ulli Beier, for the study and performance of Black African art and literature; *Poetry and Audience*, another platform for publishing poetry; *The Bug*, published to lampoon people – but it tended to concentrate on female students, which implied that its purpose was not as serious as those of the other magazines; and, *The Herald*, a more serious magazine that was funded by the university but controlled by students. Achebe was first recruited into its editorial committee, and then elected its editor in his third year.

While the university students strived to be published in any of the university magazines, some of them also wrote materials for publication in newspapers and magazines outside their campus. After graduation, they revised, reviewed, and in some cases re-envisioned some of the longer pieces they wrote as students, and published them in major local and foreign presses. In addition, some of the more controversial sociopolitical materials they wrote were published in *The West African Pilot*, a newspaper that was founded and edited by the great Nigerian nationalist, Dr. Nnamdi Azikiwe. Hence, it could be argued that the overall importance of the magazines to Nigerian literary history was the inspiration and opportunity they provided for students to produce materials that metamorphosed into the formal development of modern Nigerian/African literature. For according to Achebe, "They [the white professors] were not teaching us African literature. If we had relied on them to teach us how to become Africans, we would never have got started. They taught us English literature; they taught us what they knew."[8]

Chinua Achebe's assertion that the Nigerian students relied on their own efforts to develop African literature at the university is confirmed in Bernth Lindfors's book, *Early Achebe*,[9] where he critically narrated how Achebe (like some of his classmates) wrote short stories whose themes he later incorporated in his novels. He also revised and published others alongside the new ones he wrote during the war, which he published after the war in a collection of short stories, titled *Girls at War, and Other Stories*. Lindfors concludes his analysis as follows:

> The Nigerian-Biafran civil war was an important turning point in Achebe's literary career, so what he said then will help readers to understand better the evolution of his views on the role of the African writer in times of crisis. They will also learn a great deal from his candid reflections on his own early fiction.[10]

Their college education over, the UCI graduates found employments where they occupied high positions in the nation's civil service, radio and TV broadcasting corporations, print media houses, and teaching positions in secondary schools and teacher training colleges. Chinua Achebe stepped into the world of teaching and broadcasting from 1954 to 1966. He taught school at the Merchants of Light Secondary School, Oba, as an English teacher before landing a job at the NBS as a senior broadcasting officer in Lagos, which enabled him to observe political, social, and economic events in the country at close quarters. In playing that role, Achebe appropriated the writing and storytelling skills he had learned in secondary school and university to advantage. Ralph Opara, who joined the Talks Department of NBS three years after Achebe, described the importance of the department close to how Achebe himself could have seen it as well:

> [The] Talks Department was important, because the basis of broadcasting was the spoken word. The Talks Department was responsible for all programs, especially the informative and educative ones like "Radio Lawyer" for instance. Anyone who joined Broadcasting House as a graduate was sent to the Talks Department. It was important that the distinction between what one heard and what one read be made.[11]

While Achebe's day job was radio broadcasting, he could have been working privately on his fiction writing at night and during his vacations. I suspect that he started writing the drafts of some of his novels – the first one, at least – while he was still in college. And I also imagine how tedious it must have been for him to write and publish four groundbreaking novels, *Things Fall Apart* published in 1958, *No Longer at Ease* in 1960, *Arrow of God* in 1964, and *A Man of the People* in 1966, in eight successive years while simultaneously working full time at the NBS. It could be argued, however, that storytelling, albeit in writing, was naturally easy for him because of his innate talent plus the training he received at home and in all three levels of his Western education.

Nevertheless, three factors seem to have prompted Achebe to publish those novels in succession – namely, audience, timing, and the march for political independence in Nigeria and other African countries.

Through his university education, Achebe knew that the Western world sincerely believed that Africans lacked culture and civilization, which they used as a subterfuge and ruse to partition and colonize the continent, and to buy and sell her peoples as slaves. For that reason, Achebe needed a platform from where he could write his protest novels against those erroneous Western beliefs about Africa and her peoples. As he attempted to play the role of the novelist as teacher, he needed the right and immediate audience for his pedagogic argument, and that audience comprised Nigerian and other African students and teachers, who must clearly understand their native cultures first in order to compare and contrast them with what Westerners were telling them through their mission churches and colonial school systems. Achebe began educating his audience in Igbo culture, customs, and traditions that were in conflict with Western ways of life in his first novel, *Things Fall Apart*. For example, as we saw earlier regarding religious education, Achebe created a knowledgeable Igbo religious leader Akunna, who stood his ground while a white missionary Mr. Brown argued against the Igbo belief in what he called a polytheistic Godhead Chukwu. But Akunna firmly counter-argued that although the Igbo approach their high god through many intermediaries, such as gods and goddesses, and shrines, they too, like Christians believe in a supreme God whom they call Chukwu; he made all the world and other gods, goddesses, and deities. Achebe told the story because he was aware of the concept of the Igbo Godhead, which an Igbo Professor of Sociology, Victor C. Uchendu, contrasted with that of the Christians as follows:

> The Igbo high god is a withdrawn god. He is a god who has finished all active work of creation and keeps watch over his creatures from a distance. [Hence] The Igbo high god is not worshipped directly. There is neither shrine nor priest dedicated to his service. He gets no direct sacrifice from the living but is conceived as an ultimate receiver of all sacrifice made to the major deities. (In fact, Igbo sacrifice to any unknown and uninvited deities who might be present.) He seldom interferes in the affairs of men, a characteristic which sets him apart from all other deities, spirits, and ancestors. He is a satisfied god who is not jealous of the prosperity of men on earth.[12]

Achebe created characters who serve as priests and priestesses of gods, goddesses, and their shrines in *Things Fall Apart* and *Arrow of God* as a means of explaining the essential tenets of the traditional Igbo religion and worldview that govern their daily behavior in all areas of their lives. He succinctly makes it clear to his audience that the so-called Igbo worship of many gods and the performance of their religious rites have some correspondences in Christian performances of religious rites and use of icons, such as the cross, the altar, the Eucharist, as well as intermediaries, such as angels, saints, and priests. The differences between both religions derive from their divergent belief systems.

For Achebe's audiences to understand the correspondences and contrasts in both religions, which he romanticizes in his novels, they need to consult books that contain relevant cultural exegesis. For example, in my book *Gods, Oracles and Divination: Folkways in Chinua Achebe's Novels*, I focus on "folkways," the inclusive category of verbal performances peculiar to the world of Achebe's novels: cosmology, traditional religion; gods, divination, names; rituals, ceremonies; proverbs; tales; songs and chants; and language (See the blurb on the book, which Robert Wren wrote). The insider's exegesis should help outsiders to understand many Igbo folkways, just as Africans who embrace Christianity are taught the ways of God through catechism, Sunday school lessons, and books published on Christian theology. For the readers' benefit, however, Achebe also granted numerous interviews and published articles in which he explained concepts of Igbo culture and traditional religion, for example, the concept of "Chi in Igbo Cosmology" published in *Morning Yet on Creation Day*.[13]

The timing of the publication of the novels by Chinua Achebe was literarily and politically auspicious; for the novels can be interpreted as realizations in fiction of the same spirit that expressed itself politically in the struggle for independence by African sociopolitical leaders, who knew that unless they fought hard at that moment in history to wrest political powers from their respective erstwhile European colonial masters, their people would continue to suffer in perpetual bondage. Inspired by the vision of such leaders, Achebe became a literary legend when he founded the "modern African novel" with the publication of *Things Fall Apart* and three additional hybrid novels. All that happened because of his awareness that in 1948, when he was at UCI, political leaders were already fighting for Nigeria's self-rule, prompting British officials to draft various constitutions for the country, and inspiring Nigerians to form political parties, which eventually led to Great Britain granting them self-rule in 1957.

Like the political leaders, Achebe was waging a literary war of independence privately. One year after they won self-rule for Nigeria, Achebe published *Things Fall Apart*, which critically analyzed how the British came and colonized Nigeria, taking over the political, social, religious, and economic powers of Igbo elders. He also analyzed how the people, led by the strongman Okonkwo of Umuofia *Obododike* (Umuofia the land of the brave), made gallant but unsuccessful efforts to prevent the whites from finding a foothold in their clan. Furthermore, the Nigerian political leaders worked harder and finally won political independence for the country in 1960, a year in which Achebe's own hard work paid off through the publication of his second novel, *No Longer at Ease*. Seeing the dividends of their hard work, both the politicians and the writer continued to strive for further achievements: the politicians won a republican status for Nigeria in 1963, and Achebe published *Arrow of God* in 1964. Thus, both the politicians and the novelist had high optimism for their country and her peoples. Unfortunately, however, despite that optimism, Nigeria's march for true political and socioeconomic independence suddenly began to unravel.

With the eye of an eagle on an *Iroko* tree, Achebe foresaw the calamity that would result from the deadly political events that were precariously taking place

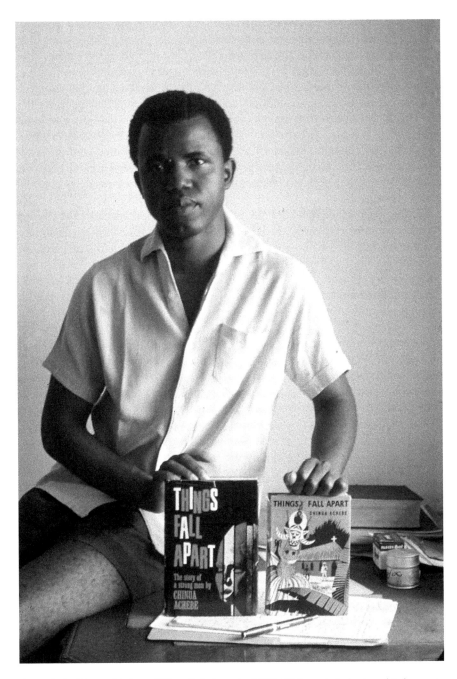

Figure 2.1 After publishing *Things Fall Apart* in 1958, Chinua Achebe is at his house in Enugu, Nigeria, 1959

Source: Getty Images

in Western Nigeria and the Plateau area of Northern Nigeria. So he published his fourth novel *A Man of the People* in January 1966, detailing the brazen corruption in independent Nigeria that the political leaders and government officials were unable to stop. As a result, the narrator called for a military intervention: "But the Army obliged us by staging a coup at that point and locking up every member of the Government" (147–48). Coincidentally, however, the coup that Achebe's narrator craved as a means of ending the corruption and social malaise in the fictive Nigeria became the first real bloody coup that took place in Nigeria on January 15, 1966. It turned into the catalyst for the waging of the Nigeria-Biafra War, from July 1967 through January 1970. Achebe did not publish any other novels during the war. Instead, he played the role of Biafran Ambassador Extraordinaire, using his storytelling skills to explain to foreign countries the emergence of Biafra as a young republic.

Finally, to conclude our brief discussion of the life and education of Chinua Achebe, we must emphasize the lessons he learned on his educational journey, lessons that budding writers should take to heart. For Achebe, the preparations he made involved acquiring first the storytelling habits of his people and their cultural folkways, and then finding the right audience and timing of his individual publications. Secondly, he developed the dual purpose of using his protest writings not only to showcase the importance and beauty of his Igbo culture but also to prove wrong the white man's claim that Africans had no culture. His acquisition of Western storytelling skills enabled him to speak in a language and manner that Westerners could understand. In the end, the combination of both native and foreign storytelling skills he acquired through two kinds of education enabled him to publish *Things Fall Apart*, the first hybrid African novel that continues to serve as a template for budding African writers.

Notes

1   Achebe, *Morning Yet on Creation Day*, p. 133.
2   Ezenwa-Ohaeto, *Chinua Achebe*, p. 13.
3   Wren, *Those Magical Years*, pp. 61–2.
4   *Ibid.*, p. 59.
5   Kalu Ogbaa, *Gods, Oracles and Divination: Folkways in Chinua Achebe's Novels*. Trenton, NJ: Africa World Press, 1992.
6   Alan Dundes, *The Study of Folklore*. Englewood Cliffs, NJ: Prentice-Hall, 1965: 37.
7   Ruth Finnegan, *Oral Literature in Africa*. Nairobi, Kenya: Oxford University Press, 1970: 12.
8   Wren, *Those Magical Years*, p. 51.
9   Bernth Lindfors, *Early Achebe*. Trenton, NJ: Africa World Press, 2003: 5–35.
10 *Ibid.*, p. 3.
11 Ezenwa-Ohaeto, *Chinua Achebe*, p. 56.
12 Victor C. Uchendu, *The Igbo of Southeast Nigeria*. New York: Holt, Rinehart and Winston, 1965: 94.
13 Achebe, *Morning Yet on Creation Day*, p. 131.

3 The Four Phases of Chinua Achebe's Writing Career

In my book, *A Century of Nigerian Literature: A Select Bibliography*,[1] I divided the literary works that Nigerian authors published during the twentieth century into four broad periods – namely, Early Colonial Period (1900–1952); Late Colonial Period (1953–1960); Early Postcolonial Period (1961–1970); and Late Postcolonial Period (1971–1999). The research I conducted for the book showed that Chinua Achebe was a dominant literary figure whose publications spanned the last three of those periods and beyond. In this chapter, however, his writing career occurred in four broad phases: Phase I (1952–1966), which was his most productive period; Phase II (1967–1970), the civil war period in which he wrote mainly shorter literary pieces, such as poems, short stories, and political speeches; Phase III (1971–1989), the postwar period in which he took up teaching appointments in one Nigerian university (the University of Nigeria, Nsukka) and in four American universities: the University of Massachusetts, Amherst, the University of Connecticut, Storrs, Dartmouth College, and City College in the City University of New York, as well as in one Canadian university, the University of Guelph. At these foreign universities, he held such positions as Distinguished Visiting Professor of English and Fulbright Professor of African Studies. At this time, he did some deep brooding and introspection on the incidents of the civil war that resulted in his writing longer pieces of literature based on the war and its aftermath, as well as critical essays on African literature and cultures; and, Phase IV (1990–2013), the late twentieth century and early twenty-first century, during which period Achebe continued to teach and give public lectures on African literature in his capacity as Professor of Africana Studies and Professor of Literature, and as Writer-in-Residence at two other American universities: Bard College (1990–2009) and Brown University (2010–2013). He also occasionally visited his native Nigeria, where he gave inspirational public speeches, especially to his ethnic Igbo people who seemed to have lost their sociopolitical bearing in Nigerian geopolitics as a result of their defeat during the Nigeria-Biafra War. Above all, Achebe published his last book, *There Was a Country: A Personal History of Biafra*, in 2012 before his demise in 2013 while still serving at Brown University.

Phase I (1952–1966): This phase of Achebe's published works began with his undergraduate writings, which he published in his final year at the University College, Ibadan. For example, one of his first essays is "Philosophy," which he

DOI: 10.4324/9781003184133-3

published in defense of philosophy lectures that had been attacked by another student's essay "Holy Devil" in a preceding issue of one of the students' magazines called the *Bug*.[2] He also published another poem in *Bug*, titled "Hiawatha," which was a stinging indictment of what Achebe considered rude, unintelligent behavior that some UCI male students exhibited toward a group of visiting secondary school female students from St. Teresa's College, Ibadan, who staged a performance of the musical "Hiawatha" at the university. The content and tone of the essay clearly demonstrated Achebe's opposition to the uncouth cultural behavior of the Nigerian college students who were supposed to be the cultural avant-garde of the whole country. The essay also glimpses the overall respect that Achebe shows for female characters, which readers often encounter in his post-graduation writings. Although the UCI students who Achebe criticized in the essay did not like what he wrote about them, he was undeterred in exhibiting the same bravado in his future writings in which he would call out people who treat others rudely or unfairly, no matter their gender, nationality, or race, all of which means that he expected students at the time to act as "Ladies and Gentlemen at Ibadan."

We see the same cultured streak in Chinua Achebe's next essay, "An Argument Against the Existence of Faculties," which he wrote for the *University Herald*. In the essay, he lamented the tendency of the UCI administration to narrow rather than broaden the education of its students by compelling them to choose between two separate and mutually exclusive streams of study.[3] After reading the essay, I was highly impressed by what Achebe did and wondered whether any other students at the time were capable of mustering up the kind of courage that he did in challenging the colonial authorities of the institution in the face of possible expulsion from Nigeria's premier university college. I doubt seriously that many students in today's Nigerian universities possess Achebe's kind of courage to speak openly against the bad policies that the administrators of their institutions make without the fear of some form of punishment from the administrators.

Nevertheless, some of Achebe's classmates and professors wrote positive reviews of his published essays and letters, which might have contributed partially to his decision to change his major from science (medicine), for which he was originally admitted to study at UCI, to arts (English, history, and comparative religion). Upon making that momentous decision, Achebe dabbled in creative writing. The outcome was that he published in the *University Herald*, a medium through which he practiced in preparation for his writing career after college. For example, drawing from his experiences of living in a village and attending church therein, Achebe wrote some essays and short stories such as "In a Village Church", "Dead Men's Path", "The Old Order in the End", "Marriage Is a Private Affair", and "The Old Order in Conflict with the New". Through these publications, Achebe reminisced about the life he lived in the village, his engagement in church activities, and the clash of cultures between the villagers and the missionaries. Those activities culminated in the entrenchment of white culture in the village that Achebe metaphorically represented as the new order in conflict with the old native order. From those publications, one can conclude that

Achebe the UCI undergraduate was obsessed with culture conflicts. Hence, he published a short story he titled "The Polar Undergraduate" in which he openly expressed his inner feelings to his audience.

Achebe later revised and re-envisioned some of the short stories and essays and added them as segments of incidents in some of his novels and critical works. For instance, the contents of "Marriage Is a Private Affair" were recreated in *No Longer at Ease* to demonstrate that marriage in Igbo country was never a private affair; instead, it is a community affair as the London-educated characters, Clara and Obi Okonkwo, sadly discovered during their ill-fated courtship. Furthermore, in the conflicts between the old and the new orders found in one story that he simply titled "Short Story" published in *University Herald* 5, No. 2 (1952–1953): 4–5, the new order won over the old. But in its recreated version, this time with a specific title "Dead Men's Path," which he published in *Girls at War and Other Stories* (pp. 78–82), the old order won over the new. When asked why he did not allow one order to win over the other in both versions of the story, Achebe gave the following response that shows how he grappled with issues generally while writing his stories:

> I never will take the stand that the Old must win or that the New must win. If I wrote two stories in which the Old man won in one, the New in the other, I would be happy. To me, that is the way life is.
>
> In Obi's story the marriage didn't come through because the woman is tabooed, and cult consideration, not tribe, is the primary issue. The fact that they failed does not mean that I believe that all young men caught in such conflicts must go the way of Obi.
>
> I never believe in taking firm positions and if I do two novels, I try to make sure that the same thing does not happen twice. . . . The point is that no single truth satisfied me – and this is well founded in the Igbo world view. No single man can be correct, all the time, no single idea can be totally correct. If you pick any proverb that seems to put forward a particular point of view, you can always find another one that seeks to contradict it.[4]

The literary critic Bernth Lindfors was highly impressed by Achebe's undergraduate publications and by those of his classmates. Hence, he did some study of the UCI student publications that laid the foundation for the growth of modern Nigerian literature. The result of the study, which gives full information on the subject to readers, was published in an article, "Popular Literature for an African Elite."[5]

The point about this aspect of our discussion is that Achebe's experimentation with creative writing and publishing at UCI can be metaphorically likened to Jesus Christ's 40-day sojourn in the wilderness where he prepared himself spiritually for his unique religious ministry, despite the fact that there were already some prophets, such as Moses, Isaiah, and John the Baptist, whose teachings were already well established before the advent of Christ. When Achebe began writing his novels, there were already other Nigerian writers, such as Cyprian Ekwensi, Bassey Etim-Okon, and Amos Tutuola, whose published works were already in the market. But unlike them, Achebe resisted the temptation of writing in the traditional style of the colonialists, which he felt would not enable him to express fully what and how he felt about his native Igbo and other African cultures that Western writers were denigrating in their "novels about Africa." And not knowing what distinguished a short story from any other form of fiction when he began his studies at UCI caused Achebe to teach himself how to do creative writing. Thus, his self-education could be seen in this regard as a blessing in disguise; for he said the following in a BBC radio interview:

> I never learnt the craft of writing. When I went to school nobody talked about writing, nobody imagined there would be writers, so there was nobody who was ready to teach it. Now an interesting thing happened when I was a student at Ibadan. I'd never written anything, really, and the English Department decided to have a competition in short story writing. And so we wrote short stories. I'd never written short stories, so I didn't know what short stories were supposed to be, really. I wrote what I thought was a short story and my teacher said, "This is interesting, but it isn't quite a short story." So I said, "What is a short story? I'd like to know," and she never told me. So that's as much teaching as I got in writing.[6]

Achebe struggled for a long time to understand what a short story really was. However, his quest eventually led him to learn, practice, and master the craft of writing not only short stories but also novels, poetry, and critical essays. In the end, his African-centered writings were so popular and well received that they became a blueprint for other budding African literary writers and critics.

To reiterate what we said earlier, Chinua Achebe's fame as a writer began with the publication of his first novel *Things Fall Apart*. Published in 1958 to great critical acclaim at the height of African political independence movements, *Things Fall Apart* is a watershed novel in which artistic achievement and cultural reeducation form a perfect balance. When it appeared in world markets and academic institutions, the novel was immediately recognized as a model for budding novelists by African writers and critics, as a literary classic by Canadian and American critics, and (not unexpectedly) as a novel of protest by British critics and press. In spite of these divergent critical evaluations of the novel, the common point of agreement is that, in developing the character of his hero Okonkwo, Achebe combined the techniques of literary modernism, the socio-literary philosophy of naturalism, and Igbo storytelling devices to recapitulate the history and consequences of the late nineteenth-century African encounter with European colonialism.

Having sold to date 11 million copies in 55 languages worldwide in 1990, *Things Fall Apart* became unquestionably the most widely read, best-selling, and influential book in modern African literature. According to Lindfors, "Indeed, it has outsold all the rest of the three hundred titles in Heinemann's African Writers Series combined. One reason this novel became such a runaway bestseller is that it was quickly adopted for use as a textbook in high school and university

English classes, particularly in Africa and notably in Nigeria."[7] Also, the novel has made a difference in the lives of its African readers, who have since begun to appreciate Achebe's message: "One big message, of the many that I try to put across, is that Africa was not a vacuum before the coming of Europe, that culture was not unknown in Africa, that culture was not brought to Africa by the white world."[8] The message has since helped to create in Africans a sense of pride in their past (however imperfect it was), as well as modifying to some extent the cultural bigotry of Europeans, for the novel forces readers to acknowledge the validity of African culture.

Part of the immediate appeal of *Things Fall Apart* lay in the fact that until its publication, no other African novel contained such a wide range of both literary and historical references; nor had any other African novelist yet displayed the kind of craftsmanship Achebe exhibits in this novel, where he holistically interweaves Igbo customary activities, the people's worldview and beliefs, and their material possessions into a rich tapestry, thereby helping to demolish the cultural presumptions of Europeans in the novels they wrote about Africa. Instead of offering a stereotypical depiction of Africa as the "heart of darkness" and its people as "primitives" and "savages," Achebe delineates Umuofia as a human community of nine villages, and his characters are human beings who possess minds, a language, a religion, and culture, with vices and virtues like other groups of people in the world. In that human community, readers find clan leaders such as the levelheaded Obierika and his friend Okonkwo, who, although not as levelheaded, is nonetheless as pious and nationalistic. In other words, despite Okonkwo's tragic flaws, the two men are able to work together for the common good of their community, their differences in character, temperament, and conduct notwithstanding.[9]

The ideas in the three preceding paragraphs are culled from the Introduction of my book *Understanding Things Fall Apart: A Casebook to Issues, Sources, and Historical Documents*.[10] The purpose of repeating them here is to reemphasize Achebe's overall objectives, narrative techniques, and craftsmanship in this novel, which he maintains in most of his other novels, especially *Arrow of God*, and which I characterize as a rural novel like *Things Fall Apart*. Furthermore, in the Introduction of the casebook, I cited Achebe's point that stories are the very center, the heart of our civilization and culture. For it is the story that conveys all our gains, all our failures, all we hold dear and all we condemn. To convey this to the next generation is the only way we can keep going and keep alive as a people. Therefore, the story is like the genes that are transferred to create a new being. It is far more important than anything else is.

Despite his obsessive ambition to tell African stories because of what they mean to him and his fellow Africans, Achebe could not have become the renowned raconteur he is today if he had not learned to write with both his right hand and his left hand, so to speak: the right hand representing the Igbo storytelling skills he acquired while growing up in Igboland, and the left hand representing the Western creative writing skills he developed while studying at the University College in Ibadan, Nigeria. His successful combination of these two apparently divergent but necessary skills resulted in the narrative techniques and craftsmanship that enabled him to extend the possibilities of the novel as a potent medium of expressing the people's folklore, oral history, and folk entertainment while simultaneously allowing him to serve as a novelist, teacher, and social critic.[11] His fame, which first rested on the publication of *Things Fall Apart* (a novel that sold 20 million copies in 57 translations worldwide before its 60th anniversary in 2018), was consolidated by his publication of three other novels in the same first phase of his writing career.

No Longer at Ease (1960), chronologically Achebe's second novel, contains a setting, incidents, and characters one would normally expect to resemble those of the first novel and precede those of the third novel, *Arrow of God* (1964), but they do not. Instead, the setting, incidents, and characters in the latter are virtually similar to those of *Things Fall Apart* (1958) and thus precede those of the second novel. For, whereas in *No Longer at Ease*, the white characters were rapidly consolidating the foothold their predecessors secured in *Things Fall Apart*, the Nigerians, while still doing everything they could to repel the British and white missionary efforts, no longer could resort to using crude military confrontation as Okonkwo and the Egwugwu did in *Things Fall Apart*. Instead, the missionaries collaborated with the British administrative and political officials to build churches and schools through which they converted some Igbo adults and trained their children through whom they created a new social order in Umuaro. In addition, the colonial officers appointed warrant chiefs through whom they ruled the natives indirectly. Consequently, the collaborative efforts of the British colonial officers and missionaries resulted in the Igbo children and adult Christian converts acquiring enough Western education to enable them to land good-paying jobs with the church and other colonial institutions, such as serving as lay preachers and readers in the church, interpreters, tax collectors, court messengers, and prison warders for the government officials. That way, a new labor force emerged in the villages, which made it almost impossible for the natives to resist the economic advantages the new dispensation provided to the people even as it was changing the old order in which the people lived and had their being before the advent of white people in their land.

Furthermore, we find that the churches the missionaries built in *Things Fall Apart* served as a precursor to the churches and schools they built in *Arrow of God*. Although Okonkwo would not allow his son Nwoye to join the missionaries, nevertheless Nwoye ran away from home and joined the missionaries in Umuru, where he was converted, renamed Isaac, and trained as a catechist. He served the church as Isaac Okonkwo in *No Longer at Ease*. The process that the British used to create a new social order in *Things Fall Apart* continued in *Arrow of God*. Ezeulu the Chief Priest of Ulu sent his son Obika "to be my eye" in the white man's church and school. He did so after realizing that the white administrator of his part of Nigeria was so powerful because of the education he acquired in his home country Great Britain. He felt that power directly when the District Commissioner summoned him and demanded that he become his warrant chief. After that encounter, Ezeulu decided that his son should acquire that kind of power which only Western education can confer on his son, which would be added to the power that his Igbo family already had. But that secret plan backfired on him, resulting in his becoming demented and shamed by rival elders of his clan. They saw through the cunning and unethical method he used to acquire personal power instead of acquiring it cleanly for the common good of his people. Hence, they concluded that his son's death and his dementia were punishments that came from their god Ulu:

> So in the end only Umuaro and its leaders saw the final outcome. To them the issue was simple. Their god had taken sides with them against his headstrong and ambitious priest and thus upheld the wisdom of their ancestors – that no man however great was greater than his people; that no one ever won judgement against his clan.
>
> (p. 230)

But as Achebe said in the BBC interview we quoted earlier in this chapter, he grappled with how to conclude each of his stories because, to him, no single truth satisfies him and no single man can be correct, all the time; no single idea can be totally correct. That is why the narration of the novel is ended with a paragraph containing an intriguing Igbo worldview, which should compel readers to pause, analyze, and have a good apprehension of Achebe's overall cultural teaching in the novel:

> If this was so then Ulu had chosen a dangerous time to uphold that truth for in destroying his priest he had also brought disaster on himself, like the lizard in the fable who ruined his mother's funeral by his own hand. For a deity who chose a moment such as this to chastise his priest or abandon him before his enemies was inciting people to take liberties; and Umuaro was just ripe to do so. The Christian harvest which took place a few days after Obika's death saw more people than even Goodcountry could have dreamed. In his extremity many a man sent his son with a yam or two to offer to the new religion and bring back the promised immunity. Thereafter any yam harvested in his field was harvested in the name of the son.
>
> (p. 230)

Although the elders found Ezeulu's act of sending his son abhorrent, what they failed to realize was that he, ironically, paved the way for other parents to follow. The passage expresses Achebe's belief in cultural dualism. For, considering his narrative technique in context, neither the Igbo traditional religion nor Christianity had absolute truth, and neither had their educational systems. That is why, as a dynamic and intellectual priest, Ezeulu not only wanted his people to maintain the good things in their folkways but also to examine all aspects of the new way of life that the British were bringing to his community. That way, they could exploit some of them to their benefit. We see that clearly in the last sentence of the novel, "Therefore any yam harvested in his field was harvested in the name of the son." The double meaning occurs in the use of the words, "field" and "son." The people did not realize that they were subverting their traditional religion by not waiting for Ezeulu to announce the day of the new yam harvest before harvesting the yams. Ironically, the yams harvested "in the name of the son" were for a sacrifice to the Son of God, Jesus Christ, the foundation of the Church and mission schools which the Igbo sons attended, and not for the promotion of their own traditional religion. Thus, the sacrifice was also metaphorically offered to quench the sons' famished appetite for the white man's religion and education, which the Umuaro clansmen were vehemently fighting against when they noticed that Ezeulu had not only befriended a British official, Captain Winterbottom but also had sent his son to acquire a foreign education and religion. That way, the Umuaro clan became the field from whence the two white institutions "harvested" Igbo sons as Christian converts and schoolchildren without their traditionally conservative parents' clear understanding of the whole conflicting situation. That is why "the Christian harvest which took place after Obika's death saw more people than even Goodcountry could have dreamed" (p. 230).

So in the end, one finds that the great effort the British started making toward total colonization of the Igbo people in *Things Fall Apart* and *Arrow of God* (both novels set in Igbo clans) resulted in well-established churches and primary schools. Thereafter a British political system flourished in *No Longer at Ease*, a novel set in a city outside Igbo country. Furthermore, Nigeria was politically on the verge of getting its independence from Great Britain. And in that novel as well, the country had already made some educational effort that produced some elementary and secondary school graduates who were seeking employment in the country's colonial civil service. That is, while some students acquired their college education at home from the University College, Ibadan, others like Clara and Obi Okonkwo acquired theirs abroad in England. Upon returning home to Nigeria, the university graduates were enthusiastic and ready to take over civil service leadership roles from British officials, like Mr. Greene, who were about to depart Nigeria for their home country. And the sociopolitical leaders from all parts of Nigeria were all hopeful that the Nigerian graduates of foreign universities would play important roles that could add to the achievements of the politicians, thereby bringing about total independence to Nigerians in all areas of their lives. Unfortunately, however, some of the university graduates in the leadership cadre of the civil service became corrupt like Obi Okonkwo and took bribes from people who sought educational opportunities in their offices. From that point on in Nigerian sociopolitical history, bribery, and corruption became an entrenched bane of society.

The focus of *No Longer at Ease* is essentially the trial of Obi Okonkwo who took bribes while working in the pre-independent Nigerian civil service, a crime that people did not expect from a highly educated man like him. However, his crime in that novel pales in comparison to the overarching bribery and corruption that political leaders committed in postcolonial Nigeria, which Achebe accurately fictionalized in *A Man of the People* (1966). Ostensibly, Achebe used Obi Okonkwo's crime to anticipate the political crimes in the latter novel. Just as the bigoted Mr. Greene asserts in *No Longer at Ease* that the African is corrupt through and through, the narrator Odili, after witnessing the political corruption in the country firsthand, laments in *A Man of the People* that the political leaders were those "who had started the country off down the slopes of inflation" (p. 2). At the time Achebe published the novel, some African countries, just like Nigeria, had won political independence from their erstwhile colonial masters, and their citizens initially believed that their poor socioeconomic conditions would improve because their native political leaders were in charge of their countries' affairs. Unfortunately, however, four years after Nigeria attained political independence, things went from bad to worse for the citizens. Achebe uses eating metaphors to describe political parties and their roles in government. For example, the politicians refer to the national treasury as national cake that they are constantly sharing without thinking of how the cake is produced in the first place. Also, he uses the acronyms of the two major political parties, POP (People's Organization Party) and PAP (Progressive Alliance Party), to connote their reckless and insatiable drinking, eating, and merriments at the expense of the masses: POP for pop soda and alcoholic drinks as when Chief Nanga asked an old man to entertain them with whiskey for him and soda for Mr. Samalu (p. 33); and PAP referring to the common man's cereal called pap, which looks and tastes like custard, that many Nigerians eat as breakfast.

The devastating politicians' corruption and misrule of the country caused the narrator to call on the army to rescue the citizens from the socioeconomic malaise they were experiencing:

> [But] the Army obliged us by staging a coup at that point and locking up every member of the Government. The rampaging bands of election thugs had caused so much unrest and dislocation that our young Army officers seized the opportunity to take over. We were told Nanga was arrested trying to escape by canoe dressed like a fisherman.
>
> (pp. 147–8)

In the concluding paragraph of the novel, a reader can feel, almost taste the narrator's revulsive reaction to the politicians' horrible and unbridled corruption and looting of the national treasury, which ostensibly justifies the military action the army took to overthrow the civilian regime:

> "Koko has taken enough for the owner to see," said my father to me. . . . But in the affairs of the nation, the laws of the village became powerless. . . . For I do honestly believe that in the fat-dripping, gummy, eat-and-let-eat regime just ended – a regime which inspired the common saying that a man could only be sure of what he put away safely in his gut or, in a language ever more suited to the time: "you chop, me self I chop, palaver finish"; a regime in which you saw a fellow cursed in the morning for stealing a blind man's stick and later in the evening saw him again mounting the altar of the new shrine in the presence of all the people to whisper into the ear of the chief

celebrant – in such a regime, I say, you died a good death if life had inspired someone to come forward and shoot your murderer in the chest – without asking to be paid.

(pp. 149–50)

Coincidentally in real life, the army staged the first bloody coup in Nigeria on January 15, 1966, which eventually led to other coups and countercoups, and the waging of the Nigeria-Biafra War (1967–1970). Consequently, the war ushered in a cycle of corruption in all the postwar military administrations of Nigeria from 1967 through 1999. Since then, all the efforts Nigeria made to re-establish democratically elected civil governments failed to produce good governance. And that has been so because ex-military leaders have been serving as presidents or working behind the scenes as advisors in all the postwar government administrations. Thus, the entrenched bribery, corruption, and brazen embezzlement of money in the postwar government systems have continued to earn Nigeria the reputation of being ranked among the most corrupt nations of the world every year. Disturbed by what he observed and hence wanting to offer a solution to it, Achebe made bold to fictionalize the roles of the military in Nigeria's governance in his postwar novel, *Anthills of the Savannah* (1987), which we examine under Phase III of his publications.

Phase II (1967–1970): This phase of Chinua Achebe's writing covers the Nigeria-Biafra War (also known as the Nigerian Civil War) period. Achebe was appointed Biafran Ambassador Extraordinaire by the government of the Sovereign Republic of Biafra to plead to the outside world the cause of the new country predominantly occupied by his native Igbo people that just seceded from Nigeria. Achebe used his literary fame to persuade international audiences in Europe, Asia, and the Americas to come and save Biafra from the brutality of three nations – Nigeria, Great Britain, and the USSR – but all to no avail. While many of his writings were comprised mostly of political speeches, others were literary, focusing specifically on such shorter pieces as poems, short stories, and essays through which he described the effects of the gruesome war on the peoples of Biafra. Although the manuscripts of many of the pieces were written during the war, they were officially published after the war. Some of the war poems appeared in *Beware, Soul Brother and Other Poems* (Enugu: Nwankwo-Ifejika, 1971). Its revised and enlarged edition was published in London by Heinemann Educational Books, in 1972. And the war short stories appear in *Girls at War and Other Stories*, which also was published in London by Heinemann Educational Books in 1972.

However, the 30-month-old Nigeria-Biafra War and the role Achebe played in it did a lot to bring diplomatic recognition to Biafra as a sovereign nation and the survival of its citizens. Achebe headed one of the directorates that His Excellency and President of Biafra, General Ojukwu, created as the Information Directorate whose functions went beyond the physical wellbeing of the troops and touched every fabric of Biafra's life. The President created it to give people information on Biafra generally and to counteract the evil effects of the propaganda warfare that

Nigeria and its British allies were waging against Biafra. Through the directorate, Biafra tried hard to offset the disinformation that Nigeria was feeding the world: that Biafrans were rebels who were fighting a secessionist war against their fatherland Nigeria; and also that the Nigeria-Biafra War was a civil war – Nigeria's internal business – which did not warrant any outside intervention and interference. In contrast, the Biafrans considered it a war between two sovereign nations that should be arbitrated by international bodies like the United Nations (UN) and the Organization of African Unity (OAU). Unfortunately, however, Biafra's argument was considered untenable by some foreign countries and by the then UN Secretary-General, Mr. U Thant, who felt that the Biafran officials should first seek diplomatic recognition of Biafra as an independent and foreign nation before fighting for any rights that its citizens were passionately craving.

To achieve the desired international recognition for his young nation, General Ojukwu quickly appointed Ambassadors Extraordinaire (including Chinua Achebe) to travel all over the world pleading the Biafran cause before foreign governments and international organizations. Moreover, Ojukwu appointed a career diplomat, Mr. Augustine S. O. Okwu, to serve as a resident ambassador to East Africa. Following the combined ambassadors' diplomatic efforts, four Black African countries – Tanzania, Zambia, Ivory Coast, and Gabon – as well as one Caribbean country, Haiti, recognized Biafra as a sovereign republic. The ambassadors' efforts also yielded some fruits in the humanitarian field. For example, with the influence of an Igbo Catholic Cardinal, Francis A. Arinze, and a former Igbo President of the World Council of Churches, Dr. Francis Akanu Ibiam, Caritas International, and the World Council of Churches respectively sent food and medical supplies unrelentingly to Biafra. But the UN Secretary-General U Thant (a Burmese), the British Foreign Minister Lord Carrington, and the head of the Nigerian military junta Major General Gowon impeded the humanitarian efforts of the church organizations. In addition, Gowon and his international supporters made it difficult for the UN organization ICRC to airlift any Red Cross medical and other relief supplies directly into Biafran territories until toward the end of the war, when they had made sure Biafra was no longer a viable military threat to Nigeria.

Politically, Achebe served as the leader of a group of Igbo university professors and intellectuals, such as Ikenna Nzimiro, Emmanuel Obiechina, Michael Echeruo, Donatus Nwoga, and Adiele Afigbo, as well as some sociopolitical leaders who worked on a famous document known as the "Ahiara Declaration," which General Ojukwu delivered to the citizens of Biafra as a means to explain the principles of the Biafran Revolution with the hope of creating a better society for his people when fully implemented. Radio Biafra, which Achebe also helped to develop, became an indefatigable mouthpiece of the young republic, which broadcast news from Biafra to the outside world. It consistently broadcast the impassioned speeches that President Ojukwu made to Biafran citizens and to foreign countries and organizations, appealing for their recognition and support of Biafra. The Ahiara Declaration, which became the bedrock of the Biafran Revolution, was carried live as the President delivered it. In a word, it succinctly explained to Biafran citizens and the world at large the Biafran spirit, its social, economic, and political philosophy. It also glimpsed the style of governance that future rulers would adopt in postwar Biafra.[12]

Phase III (1970–1989): After the war officially ended on January 15, 1970, Chinua Achebe, like other surviving ex-Biafrans, returned with his family members to his hometown of Ogidi to start a new life, including resuming his writing career, which was greatly stalled by the war situations. First of all, he revised and published some of the shorter pieces of literature he wrote during the war, which he followed up with the writing of more poems, short stories, and children's books. Thereafter, he wrote some essays, articles, and books on politics in which he expressed his personal views on the war, as well as on the postwar reconstruction of the reunited Nigeria. In addition, his literary output at this time included some critical articles and essays that revealed his inner thoughts on the themes of African cultures and civilizations through its literature. Moreover, in his zeal to ensure that some of the ideas and visions of governance that he and other members of the Biafran Information Directorate enunciated in the Ahiara Declaration document during the war were implemented in postwar Igbo communities, Achebe sought a job at the University of Nigeria, Nsukka (UNN), and was appointed the Director of the African Studies Center.

Throughout the war years though, a renowned Igbo scholar, Professor Eni Njoku, served as the nominal Vice Chancellor of the university, replacing its British and American administrators who left Nigeria on the eve of the outbreak of the war. At the end of the armed conflict, however, the federal military government of Nigeria invited another Igbo academician who was living in London, Professor Herbert C. Kodilinye, to come home and serve as the first postwar Vice Chancellor of the institution. His appointment was considered unfortunate for the Igbo people; for because of his colonialist mentality, the federal government intentionally used him as a stooge – a black man with a "white" mind – to wreak vengeance on his own Igbo people who dared to fight what the Nigerian military authorities characterized as a war of secession against their fatherland Nigeria. In essence, Kodilinye was there to perform his administrative roles according to the dictates of his employers, policies that were against the wishes of the Igbo people, the real owners of the university. However, after a month or two into his vice-chancellorship, it became crystal clear to Igbo academic faculty and administrative staff of the university that, if not challenged, Kodilinye could run down the only Nigerian university in Igboland at the time, thereby fulfilling the objectives of the federal military government. Resultantly, Professors Chinua Achebe, Ikenna Nzimiro, and Emmanuel Obiechina created a weekly pamphlet, titled *Nsukkascope*, which offered stinging indictments against the policies and actions of the Kodilinye administration that were inimical to the students' interests and progress. Hence, the fighting troika brought so much pressure on the VC that he barely survived the full tenure of his office, from 1971 to 1975. Thereafter, following intensive negotiations between the federal government and the then-East Central State government officials, a true Igbo academic luminary, Professor James O. C.

Figure 3.1 1974, Visiting Professor Chinua Achebe at UMass

Source: UMass

Ezeilo, was appointed to replace Kodilinye. Ezeilo served as Vice Chancellor of the university from 1975 through 1978. Under his administration, UNN gradually regained its preeminent prewar academic leadership in Nigerian higher educational system as it engaged in viable academic competition with Nigeria's premier university, the University of Ibadan. Since then, UNN has striven to live by its motto, "To Restore the Dignity of Man."

Between 1973 and 1976, Achebe took a leave of absence from Nsukka to sojourn at the University of Massachusetts at Amherst and briefly at University of Connecticut, Storrs, where he gave many public lectures on modern African literature, culture, and civilization, as well as researching and writing articles through which he challenged Western critics' positions on Africa and its peoples. He focused especially on the cultural theory and content of Joseph Conrad's novella *Heart of Darkness*, which depicted continental Africa as a center of evil, and that its peoples had no cultures, civilizations, and any intelligible human languages. Moreover, he criticized the African characters in the novella as mere caricatures of human beings when compared to their European counterparts. The work Achebe did during his brief sojourn abroad caused Tijan M. Sallah and Ngozi Okonjo-Iweala to give him the moniker, "Chinua Achebe: Teacher of Light," which they adopted as the title of their biography of him in contrast to the darkness and gloom in Joseph Conrad's *Heart of Darkness*.

The essays he wrote to challenge Conrad's views on continental Africa and its peoples, as well as those of other European colonial writers like Joyce Cary, the author of *Mister Johnson*, and racist teachers include such titles as "Colonial Criticism", "Africa and Her Writers", "Language and the Destiny of Man", "What Do African Intellectuals Read?", "The Novelist as Teacher", "Where Angels Fear to Tread", "Thoughts on the African Novel", "The African Writer and the English Language", "Publishing in Africa: A Writer's View", "Named for Victoria, Queen of England", "Tanganyika – Jottings of a Tourist", "The African Writer and the Biafran Cause", "Dear Tai Solarin", "Onitsha, Gift of the Niger", and "Chi in Igbo Cosmology". Achebe later collected and published the essays in a book, titled *Morning Yet on Creation Day*, in New York, issued by Anchor Press/Doubleday, 1976. In those essays, Achebe played indeed the role of the novelist as teacher, refuting the European notion that Africans did not have viable cultures and civilizations until the Europeans came to "civilize" them. Achebe warned Africans to beware of what European writers and teachers offered to them, emphasizing the need for them to write from their own indigenous cultural experiences, and to build their own printing presses that would facilitate the publication of their literary works.

Furthermore, during some of the conferences on African literature in which he made presentations, Achebe warned that until Africans are able to embrace fully their cultural and historical experiences in their minds and thoughts, they would continue to be colonized intellectually through the writings of foreigners despite the fact that they had regained their political sovereignty from their former colonial masters. To date, his writings on the subject continue to resonate with, and inspire, budding African writers who use his novels, especially *Things Fall Apart*, as a template for writing novels that romanticize their individual countries' issues. In fact, one of the essays that Achebe presented in 1964, titled "The African Writer and the English Language" so provoked heated but necessary seminal arguments between Achebe from West Africa and Ngugi wa Thiong'o from East Africa, to the extent that other African writers began to ponder whether they should be writing solely in their indigenous languages or continue writing in English. Although Ngugi is a renowned, leading African writer who initially published most of his fiction in English language, he later led those who feel that African literature should be written primarily in indigenous African languages; he has also been writing in his native Gikuyu language since 1977, as well as in the widespread Kiswahili language – a tactical move that liberalized literary education in East Africa, an important sub-Saharan region.

Achebe, on the other hand, expressed a contrary view on the subject, saying that African writers must first understand the complex nature and definition of African literature before deciding in what language or languages it should be written:

> [What] all this suggests to me is that you cannot cram African literature into a small, neat definition. I do not see African literature as one unit but as a group of associated units – in fact the sum total of all the *national* and *ethnic* literatures of Africa.

A national literature is one that takes the whole nation for its province and has a realized or potential audience throughout its territory. In other words, a literature that is written in the national language. An ethnic literature is one which is available only to one ethnic group within the nation. If you take Nigeria as an example, the national literature, as I see it, is the literature written in English; and the ethnic literatures are in Hausa, Ibo, Yoruba, Efik, Edo, Ijaw, etc., etc.

Any attempt to define African literature in terms which overlook the complexities of the African scene at the material time is doomed to failure. After the elimination of white rule shall have been completed, the single most important fact in Africa in the second half of the twentieth century will appear to be the rise of individual nation-states. I believe that African literature will follow the same pattern.

[. . .]

I have indicated somewhat offhandedly that the national literature of Nigeria and of other countries of Africa is, or will be, written in English. This may sound like a controversial statement, but it isn't. All I have done has been to look at the reality of present-day Africa. This "reality" may change as a result of deliberate, e.g., political, action. If it does, an entirely new situation will arise, and there will be plenty of time to examine it. At present it may be more profitable to look at the scene as it is.[13]

Achebe felt that the English language would be able to carry the weight of his African experience. But it would have to be a new English, still in full communion with its ancestral home but altered to suit its new surroundings.[14]

On the other hand, in his counterargument to that of Achebe, Ngugi makes a radical demand for African writers to express their writings in indigenous African languages instead of English, insisting that his own early choice of the latter was based on European cultural imposition. Part of his argument reads as follows:

[I believe that] my writing in Gikuyu language, a Kenyan language, an African language, is part and parcel of the anti-imperialist struggles of Kenyan and African peoples. In schools and colleges our Kenyan languages – that is the languages of the many nationalities which make up Kenya – were associated with negative qualities of backwardness, underdevelopment, humiliation and punishment. We who went through that school system were meant to graduate with a hatred of the people and culture and the values of the language of our daily humiliation and punishment. I do not want Kenyan children growing up in that imperialist-imposed tradition of contempt for the tools of communication developed by their communities and their history. I want them to transcend colonial alienation.[15]

Ironically, however, it should be noted that without his adequate training in English, Ngugi could not have successfully acquired his high school education in Nairobi, Kenya, and college education in Makerere and Leeds, respectively, because none of the tertiary institutions he attended offered instructions in his native Gikuyu language. Without the superior knowledge of the English language, he might not have come across and understood some of the political and socioeconomic concepts that enabled him to fight imperialism critically in the works he wrote in standard English language. This is the "Caliban motif" in African literature: the colonized Africans learn the colonizers' foreign languages, which enable them to understand all the ramifications of colonialism, thereby empowering them to fight their colonizers in the languages they understand.

Because of the hegemonic influence that foreign education has had on former African colonial countries, the literary works of both renowned African writers – Achebe and Ngugi – are written primarily in the English language; they continue to resonate and attract more readership worldwide than the literary works written in any of the African indigenous languages.

Despite the advantage that the English language continues to have over the indigenous African languages, Achebe, like Ngugi, also wrote some important speeches in the Igbo language during the first decade of the twenty-first century, which he delivered to his native Igbo communities. However, such public speeches and lectures were presented in the form of what he preemptively defined as *ethnic* literature in his 1964 article, which were mentioned earlier. And presenting them in Igbo was an opportunity for him to talk specifically to the Igbo ethnic group on sociocultural and political issues because of the way they were marginalized after the Nigeria-Biafra War. But if the issues were of general concern to all Nigerian ethnic groups, he made his presentations in English as part of their *national* literature. An example of that shift in his use of language of expression is found in his last published book, *There Was a Country: A Personal History of Biafra* (2012). Achebe, writing belatedly in his native language, has since inspired some Igbo literary scholars to translate the literary pieces he wrote in English, especially the famous novel *Things Fall Apart*, into Igbo versions, which helps the Igbo masses to read the works easily for better understanding and appreciation of their themes. To that end, Chinua Achebe was a writer who played heroic roles that other Igbo, Nigerian, and African writers are trying to emulate.

It was during his foreign sojourn to America that Achebe wrote and presented many conference papers that critically shed light on the literature and cultures of continental Africa, "the heart of darkness," which impressed foreign scholars and researchers of African literature who gave him many accolades and awards that will be discussed later in this book. Nevertheless, commenting on Achebe's presentation in one of the world conferences he attended, Ezenwa-Ohaeto wrote:

> While Achebe was contemplating disconcerting realities at home, he also found himself compelled to address issues of continental scope, especially in the area of literatures from Africa. One continental forum was the Association of Commonwealth Literature and Language Studies conference in Kampala, Uganda in January 1974 which Achebe was invited to attend. It was the fourth conference of the association since its foundation in England in 1964, when Achebe had also been a keynote speaker. In Kampala he presented a

paper on "Colonialist Criticism" which, as usual, created much interest with the participants reacting in varied ways. Achebe's views are presented in a manner likely to affect even the most insensitive critic, which must account for the constant stream of references that resulted. He fears that his use of the word "colonialism" in his title may be inappropriate because it is "associated in many minds with that brand of cheap, demagogic and outmoded rhetoric" which rests on "a tendency to blame other people" and also because "it may be said that whatever colonialism may have done in the past," it has "become a symbol of a new relationship of equality between peoples who were once masters and servants." The latter-day colonialist critic "sees the African writer as a somewhat unfinished European who with patient guidance will grow up one day and write like every other European." While

> most African writers write out of an African experience and out of commitment to an African destiny. For them that destiny does not include a future European identity for which the present is but an apprenticeship.

Thus, he criticizes the idea of creating "universal" African literature as well as the cultivation of self-contempt in some African novels as part of that colonialist perspective. At the same time, Achebe protests "meanwhile the seduction of our writers by the blandishments of colonialist criticism is matched by its misdirection of our own critics." One of the major flaws he identifies is the fact "that the colonialist critic, unwilling to accept the validity of sensibilities other than his own, has made particular point of missing the African novel" with "lengthy articles to prove its non-existence largely on the grounds that it is a particular Western genre, a fact which would interest us if our ambition was to write 'Western' novels." Instead of prolonging Western parochialism, he suggests,

> let every people bring their gifts to the great festival of the world's cultural harvest and mankind will be all the richer for the variety and distinctiveness of the offerings.[16]

Ezenwa-Ohaeto's summary of the thesis and overall argument of Achebe's paper in that conference – that Achebe's conclusion does not deny the achievements of the responsible and insightful foreign critics, but it suggests that there is a need to rid criticism of prejudices and also racist notions – emphasizes Achebe's call on African writers to publish novels that reflect authentically African issues and experiences without portraying themselves as "somewhat unfinished European writers." The paper also emphasizes Achebe's call to critics of the African novels – a hybrid genre – not to criticize those novels from a colonialist critic's point of view, which is full of prejudice and is racist by nature. Instead, they should be willing to accept the validity of sensibilities that might be at variance with the Western critical tradition. In that case, both the writers and the critics of the African novel will have established their own literary independence. That is why Chinua Achebe, who practices what he preaches as both a creative writer and critic of the African novel, is dubbed by many as the father of the modern African novel.

Ernest Emenyonu, a renowned African literary critic, emphasizes such invaluable roles Achebe played in the development and practice of modern African literature as follows:

> Chinua Achebe's remarkable influence on contemporary African Literature is as much in the establishment of the art of the African novel in his fiction, as it is in the articulation of African poetics and aesthetics in his extra-fictional pronouncements. He is as much the father of the modern African novel, as he is the forerunner-theoretician of African literary criticism. Such philosophical and theoretical articles as "The Role of the Writer in a New Nation", "The Novelist as Teacher", "English and the African Writer", "Thoughts on the African Novel", "Colonialist Criticism", "The Black Writer's Burden", and "The African Writer and the Biafran Cause", among others, read like blueprints for both creative writers and critics of African literature. They are as imaginatively versatile as they are theoretically profound. In his role as Philosopher-critic, Achebe has bequeathed to critics of African literature a legacy of ideas and theories, which has helped to shape the trends in contemporary African literary criticism.[17]

Achebe's role as a writer-critic of African literature took him to many places in three continents, such as France and London in Europe, Australia in Asia, and Uganda in Africa. He also traveled to other states beyond Massachusetts and Connecticut, where he was sojourning in the United States at the time, to visit other places such as the University of Missouri, Kansas City. In those places, he granted numerous interviews to students, researchers, scholars, and critics of the four novels that he had published during the second phase of his writing career, shedding light on the culture and civilization of the "dark" African world, just as he did while serving Biafra as its roving Ambassador Extraordinaire during the Nigeria-Biafra War. His mission entailed using his renowned fame as a writer to explain the Biafran cause to various world bodies. In the end, his accomplishments on both fronts increased readers' understanding and appreciation of his fiction in particular, and the nature and essence of African literature in general. And as we noted earlier in this discussion, his clear explanation of the Biafran cause (alongside the effort of other Biafran diplomats) enabled four African countries – Gabon, Tanzania, Ivory Coast, and Zambia – and one Caribbean country – Haiti – to accord diplomatic recognition to the young Republic of Biafra, which was struggling to survive right from its creation.

For instance, in a conference that took place at the University of Missouri from January 9 through 23, 1973, on an intensive study and discussion of African and Caribbean literatures, there was a session that focused on a dialog between Chinua Achebe and the famous Guyanese writer Wilson Harris. The two black writers from different continents were able to discuss the great importance of using their writing skills and philosophies to dispel Western readers' preconceived, simplistic notions of third world writers' fiction, which helped in no small measure to sell the culture and civilizations of the universal Black World to outsiders. I witnessed a similar eye-opening dialog between Chinua Achebe and James Baldwin that took place at the University of Florida at Gainesville on April 11, 1980. A copy of my interview with Achebe on that occasion is reproduced elsewhere in this book because it covers part of the general vision and theme of Achebe's fiction.[18] Thereafter, I interviewed Wilson Harris, who was a visiting professor in 1981 at the University of Texas at Austin, to gain further understanding of comparative Africana literatures.[19]

Furthermore, during his visit to Australia, Achebe met and discussed his writing with A. D. Hope, one of Australia's leading poets. Achebe recollects Hope saying wistfully, "the only happy writers were those writing in small languages like Danish. Why? Because they and their readers understand one another and knew precisely what a word meant when it was used." Although Achebe had not thought of writing that way, he believed that there was an important sense in which Hope was right – that every literature must seek the things that belong unto its place, must in other words, speak of a particular place, evolve out of the necessities of its history, past and current, and the aspirations and destiny of its people.[20]

Still reflecting on his Australian visit, which he said was quite enlightening, Achebe tells of how he handled the reaction of another Australian, a female student who attended his lecture on African fiction writing as follows:

> On another occasion, a student at the National University who had taken a course in African Literature asked me if the time had not come for African writers to write about "people in general" instead of just Africa. I asked her if by *people in general* she meant *like Australians* and gave her the bad news that as far as I was concerned such a time would never come. She was only a brash sophomore. But like all the other women I have referred to, expressed herself with passionate and disarming effrontery. I don't know how women's lib will take but I do believe that by and large women are more honest than men in expressing their feelings. This girl was only making the same point which "serious" critics have been making more tactfully and therefore more insidiously. They dress it up in fine robes which they call universality.[21]

Some of these quoted passages come from Achebe's reflections on his Australian visit; they are excerpted from the article, "Colonialist Criticism," which is one of the 15 articles he published in *Morning Yet on Creation Day*, a book whose overall contents not only reveal the literary philosophy, artistry, and commitment of Chinua Achebe the writer-critic as a teacher, but also show the direction and form the contemporary African literature had to take in order to qualify as a viable corpus in World literatures. Those articles and other literary works he published thereafter established him as an undisputed guru in the history of modern African literature.

One of the important literary activities that Chinua Achebe engaged in while sojourning in the United States was establishing a new headquarters of *Okike* magazine in his office in the African Studies Building at the University of Massachusetts, Amherst. It used to be edited in the African Studies Building at the University of Nigeria, Nsukka. Working in the Amherst office one or two days a week with his secretary, Kathy, enabled Achebe to publish three issues of *Okike* magazine per year, unlike its irregular publication in Nigeria one year before it found a new home in Amherst. Achebe's success in this regard was due in part to the many resources he found and used, including the assistance of some scholars such as C. L. Innes he employed to work with him on some of the articles submitted to him for inclusion in the magazine. As a result, he published many articles by scholars of African literature from countries in Africa and Europe in the first American issue of *Okike*, No. 4, in December 1973. Coupled with the many public lectures he was giving, Achebe's devotion to working on *Okike* was so intense that it slowed down the pace of the work he was doing while writing his fifth novel, *Anthills of the Savannah*, which later appeared in the market in 1987, 21 years after publishing his fourth novel *A Man of the People* in 1966.

In a published interview, Innes, who worked closely with Achebe on *Okike*, revealed to the public something about his life and relations with those he worked with:

> Chinua [Achebe] treated all those who worked with him with a deference and courtesy unusual in the States . . . or anywhere else for that matter, and I think Kathy [the secretary] felt that was an important and efficient part of the *Okike* enterprise. The article was a center of work, discussion, occasional social gathering for others in the Africana Studies Center – Michael Thelwell, the novelist and critic, John Bracey the historian, Esther Terry who taught drama and produced a dramatic version of *Things Fall Apart* at the University Theater, Nelson Stevens, an artist whose work was sometimes printed in *Okike*, Irma McClaurin, a young poet and teacher who was to become United States representative for *Okike* when Chinua returned to Nigeria. Letters and contributions came from many well-known authors – John Updike, Ezekiel Mphahlele, Doris Lessing, Nadine Gordimer.[22]

In all the years I interacted with Achebe as an ardent student of his works, he exhibited the same deference, kindness, and puritanical streak of humility toward me, which are definitely unusual for an Igboman to show to a small Igbo boy like me in his presence. Every time we met, he always spoke to me in our native Igbo language, not minding that he was *the owner of the English language*, so to speak. But as time went on, I was not surprised by his uncommon admirable behavior because as the Igbo say, *Agu nwe uzo na aga ya nakuku* [The tiger that owns the road treads carefully on its sidewalk]. And I reciprocated his behavior by adopting the Igbo maxims, "As our people say, a man who pays his respect to the great paves the way for his own greatness," and "Age is respected but achievement is revered." Furthermore, Achebe knew and wrote, "As the elders said, if a child washes his hands, he could eat with kings."[23] In the end, Achebe lived to see me as his fervent *kotma* [cultural messenger]. Proverbially, when all was said and done, the dog of the king became the king of dogs in Achebe's studies.

Notes

1 Kalu Ogbaa, *A Century of Nigerian Literature: A Select Bibliography.* Trenton, NJ: Africa World Press, 2003.

2 A. C. Achebe, "Philosophy," in *Bug* (February 1951): 5; and "Hiawatha" also in *Bug* 4 (November 29, 1952).

3 For the full text and a brief analysis of the essays, see Lindfors, *Early Achebe*, pp. 12–16.

4 Ernest N. Emenyonu and Pat Emenyonu, "Achebe: Accountable to Our Society," *Africa Report*, Vol. 7, No. 5 (1972): 26–7.

5 Bernth Lindfors, "Popular Literature for an African Elite," *Journal of Modern African Studies*, Vol. 12 (1974): 471–86.

6 Achebe, "The Role of the Writer in a New Nation," 158.

7 Bernth Lindfors, ed., *Conversations with Chinua Achebe.* Jackson, MS: University Press of Mississippi, 1997: ix. and the blurb.

8 Kalu Ogbaa, *Understanding Things Fall Apart: A Student Casebook to Issues, Sources, and Historical Documents.* Westport, CT: Greenwood Press, 1999: xv.

9 *Ibid.*, p. xxii.

10 *Ibid.*, p. xvi.

11 *Ibid.*, p. xvii.

12 Kalu Ogbaa, *General Ojukwu: The Legend of Biafra.* New York: Triatlantic Books Ltd., 2007: 275–317.

13 Achebe, *Morning Yet on Creation Day*, pp. 75–6.

14 *Ibid.*, p. 84.

15 For the full speech, see Ogbaa, *Understanding Things Fall Apart*, pp. 198–200.

16 Ezenwa-Ohaeto, *Chinua Achebe*, pp. 183–4.

17 Ernest N. Emenyonu and Iniobong I. Uko, eds., *Emerging Perspectives on Chinua Achebe, Volume 2: ISINKA, the Artistic Purpose: Chinua Achebe and the Theory of African Literature.* Trenton, NJ: Africa World Press, 2004: xv.

18 The interview was published in *Research in African Literatures*, Vol. 12, No. 1 (Spring 1981): 1–13.

19 The interview, "Exile, Philosophic Myth, Creative Truth, Thrust and Necessity: An Interview with Wilson Harris," was published in *Caribbean Quarterly*, Vol. 29, No. 2 (June 1983): 54–62.

20 Achebe, *Morning Yet on Creation Day*, p. 9.

21 *Ibid.*, p. 10.

22 Ezenwa-Ohaeto, *Chinua Achebe*, pp. 181–2.

23 See Ogbaa, *Gods, Oracles and Divination*, p. 116.

4 Leave of Absence Abroad Interrupted for Patriotic Duties at Home

Toward the end of his employment at the University of Massachusetts at Amherst, Chinua Achebe was appointed Professor of English at the University of Connecticut, Storrs, as part of his leave of absence, which occurred during the third phase of his writing career. All the while, he managed to maintain regular communication with his compatriots, who constantly gave him information on important issues and incidents taking place in his absence, some of which disturbed him as a patriotic Nigerian. In fact, not many people knew the depth of his patriotism because whenever his name was mentioned, scholars, students, and general readers of his works usually focused their attention on his literary achievements. For that reason, they may not have imagined the extent to which he was committed to using his writing and oratory to render sociopolitical service to his nation – service that came to public awareness the first time in the Republic of Biafra during the civil war, and then in Nigeria generally after the war. When he was just beginning his new appointment at Storrs, he learned of a brutal incident that took place in Nigeria, which disturbed him so much that he thought of interrupting his leave of absence to resume work in Nigeria – a move that surprised his host institution as well as his friends and colleagues. Achebe heard of the military coup of July 29, 1975 that toppled the former head of the Military Government of Nigeria, General Yakubu Gowon, who was attending a summit of the OAU in Kampala, Uganda. The more he studied the impact of the coup on the lives of his fellow Nigerian citizens and brooded over it, the more his attention was diverted from teaching and writing. Consequently, he decided to return to Nigeria to confront the reality of his country and thereby contribute to the ongoing postbellum reconstruction effort. After all, as the Igbo say, "*Nwoke madu anaghi ahapu ulo ya nagba oku wee gaa ichu oke*" [A man does not leave his burning house to pursue a rat fleeing from the flames]. Ostensibly, Achebe made that decision because the military coup was bloodless, unlike other previous coups in Nigeria, and because the man who succeeded Gowon as head of state, General Murtala Mohammed, demonstrated initially up to the end of 1975 that he had a clearer vision of how he would govern the country and, also, more purpose leadership qualities than the man he had just overthrown. Moreover every citizen to get involved in the reconstruction ef tary government was undertaking encouraged Acheb

DOI: 10.4324/9781003184133-4

toward the much-needed restoration of a civilian governance that would replace the military regime.

What is noteworthy and laudable about Achebe's decision to return to Nigeria in the heat of the military revolution is that while other less patriotic Nigerians were leaving the country in droves for greener pastures in the United States, Canada, France, and Great Britain (if they had the chance and opportunity to do so), Achebe the Eagle on Iroko could not have stayed back in America and lived with good conscience.

He eventually left the United States in late 1976 for Nigeria, where he resumed work at the University of Nigeria, Nsukka, this time, however, not focusing only on teaching and writing fiction. Instead, he got more involved with sociopolitical issues after the abortive countercoup of February 1976 by B. S. Dimka, which took the life of General Mohammed. The General was immediately replaced by his second-in-command, General Olusegun Obasanjo, who claimed that he was taking over the governance of Nigeria against his will and personal conviction – an assertion that implied that he was still covertly paying allegiance to the ousted military head of state, General Gowon, who hails from the North. In fact, many Nigerians believed that Obasanjo had another motive for wanting to relinquish power so soon. For example, Dubem Okafor argued:

> Because that coup was unsuccessful, Murtala was succeeded by his-second-in-command, General Obasanjo, a Yoruba, whose regime was characterized by extreme haste to hand power over to those whose birthright it was to rule Nigeria, the Hausa/Fulani House, that is. I had tried to convey this sense of hurry of an uncomfortable ruler in my poem "Ulysses' Bastard."
>
> [. . .]
>
> It is interesting to note that while his discomfiture as a Southerner/Yoruba was responsible for his haste to relinquish power as Head of State, it still left General Obasanjo enough time to promulgate the Land Use Decree, which made it possible for him to acquire vast tracts of land, which with his "savings" and "bank loans," he was able to transform into the largest individually owned agricultural business in the whole of West Africa. He was now ready to hand over power to the newly elected political elite, with Shehu Shagari, a Fulani, as President.[1]

Put differently, Obasanjo did not want to offend people from the Northern and Western states; yet, on the other hand, he was blatantly overbearing to the Igbo people of the South Eastern states (Achebe's home region), who were defeated by Nigerian troops during the civil war. As a matter of fact, that difference in Obasanjo's treatment of the Igbo, who were hoping for true reconciliation and peace with other indigenous peoples of Nigeria, served as another incentive for Achebe to return home to continue working for the acceleration of democratic processes aimed at pressuring the military brass to hand power over to a civilian government.

Furthermore, even though the Obasanjo military regime tried so hard to instill in people the same kind of fear as its predecessor, the public servants' attitude to work and discipline was less rigorous, and the change that occurred during the brief Mohammed regime was beginning to fade. A few years after, as Achebe recalled in *The Trouble with Nigeria*,[2] an encouraging change took place in public servants' attitude to work during the Mohammed regime:

> On the morning after Murtala Mohammed seized power in July 1975 public servants in Lagos were found "on seat" at seven-thirty in the morning. Even the "go-slow" traffic that had defeated every solution and defied every regime vanished overnight from the streets! Why? The new ruler's reputation for ruthlessness was sufficient to transform in the course of only one night the style and habit of Nigeria's unruly capital. That the character of one man could establish that quantum change in a people's social behavior was nothing less than miraculous. But it shows that social miracles can happen.

But Achebe also surmised then that such a change could endure only under certain conditions:

> We know, alas, that that transformation was short-lived; it had begun to fade even before the tragic assassination of Murtala Mohammed. In the final analysis a leader's no-nonsense reputation might induce a favorable climate but in order to effect lasting change it must be followed with a radical program of social and economic reorganization or at least a well-conceived and consistent agenda of reform which Nigeria stood, and stands, in dire need of.
>
> (p. 1)

It was to the general development of the radical program of social and economic reorganization that Achebe conscientiously devoted his writing and public speeches at the time. As we observed in the preceding chapter, Achebe expressed in *A Man of the People*, his fourth novel, the idea of inviting the army to come and combat the overall corruption that politicians at the time had entrenched in the governance of prewar Nigeria. Unfortunately, however, the army came and launched the civil war, and enthroned more corruption as the order of the day that spanned the tenures of various military regimes. This time around, though, Achebe's homecoming helped him to assess accurately the traumatic, as well as the beautiful, experiences in the life of his native Igbo people before and after the war. Thus, his keen awareness of both types of experience enabled him to create and edit a new journal, titled *Uwa Ndi Igbo*, with Chukwuma Azuonye. In addition, Achebe wanted to finish writing the fifth novel he began working on while he was on leave of absence abroad in which he would romanticize the causes, courses, and effects of the war on the people, as well as the roles that military administrations played after the war to prolong the people's suffering. But the burning issues of the day vis-a-vis what happened to the Igbo people took precedence in the choice and course of action that he took in his writing career. This involved devoting time to learning about Igbo culture in greater detail, which led him to solicit more articles on Igbo cultural life for publication in future volumes of *Okike* (Figure 4.1).

Figure 4.1 Chinua Achebe brooding over Igbo war and political situation

Source: Getty Images

Returning to Nsukka in 1976, when Nigeria was preparing to host the Second World Black and African Festival of Arts and Culture (FESTAC), thrust Achebe into performing another form of patriotic service to Nigeria. The organizers of the festival sent a delegation to Nsukka to request that he write the words of the anthem that would be used for the festival. When he asked the delegation why he was chosen to write the words, they told him that Fela Sowande, the famous Nigerian musicologist, had been approached to provide the music for the anthem, and he agreed to do it but insisted that Achebe should write the words. To fulfill that condition, the delegation came to see Achebe so Sowande could play the anthem at the FESTAC celebration. Out of his usual patriotic feeling, Achebe obliged them with a well-written lyric for the anthem. However, when the delegation returned to Lagos from Nsukka with a promise to pay Achebe for his work, it turned out that the words he wrote were not used by the organizers of FESTAC. Even though the issue was disappointing to Achebe, he was not discouraged from rendering other services to Nigeria wherever and whenever he was called upon to do so.

Very soon, Achebe settled down to work at Nsukka with a new zeal because his position in the university changed from Senior Research Fellow in the Institute of African Studies to Professor of Literature. The change was due in part to the recognition he received worldwide during his leave of absence in America, and in part to the more conducive working milieu under the administration of Vice Chancellor J. O. C. Ezeilo, which, unlike that of his predecessor Kodilinye, gave Achebe the opportunity and freedom to do things differently. That way, he was enabled to express in practical terms his vision of working for the progress of the university and the country at large. For example, when Achebe was first appointed to the university, the administration erroneously did not allow him to teach courses in the English Department while I was a student there (1970–1973), ostensibly because he did not have a Ph.D. in English, even though we were studying the novels he wrote as a creative writer. It was only after some American universities appointed him Professor of English and Africana Studies, and after he was awarded many honorary doctorates by Ivy League schools and top state universities, did Nsukka recognize their own native son as the renowned Professor of Literature he had been all along. Shortly thereafter, the university administration appointed him Chair of the English Department. Serving in that capacity, Achebe made significant changes that resulted in noted improvements in curricular offerings.

Achebe quickly began playing again the role of "the novelist as teacher" but not with the publication of a fifth novel as readers had anticipated. Instead, he published two children's books – *The Drum: A Children's Story* and *The Flute* – both in 1977. These two books were a sequel to the children's book, *How the Leopard Got His Claws* (coauthored with John Iroaganachi), which he published in 1972. As many scholars of his writings know, Achebe learned informally as a child how to tell stories at home from his mother and elder sister. So when he later enrolled for formal education at the primary school level in Ogidi and Nekede, at the secondary school level in Government College, Umuahia, and at the college level in University College, Ibadan, his recollection of the importance of storytelling guided him to choose and pursue creative writing as an area of interest. And as we saw in an earlier discussion of his career, Achebe wrote shorter literary pieces comprising children's literature and poems during the war, some of which were published in *Girls at War and Other Stories*, 1972. Moreover, he considered storytelling a serious and powerful medium for teaching early childhood education formally and informally in Igboland and other Nigerian communities. The culture, language, and civilization of the people, as well as their ethos, mores, morality, and worldview were all transmitted to children from one generation to another by adults and parents as a pedagogical system that some educationists dub the Igbo vernacular tradition, one in which storytellers serve as teachers of the people's culture and tradition, both at home and in the classrooms.

The Drum: A Children's Story, for instance, is the story of the trickster Tortoise's adventure to find food during a time of drought and famine in the animal kingdom. Wandering hopelessly in the forest for many days, he accidentally enters the world of the spirits underground, where he is rewarded with a magic drum that produces food and drinks. When he returns to his village with the drum, Tortoise beats it at every mealtime to feed the entire village of animals who gathered in front of his compound. Achebe explained why he wrote the story as a political satire:

> So far I have kept reasonably close to the original tradition tale. But I want to turn the story more sharply into a contemporary story. And so my Tortoise now has political ambitions. He considers the power he has over the animals and the debt of food they owe to him. He considers all the suffering and danger he endured to go to the land of spirits and bring them the magic drum. And he decides that he deserves to be made king of the animals. And his plan is succeeding. But we can already see the kind of king he would become by the way he is carrying on. Whenever he wants to say *my place* he makes a slip of the tongue and says *my palace, I mean my place!* He sets up a committee to plan his coronation and appoints the biggest animal in the village, the elephant himself, as the ceremonial drum beater.
>
> Naturally the elephant beats the drum too heavily and breaks it. And the free meals come to an end; and there is consternation in the village.
>
> "Never mind," says the Tortoise with royal confidence. "After the coronation I shall send for a bigger and better drum."
>
> But the animals are wise. "Oh no!" they say. "No drum, no coronation!"
>
> For the rest of the story I return to oral tradition. Tortoise is compelled to leave the village a second time. But this time his adventure is no longer genuine; it is contrived. Which is the main point of the traditional tale – adventure, yes; fake adventure, no!
>
> In Tortoise's second journey everything that happened by chance before is now forced and false. His reward is a drum that dispenses not food but an assortment of punishments.
>
> Now some people might take exception to my turning an innocuous tale into a political parable. There is a strong feeling in some quarters that art and politics mix no more easily than oil and water.[3]

Achebe's explication of the theme of *The Drum: A Children's Story* helps readers to understand how they too can appropriate traditional tales to create contemporary children's stories so as to maintain the traditional Igbo codes of conduct and values. In other words, teaching such stories to children helps communities to inculcate good moral and ethical values in the children who could become their future sociopolitical leaders.

Talking about the second story, *The Flute*, Achebe explains further how he applied his artistry to recreate a traditional African story to fit a new situation:

> I have used oral tradition in two kinds of stories; one is called *The Flute*. Now this is the story of a child who forgets his flute on the farm. It is a fairly common story in Africa. When the child and family reach home at dusk he remembers his flute and wants to go back for it. But that is not permissible. You see, the world is divided. Spirits have their own time. So if you go there at night, you are breaking the law of jurisdictions and you can expect all kinds of problems. So when this boy wants to go to the distant farm at night his parents beg him not to go. But still he goes. And so in a sense this is a story about disobedience. And true enough, the boy meets the spirits. All of this is in the tradition. What is not there is the king of the spirits saying to the boy: "Why did you disobey your parents?" Being a spirit, you see, he has seen far away right into the boy's home, before he came. So he says, "What about your mother?" Didn't she offer to buy you another flute on the next market? Why did you disobey your mother?" The boy looks down, he knows he is beaten, you see, he knows about disobedience. He rallies and says, "The flute, I made it myself. It is the only thing that I could call my own." Now I put that in, quite shamelessly, you see, because I think you require that kind of justification for disobedience. Children may not ask you, but it will be bothering them, you know. If you tell them, "You should obey your parents." Why is it that this boy didn't and yet he is rewarded in the end? Now I insist the question should be asked. So the boy gives a good answer and the spirit says indulgently: "Well that is not good enough. But I like your spirit. I like your guts." So the point is made that obedience is still the rule, but courage is also important. And we make the point that the song which the boy makes about his flute lying out there all alone, in the cold, is another saving grace. And so. Making a thing – a flute or song – adds to build up a story, I think. And that way, the idea of making things which I feel very strongly about is injected into the story without destroying it.[4]

In this recreated version of the old story, the original disobedience of the trickster is expanded to include the rewards of courage and taking responsibility for one's actions.

Earlier on, the Nigerian civil war had brought a lot of devastation to the Igbo country physically, economically, mentally, and spiritually, especially to children. For that reason, Achebe the master storyteller and teacher was compelled to write children's books as a means of educating them on the Igbo ethos of hard work, respect for elders, and constituted authorities, as well as the value of human lives, of harmonious, moral, and ethical coexistence, and of belief in the Igbo high God Chukwu, all of which constitute the cosmic center and worldview of the Igbo, which have distinguished them as a special ethnic people of Nigeria. Achebe knew that Igbo children and young adults who had never experienced the Igbo ethos before, during, and immediately after the war could never embrace it unless they were taught or reminded of it by experienced and committed elders like himself. Nevertheless, the lessons of the children's books that he wrote were also intended for Igbo adults and other Nigerians and Africans. That is because these great and acceptable qualities characteristic of Igbo life and values had to be promoted and preserved to guide their people at home and in the Diaspora. It seems to me that Achebe saw it as his mission in life to preserve Igbo ways and culture (as well as those of other West African peoples) in all his fiction. This is why his close friend Emmanuel Obiechina praised him profusely in "In Praise of The Teacher," a paper he presented in "The Chinua Achebe International Symposium 1990," organized by Achebe's university peers to honor him as a pre-eminent African literary guru, on the celebration of his 60th birthday. Iniobong I. Uko highlighted some of the ideas found in Obiechina's paper as follows:

> Chinua Achebe has been consistent in making his literary works serve peda-gogical purposes among the Igbo people, specifically, and other African peo-ple in general. He demonstrated the fact that being the "critical conscience" of his society, and a chronicler of events within the society, he has the duty of recreating the events in artistic forms. This preoccupation necessarily entails utilizing the real events as different colors of thread to weave a fictional-ized fabric that is relevant to the people and gives them a sense of dynamic hopefulness and profound identity in history. Achebe's writings constitute a tremendously useful storehouse of cultural values in Igbo cosmology. It tran-scends the static framework of "art-for-art's sake" within which some liter-ary works are trapped, thereby not serving the sociocultural, economic and political needs of the people. Many African writers function largely as intel-lectuals and teachers of the people, and are also impelled to provide ethical guideposts and moral signboards to reveal the hidden snares and treacherous quick sands that constitute the hazards that people perpetually live in.[5]

Furthermore, some episodes in the children's books are also found in some of his novels meant for adult education as well, but he wanted parents and other adults to use the children's books, which contain etiological animal tales to teach children about human life generally. Such tales involve investigating the cause or reason for something, often expressed in terms of historical or mythological explanations of the world. Some animals in the children's books are used as paro-dies to exhibit characteristics that mirror human behaviors. When the stories are dramatized, children participate actively as characters who sing, clap, and dance during evening storytelling sessions at home or in schools during the day. It is from the morals of the stories that the children learn how to work collaboratively with one another in villages and clans when they become adults. Achebe empha-sizes the need for unity among Igbo people through the onomastic implications of the names he gives to communities in his fictions, for example, Umuofia *obodo dike* (Umuofia the fearsome clan) in *Things Fall Apart*, noting their warrior attributes, and Umuaro (Umuaro the weighty clan) in *Arrow of God*, a six-village clan obedient to their god Ulu. Both Igbo clans are so described because they have inhabitants who were patriotically trained as young men to fight and protect their clans against internal and external aggressors. Such great warriors include Okonkwo and Obierika in *Things Fall Apart*, and Ezeulu and Nwaka who are known to be savvy religious and political leaders in *Arrow of God*.

Moreover, the adult education found in the novels – just like the themes of some of the children's books – can only be understood if their readers are guided by their teachers to read any work of fiction critically. At first, Achebe did not really know how well Nigerian college students were reading his novels. It was not until he taught classes in fiction in early 1970s that he discovered that some secondary school graduates who gained admission into the University of Nigeria, Nsukka, and who took his modern African fiction course were ill-prepared to read critically and understand the novels he adopted as textbooks for the course. Achebe revealed this discovery in his interview with Jane Wilkinson:

> To many students coming to the University, reading a novel is a huge chore. To plough through a novel is intimidating to many of them. Some will even run away to go to study linguistics because they imagine there is very little reading required there. So you have to coax them into literature. Many of them had never read before except for what they had to read for their school certificate. What I did was to introduce short stories. African short stories that anybody could manage: the scope is small, the time required is small and there are some stories that can really trigger off discussion and interest. People could really come alive in discussing what happened in this story in a way that they would never have imagined before: they had thought of these stories as something dead, that you had to struggle to master. Once this was done with the shorter things then they were readier to tackle a longer novel.[6]

As one can see, Achebe's discovery led him to change not only his pedagogical approach, but also the textbooks he used, from novels to short stories that took a shorter time to read, because their contents were briefer and less complex in scope than those of the novels. However, that is not to say that the appreciation of short stories was less critical and rigorous; instead, as shorter literary pieces, it gave the students more focused time to read. Over time, Achebe trained the students to gradually transition from critical reading of short stories to critical reading of novels. That way, Achebe whetted the student's appetite and encouraged them to discover the fictive worlds in short stories and novels with confidence.

In addition, Achebe's early detection of the deficiency in his students' reading abilities and habits caused him to correct such problems within and outside the Nsukka campus of the university, fully aware that students in other Nigerian universities had similar difficulties due to the way they were taught in secondary schools before coming to college. Keenly aware that the quality of secondary school education had declined, he saw the need to work toward remedying the deficiency in the teaching and study of literature by students who would graduate and go to teach students like themselves in secondary schools. That is why when S. O. Biobaku, an educator from another part of Nigeria, invited him to contribute to his book, *The Living Culture of Nigeria*, Achebe did not hesitate to accept the invitation as an opportunity to contribute an essay on "Contemporary Literature". In this essay, Achebe offered a survey of Nigerian literature, which included a critical examination of works by Nigerian novelists, poets, and playwrights. He suggested new ways of enhancing the teaching and study of literature in Nigerian secondary schools and universities. Consequently, the issues he raised in the essay, as well as contributions by others to *The Living Culture of Nigeria*, provoked useful debates on the teaching and study of literature in many Nigerian tertiary institutions.

Many university teachers noticed and appreciated his pedagogical recommendations and appointed him as an external examiner of their graduating students. The University of Lagos, for instance, not only made him the external examiner for their English Department in 1977, but also recruited him to serve as Chair of the university's Ceremonial Committee and as public orator. Although these two latter roles are usually reserved for internal professors of the university, the administration and faculty made this exception to the tradition because they thought that Achebe's fame would benefit the university by creating an aura of unity among Nigerian universities. Many other Nigerian universities followed suit in making guest professors members of their university ceremonial committees and public orators.

Moreover, Chinua Achebe, a member of one of the three dominant ethnic groups of Nigeria – Igbo, Hausa/Fulani, and Yoruba – was always keenly aware that in discussing the living cultures of Nigeria, he had to showcase Igbo culture through his writings and lectures.

While Achebe was performing these good works within and outside Nigerian universities, he did not forget the contributions that his fellow Igbo writer and warrior, Christopher Okigbo made toward literary development and the celebration of the African (indeed Nigerian) literature. Okigbo did this by addressing the survival of the Igbo people when facing imminent danger from Nigerians who were aided and abetted by Great Britain and the USSR during the Nigeria-Biafra War. In his book of poetry, *Labyrinths with Path of Thunder*, Okigbo had written poems in which he warned Nigerians of a looming civil war, which began with the bloody military coup of January 15, 1966. When Nigerian authorities refused to heed his warning, choosing instead to wage a war against Easterners living in the seceding Republic of Biafra enclave, Okigbo fought on the side of Biafra as an army major, and was killed in combat in the early months of the war in 1967.

Soon after the war, some literary critics began to publish articles and books, condemning Okigbo for leaving his role as a writer to take part in a war of secession against his fatherland. Some also misinterpreted the themes of his poems. Ali Mazrui, for example, published *The Trial of Christopher Okigbo* "in which the greatest charge against the poet is that he was forced, and also chose, to be also a man, a citizen, a member of an historical time and place caught, as it was then, in a very tragic impasse;" and Elain Savory Fido, asserted in her own criticism of the poet that "in his life Okigbo had problems with women," which resulted in "the imposition of inapplicable psycho-sexual theory on the poetry of Okigbo, in order to make unbelievable biographical extrapolations."[7]

Unfortunately, such critics forgot that Okigbo saw himself as an Igboman first and secondarily as a Nigerian, just as all ethnic peoples of Nigeria see themselves, even though some of them hypocritically claim to be detribalized. So when he made the decision to join the army in order to save his fellow Biafrans from being annihilated, Okigbo was very much aware that he could be killed; and that neither stopped him from writing against the prospective war nor enlisting to fight it as a patriot. His bravery in writing to criticize the Nigerian government and his determination to face its mighty army are expressed in his poem "Hurrah for Thunder" before the war broke out:

> Whatever happened to the elephant –
> Hurrah for thunder –
>
> The elephant, tetrarch of the jungle:
> With a wave of the land
> He could pull four trees to the ground;
> His four mortal legs pounded the earth:
> Wherever they treaded,
> The grass was forbidden to be there.
>
> Alas! The elephant has fallen –
> Hurrah for thunder –
>
> But already the hunters are talking about pumpkins:
> If they share the meat let them remember thunder.
>
> The eye that looks down will surely see the nose.
> The finger that fits should be used to pick the nose.
>
> Today – for tomorrow, today becomes yesterday:
> How many million promises can ever fill a basket . . .
>
> If I don't learn to shut my mouth I'll soon go to hell,
> I, Okigbo, town-crier, together with my iron bell.[8]

Chinua Achebe was aware of the critics' misreading of the contents of Okigbo's poetry as well as his reason for fighting the Nigeria-Biafra War on the Biafran side. Hence, in 1978, he founded and edited with Dubem Okafor an anthology with the emotional title, *Don't Let Him Die: An Anthology of Memorial Poems of Christopher Okigbo (1932–1967)*, to lionize and memorialize the great poet, who could have become to the Igbo people what William Butler Yeats was to the Irish people, had he lived to continue writing his patriotic poems after the war. And so in the "Preface" to the memorial anthology, Achebe wrote among other things:

> Christopher [Okigbo] . . . had friends, admirers, fans, cronies of both sexes, from all ages, all social classes, all professions, all ethnic groups, in Nigeria and everywhere. . . . The variety of tributes assembled here bears witness to the power of his personality, his poetry, his life and death. Some of the contributors were close friends of his; some only knew him slightly, and others not at all. Some were his fellow countrymen, sundered at the time of his death by a horrendous fratricidal conflict and today divided still by its memory, repercussions and the hypocrisy it engendered. Some are fellow Africans who may have heard Okigbo declare at Makerere in one of his impish moods that he wrote his poetry only for poets. And some are from faraway West Indies, U.S.A., Canada, and Great Britain.[9]

The submissions in that anthology have since kept the memory of Okigbo alive, and his book of poetry has been prescribed as an essential textbook for studies in many English and Africana Studies Departments in Nigeria, continental Africa, Canada, the United States, and Great Britain.

Over time, what Achebe did during this transitional period, and continued to do thereafter, in his writing career earned him the admiration of one of the most renowned professors of English and Africana literatures, Emmanuel Obiechina, who gave him the moniker "The Teacher" when he presented the following tribute in 1990 to mark Achebe's 60th birthday:

> I will call my tribute to Professor Chinua Achebe "In Praise of THE TEACHER" because I regard Achebe as a quintessentially a teacher. I respect and honor him as a great writer and a consummate artist, but when I consider the totality of his creative and intellectual output and profound impact which his work has made upon the world of literature and humane learning in Nigeria, Africa and everywhere his writing is known, then I tell myself that there is something more significant in the man and his work than is encountered in the generality of writers and artists. We appreciate our artists and we respect our writers, but we approach Chinua Achebe with more than appreciation and respect; we approach him with gratitude and a kind of awe bordering on reverence.
>
> And yet, we do not regard him as an icon, as a sacred object set apart on a pedestal for the purpose of periodic adoration of celebration. Chinua Achebe is so much one of ourselves and part of our active world and concerns, so much a part of the landscape of our minds and responses that we see him as an indispensable reference point in our everyday social interactions. Find any group of educated Nigerians in a street corner arguing irrepressibly as only Nigerians know how to argue about anything social, ethical, cultural, or political and Chinua Achebe is bound to be introduced from time to time

to set off an idea or support a point of view. "According to Chinua Achebe," "In the words of Chinua Achebe," "As Chinua Achebe said" have become the regular gambits in educated Nigerians' conversations and discourses. He is the most quotable and quoted Nigerian writer. We quote him as our elders quoted proverbs. Among Nigerians, appropriate quotations from Chinua Achebe are a palm oil with which conversations are eaten.

Nor is Chinua Achebe's fame and popularity limited to Nigeria. Unlike Okonkwo Unoka whose fame is said to be known throughout the nine villages of Umuofia and their neighborhood, Chinua Achebe's fame as a writer has spread all over the world. Judging by the large number of academic honors and awards which he has amassed from famous institutions of higher learning and from learned academics all over the world, from Europe, America and elsewhere, it is clear that the world also recognizes him as one of the great contemporary men of letters. And let me add here that in spite of our built-in skepticism about the rationales and hidden or open motives for honorific awards of the sort we speak about, the world does not part with its recognition and its awards merely for a song. It is also obvious, judging by the scores of Ph. D. degree candidates who have ascended to academic glory on Achebe's writing in the last thirty years, that Achebe enjoys full and unreserved endorsement by academia. And most importantly, it should be recognized that the immense spread of the international audience of his writing through translation is further proof of his acceptance as not only a world-class writer but as one of the most illustrious of modern authors.[10]

The tribute contains the essential attributes of Chinua Achebe the writer and teacher I knew, and they express the candid opinion of the literary critic and teacher Emmanuel Obiechina I knew as well; for I had the rare fortune and privilege to have had both of them as my university professors. Above all, it was deeply important for Chinua Achebe that he received the praises of his colleagues from Nigeria and beyond while he was still alive; for such praises are usually given to renowned writers like his friends Emmanuel Obiechina and Pius Okigbo posthumously.

In face of the praises that erudite literary luminaries like Obiechina showered on Achebe, on a hindsight one wonders why a budding Igbo critic, Charles Nnolim, would publish in 1976 a pamphlet, *A Source for Arrow of God*, in which he claimed that Chinua Achebe used without acknowledgment his uncle Simon Alagbogu Nnolim's 17-page pamphlet, titled *The History of Umuchu*, as a source for writing his novel, *Arrow of God*, which is 230 pages long. He was teaching in the English Department at Alvan Ikoku College of Education, Owerri, Nigeria then, and compelled his students to purchase copies of the pamphlet with tacit approval of Ernest N. Emenyonu, the department chair. Some lecturers in the department who read the pamphlet questioned the academic value that warranted its compulsory adoption; for Nnolim did not critically and persuasively address the Igbo sociocultural and political issues that Achebe expertly discussed in *Arrow of God*. For that reason, they were left with the impression that Nnolim was just calling attention to himself as an emerging literary critic without any consideration whatsoever for the damage the publication would do to Achebe's own reputation as a renowned novelist.

Although Emenyonu seemed to have ignored people's complaint on the matter, his own subsequent publication showed that he was a more serious literary critic of Achebe's fiction. I personally discovered the fact when he gave me a copy of the manuscript of his book, *The Rise of the Igbo Novel*, to proofread before giving it to the acquisition editor of Oxford University Press to publish. From the manuscript, I learned a lot about the important role Achebe played in establishing Igbo (indeed, Nigerian) modern novels as a viable corpus in African literature. In the end, both publications from Nnolim and Emenyonu inspired me to pursue the study of Achebe's fiction in great detail during my graduate studies.

In the Black Studies Department at the Ohio State University, Columbus, I studied the four novels of Chinua Achebe and a few others by black authors from continental Africa, America, and the Caribbean. While doing so, I later discovered that, in spring 1977, Nnolim published in *Research in African Literatures* an article, "A Source for *Arrow of God*," which is the same title of the pamphlet he sold to students in Owerri in 1976. In the article, he reemphasized the damaging argument that Achebe used his uncle's pamphlet as a source for writing *Arrow of God*:

> [Although] Achebe has never admitted it publicly, the single most important source – in fact, the only source – for *Arrow of God* is a tiny, socio-historical pamphlet published without copyright by a retired corporal of the Nigeria Police Force. His name was (he died in 1972) Simon Alagbogu Nnolim and the title of his pamphlet was *The History of Umuchu*, published by Eastern Press Syndicate, Depot Road, Enugu, Nigeria, in 1953. It was while I was preparing a second, enlarged edition of this booklet . . . that certain passages began to remind me of *Arrow of God*. One such passage was the story of the priest who refused chieftaincy, was imprisoned, and stubbornly refused to roast the sacred yams.
>
> [. . .]
>
> In conclusion, the reader must be warned that the foregoing is in no way intended to denigrate the great artistic achievements of Achebe as a creative writer and novelist. But my study does establish a few facts about Achebe and his sources. First, we must admit that Achebe is a careful researcher of his facts, which shows great intelligence, for no one has been able to complain that his depiction of Igbo society is distorted or falsified. Secondly, one must admit that it takes painstaking and diligent research to organize and bring alive such complex material. Thirdly, though Achebe is a great observer of Igbo cultural life, the evidence tends to show that his sources are not solely oral; Achebe did not write from personal observation alone, nor merely from a combination of personal observation and the great stories told to him by his father and grandfather. He definitely made use of printed sources in writing *Arrow of God*.[11]

In spring 1978, several months after Nnolim's article was published in *Research in African Literatures*, C. L. Innes published in another volume of the same journal her own article titled "A Source for *Arrow of God*: A Response," to rebut Nnolim's claims as follows:

> In his article "A Source for *Arrow of God*," in *RAL*, 8 (1977), pp. 1–26, Charles Nnolim makes some rather bold claims: "the single most important source – in fact, the only source – for *Arrow of God*," he declares, "is a tiny socio-historical pamphlet," entitled *The History of Umuchu* by Simon Alagbogu Nnolim, although Achebe has "never admitted it publicly." He promises to provide "overwhelming" evidence that Achebe "had Nnolim's book before him as he wrote *Arrow of God*, and further maintains that "Achebe did not merely take the story of the High Priest and blow life into it as Shakespeare did when borrowing material for Julius Caesar from Plutarch's *Lives of the Noble Grecians and Romans*; Achebe went much further. He lifted *everything* in *The History of Umuchu* and simply transferred it to *Arrow of God* without embellishment" (Nnolim's italics).
>
> Such claims led me to read on with great interest and, indeed, some concern for the reputation of Achebe, against whom these accusations of artlessness, lack of creativity, and failure to "admit sources publicly" were being leveled. The evidence, however, was far from "overwhelming." Despite repeated statements by Nnolim that passages from *The History of Umuchu* were rendered "verbatim" or "set down almost verbatim" in *Arrow of God*, or were "lifted from Nnolim" or were "artlessly faithful" to their source, or showed that Achebe "forgot even to disguise his source," or simply "defied comment," a quick reading of the passages compared revealed that they were neither "verbatim" nor "almost verbatim" copies. On the contrary, they varied significantly in detail, structure, length, and phraseology.

After rebutting with convincing evidence Nnolim's claims point by point, Innes concludes:

> As Charles Nnolim himself tells us, Achebe "admitted" that he had met Simon Alagbogu Nnolim in 1957 and interviewed him in Umuchu where he spent three days with the Eastern Nigeria Broadcasting Company. Given Achebe's interest in Igbo history and culture, one can assume that his questions and notes during that visit were not limited to the formal subject – Night Masks. It is probable that it was on this visit that Achebe heard further details of the story of Ezeagu, of the founding of Umuchu, and of local ceremonies such as the Festival of the Pumpkin Leaves (still performed, Simon Nnolim tells us, in 1952) from Nnolim and others. From this germ, the novel must have taken shape over the years with the addition of a multitude of other sources, oral or written. One of these sources *might* have been *The History of Umuchu*, but Charles Nnolim's claims that it is the only source and that Achebe must have had it before him as he wrote are unconvincing and

irresponsible. Like Achebe's Ofoedu at the meeting to discuss the road labor, he appears to have "opened his mouth and let out his words alive without giving them as much as a bite with his teeth."[12]

As a man raised in Igboland, Charles Nnolim should have known that making such serious allegations against Achebe without talking with him first was not an appropriate Igbo way of doing things, and yet he went ahead to publish the article. For on page three of the article he wrote, "My first impulse was to take up a phone and call him, since we were not more than sixty miles from each other, but I resisted the impulse: he would think it sheer effrontery." If he had followed his impulse to do the right thing, he could have avoided the public criticism that he subjected himself to. As an Igboman myself, I was not only embarrassed by what I saw as an irresponsible behavior but also by the fact that our older and more experienced Igbo literary scholars did not do what Innes did to condemn what a fellow Igboman did to bring down our literary hero, even though his attempt failed woefully. And I ask, "Could a Yoruba man have done so to a Yoruba (indeed, a Nigerian) literary hero like Wole Soyinka without Yoruba scholars condemning him instantly?"

Nevertheless, in 1978, I began my journey into learning how to work critically on Achebe's fiction. My professor and would-be dissertation director, Bernth Lindfors, gave me the final manuscript of *Critical Perspectives on Chinua Achebe*, which he and C. L. Innes were editing, to proofread to ensure that Igbo words and cultural issues in the book were written accurately. I learned so much from the articles in it that I decided finally to write my dissertation on Chinua Achebe's novels. Furthermore, in spring 1980, I attended with Lindfors a conference of the African Literature Association (ALA) holding at the University of Florida at Gainesville. During the conference, I had an interview with Achebe that helped me to learn how to do critical analyses of his works, and to find out from him how well we Africans (indeed, Igbo scholars) were doing cultural exegesis of his novels for the benefit of foreign readers of his works. That interview also gave Achebe an opportunity to comment briefly on Charles Nnolim's allegations. Considering its overall importance, I have reproduced the entire interview as the next chapter of this book.

Finally, after interrupting his leave of absence at American universities to return to Nigeria, Achebe went back to the University of Nigeria, Nsukka, where he gradually settled down to carry out his self-imposed duty of the writer as a teacher. He started that aspect of his role by publishing children's books through which he taught children how to grow up to become patriotic leaders of their villages, clans, and country when they grew up as adults. He also collaborated with other Nigerian educators within and outside university campuses to reform tertiary education in Nigeria. That task included setting a template for teaching critical reading courses in fiction for freshmen in those institutions, so they could be enabled to discover and enjoy the fictive worlds contained in short stories and novels. But he also delved into the area of Nigerian cultural and political education, which prepared him to write the book *The Trouble with Nigeria*. In a word,

Achebe was at this time both a writer and a teacher of fiction that earned him the well-deserved monikers, "The Teacher" and "Teacher of Light," from Emmanuel Obiechina, and from Tijan M. Sallah and Ngozi Okonjo-Iwuala, the coeditors of one of Achebe's biographies.

Notes

1   Dubem Okafor, *The Dance of Death: Nigerian History and Christopher Okigbo's Poetry.* Trenton, NJ: Africa World Press, 1998: 42–3.
2   Chinua Achebe, *The Trouble with Nigeria.* Enugu, Nigeria: Fourth Dimension Publishers, 1983: 1.
3   Quoted in Edith Ihekweazu, ed., *Eagle on Iroko: Selected Papers from the Chinua Achebe International Symposium 1990.* Ibadan, Nigeria: Heinemann Educational Books (Nigeria) Plc., 1996: 208.
4   Chinua Achebe, "Achebe on Editing," *World Literature Written in English,* Vol. 27 (1987): 1–5.
5   Emenyonu and Uko, eds., *Emerging Perspectives on Chinua Achebe, Volume 2,* p. 57.
6   Jane Wilkinson, "Chinua Achebe," in *Talking with African Writers.* London: James Currey, 1992: 55–6.
7   Okafor, *The Dance of Death,* pp. 100–3.
8   Christopher Okigbo, "Path of Thunder: Poems Prophesying War," *Black Orpheus,* Vol. 1, No. 2 (March 1968).
9   Okafor, *The Dance of Death,* p. 104.
10 Emmanuel Obiechina, "In Praise of the Teacher," in Ihekweazu, *Eagle on the Iroko,* pp. 22–3.
11 Charles Nnolim, "A Source for *Arrow of God,*" *Research in African Literatures,* Vol. 8, No. 1 (Spring 1977): 1–26.
12 C. L. Innes, "A Source for *Arrow of God:* A Response," *Research in African Literatures,* Vol. 9, No. 1 (Spring 1978): 16–18.

5 My Interview with Chinua Achebe*

Culled from *Research in African Literatures*, Vol. 12, No. 1(Spring 1981): 1–13.

Many foreign readers are greatly attracted by the cultural information they get from your novels about traditional Igbo society. Do you consider these novels a competent source of that kind of information?

Yes. What I'm doing is presenting a total world and a total life as it is lived in that world, and you cannot do that in a vacuum; I cannot do it in a vacuum. I am writing about my people in the past and in the present, and I have to create for them the world in which they live and move and have their being. If somebody else thinks, as some do, that this is sociology or anthropology, that's their own lookout. It is the life of the people I am writing about. Therefore, if someone is in search of information, or knowledge, or enlightenment about the total life of these people – the Igbo people – I think my novels would be a good source.

How would you advise foreign readers, who are alien to the culture about which you are writing, to approach your novels?

I don't advise them at all beyond the novels. I think just in the same way as I got myself sufficiently informed to the understand the culture in which Dickens set his characters or the environment in which James Joyce situated his stories, in the same way anybody who is genuinely after whatever virtues literature gives and wants them to get them from my books, indeed from African books, he must be prepared to get himself immersed in the life of the Africans. How he does it is not for me to say, but I think he would fail unless he displayed an openness of mind and a readiness to accept another way of looking at reality. This turns out to be difficult for many people in the West, but that's not my fault; it's their fault. And it's up to them to do something to correct that defect – the defect of self-centeredness.

I say that it's not a universal fault because, as you yourself know, the Igbo culture lays a great deal of emphasis on differences, on dualities, on otherness. This is why we do not find it difficult to accept that other people somewhere else might be doing one thing differently from ourselves. Look at our proverbs; they are full of statements like "*Odi be ndi adiro be ibe fa*" ("What there

DOI: 10.4324/9781003184133-5

is among one people is not among another"). It's as if Igbo culture is constantly anxious to remind you of the complexity of the world. And so you are ready for it. Now, if you're brought up in a culture which is fanatically single-minded in its own self-centeredness, then you've got a job to do to correct it.

As a creative writer, you have done much in the way of correcting misinformation about Igbo culture. How do you regard the work of Igbo literary critics? Do you think that they have done enough to interpret the messages borne in your novels?

I think some of them have. I mean, there have been outstanding examples. It would not be proper, in fact, to get into names, but I think I should mention that there are people like Emmanuel Obiechina and Donatus Nwoga who have done very serious work on my novels or generally on Igbo culture as seen through our literature. But there have been others who have been somewhat casual or even negative in their attitude. I'm thinking, for instance, of a certain fellow who was claiming that *Arrow of God* was written by his uncle, which led to the rather curious situation in which the fellow was dismissed as irresponsible by a white critic! It really should have been expected that some Igbo critics would have shown as much concern as the white critic about matters of critical responsibility in our literature.

I do think that what you need is a fair number of indigenous critics who are on the ball because they see literature as a serious matter (our people do not take it seriously enough; I think we are still too complacent). And the next thing you know we will be complaining about Americans, about the British, running around telling us about our writers. And yet there is not enough dedication and diligence among our own critics. I'm looking forward to a change in this for it is absolutely important. If literature is important, then criticism of literature is also important, and we should get more and more people who are ready to read the books. Read the books first. It's not enough to say, "I am a Nigerian therefore I understand Achebe." No, you've got to read what I have written. If not, an American who has read it would be a better critic than yourself.

Do you think the white man's culture succeeded in destroying Igbo culture completely, or did it just injure it a little bit?

Culture is not as fragile as we sometimes think, but it is not granite, either. A culture can be damaged, can be turned from its course not only by foreigners. Let's get this absolutely clear: a culture can be mutilated, can be destroyed by its own people, under certain situations. Maybe we could return to this later on because I think the Igbo people are in many ways today doing as much as, or more than, the British ever did to destroy their own culture. Take the question of these comical chiefs that you have now – 400 in Anambra State and 400 in Imo State. This goes against all the history and tradition and philosophy of Igbo people. But that's by-the-way – no, I mean that's a digression.

The Igbo culture was not destroyed by Europe. It was disturbed. It was disturbed very seriously, but this is nothing new in the world. Cultures are constantly influenced, challenged, pushed about by other cultures that may have some kind of advantage at a particular time – either the advantage of force, persuasion, wealth, or whatever. But as I said initially, a culture which is healthy will often survive. It will not survive exactly in the form in which it was met by the invading culture, but it will modify itself and move on. And this is the great thing about culture, if it is alive. The people who own it will ensure that they make adjustments: they drop what can no longer be carried in transition; they drop whatever seems like excess baggage so that they can continue their journey. We're all engaged, we're all embarked on a journey through history. So I think what has happened is that we still have the fundamental principles of the Igbo culture. Its emphasis is on the worth of every man and woman. Every man has his *chi* and every woman has her *chi*. Nobody is useless; that's one thing we have not jettisoned. I am as good as the next man.

From this flows the idea that in the deliberations of the people everybody should participate. It's a democratic principle which is very deeply embedded in our culture. We don't send representatives – you go yourself. But that was all right in the microstate of the village. Today our situation is different; we can no longer all appear in person. So our culture has to make some adjustments to find a way of dealing with this new threat to its egalitarian philosophy. This is what I mean: How do you send a representative? And you can see that our people don't know. From recent experience in politics, you can see that our people simply have no idea how to choose their representatives. And it's not that surprising because we didn't have representatives in the past. So this is something our culture has to learn. Like the adaptable bird in our proverb, we must learn to fly without perching or perish from man's new-learnt marksmanship. So there is the need for a culture to be alive and active and ready to adjust, ready to take challenges. A culture that fails to take challenges will die. But if we are ready to take challenges, to make concessions that are necessary without accepting anything that undermines our fundamental belief in the dignity of man, I think we would be doing what is expected of us.

So, in other words, when people describe your novels as protest novels, you accept the term protest *to mean that you are protesting against the European disturbance of African culture as well as the disturbance that comes from within?*

Yes, yes. I think that protest is not a very good word, but we use it quite often, and whenever I use it, I use it in a very general sense, the sense in which we all admit that there is a lot to protest against in every life, in every community, in every civilization. If things were perfect, there would be no need for writers to write their novels. But it is because they see a vision of the world which is better than what exists; it is because they see the possibilities of man rising higher than he has risen at the moment that they write. So, whatever they write, if they are true practitioners of their art, would be in essence a protest against what exists, against what is.

All your novels contain incantations, proverbs, and aphorisms used by priests, chiefs, and elders. Were you very conscious of their poetic qualities or were you more interested in the traditional philosophy they convey as you wrote these novels?

There is no need to separate the two. You see, this is a Western attitude to things. Our people have always taken a more holistic approach. So when people ask me, "Is it this or that?" It's both, it's both. A proverb is both a functional means of communication and also a very elegant and artistic performance itself. I think that proverbs are both utilitarian and little vignettes of art. So when I use these forms in my novels, they both serve a utilitarian purpose, which is to reenact the life of the people that I am describing, and also delight through elegance and aptness of imagery. This is what proverbs are supposed to do.

What of the dramatic values of the costumes and postures of the Egwugwu?

I do not attempt too much description in my writing of the actual physical appearance, the face or faces. I do a certain amount, but it's not a preoccupation with me. I go over this rather fast because I am concerned about other things. But when it's absolutely essential to draw attention to the physical appearance of the person or spirit or how he is dressed, then I would do so. But basically, I think that costume belongs to drama. You can only give an impression, some kind of impression, that something looks like this. I do not know whether I'm making myself clear. It's not basically my function as a novelist to concentrate on the appearance except where it is absolutely essential for the story.

But we must not attempt to be too prescriptive or dogmatic. Rigid distinctions tend to put us into difficulties because *drama* is an abstraction from something which is total. Take, for instance, the appearance of Ezeulu to reenact the coming of his God and the consecration of the first chief priest. He has to explain who he is and he goes back to history and myth. That whole episode is drama. But if you ask an Igbo man what is going on, he won't say that this is drama or that is religion. It is all: religion, drama, and mythology. Everything is rolled into one in the service of art and society.

Do you consider the Igbo rituals and ceremonies in your novels a photographic reenactment of traditional Igbo rituals and ceremonies? If so, does your writing them down vitiate or promote their oral performance? Put differently, some people are talking about oral literature, others call it oral performance, and still others believe we are simply dealing with literature.

I don't mind what anybody calls anything as long as we are up and doing. I think the people in oral literature have a lot of work to do in collecting, analyzing, and presenting what we have. They cannot stop a novelist from using what he wants to use from this tradition. Such borrowing doesn't prevent scholars from doing their own job. The fact that I have a pumpkin ceremony in *Arrow of God* does not prevent an oral literature scholar from going to Umuchu where – and only where, according to Nnolim – the thing exists and recording it; or going to Ngwa where, according to Amankulor, a pumpkin festival happens one month before the New Yam Festival and is dominated by women. So the novel does not prevent a documentation or presentation of what we have in other art forms. I think that, on the contrary, it should encourage such documentation.

You are saying literature encompasses all these variations?

Yes, yes, yes!

Many African scholars, especially those who receive their higher education in Europe and America, come back to African countries disillusioned with the white man's religion. Do you think there will be a time in the future that they will consider going back to practice traditional African religion such as the society of Okonkwo had before "things fell apart" for them/us?

I don't think people go back, if you see what I mean. It's not really a question of going back. I think if one goes back, there's something wrong somewhere, or else a misunderstanding. In other words, you assume already that he is ahead and returning. When we talk of going back, I suppose we mean metaphorically. I guess we mean searching around for alternatives. There are alternatives which say something about religion, morality, in a way other than the Christian-Western-European, which are indigenous to our culture and which some of our best people, even the Christians, never abandoned. There is really no question, in my mind, of going back. If one religion fulfills a certain need for some people, I'm not about to prescribe how they will make use of it. Other people may not need it all. As we know now, some people feel they can do without any kind of formal religion. So you can't say, "oh, let us all go back," because our attitude towards religion and what religion does for each and every one of us is different.

But that's not what we're talking about. We are not talking about the forms or manifestations of religion – like whether somebody has a sacrament with God through Christian communion or somebody else has another sacrament in which he breaks kola in the presence of his guests and his God and ancestors. I don't think these two things conflict. We must realize that our ancestors were wiser than is often made out. They were around in our environment for thousands and thousands of years. They learned a lot about that environment. And if we think that we are wiser than they because of 30 years or so of mixing with Europe, I think we are sadly mistaken. And the day will come when we will rediscover some of their values and attitudes – for instance, their attitude to family. We see the Western people that we are copying are in trouble with their families. So why go and copy people who are in trouble? It may be, in fact, that what they need is help from us. If you meet someone who is in distress and has collapsed, do you collapse beside him? No, what you should really do is give first aid or send for a doctor.

What kind of trouble do you have in mind? Is it the problem of one man having one wife? Or do you mean the kind of moral support that somebody receives as a result of the extended family system?

All that, all that! I think that the respect that fathers and mothers had and still have in Africa (and this extends to all old people, not just one's parents) is very valuable. The respect you give to age is very valuable to you because an old person has been around a long time and has encountered a whole lot of things you haven't seen. You may think, "This is an old man; what does he know?" But you are wrong. Respect is not only valuable to you, it's also valuable to the old people for they are senior members of the society. If they feel they are needed and that their advice is useful, they will remain alert. They will not simply go to pieces. I've known old people in my village, some of whom were said to be 100, who were still very alert in their minds because they knew that if there was any land quarrel, they would be called. They had a job; they were not useless. If you render somebody useless – that is, everybody above 50 – then they become useless. They grow senile, they lose their mind, and they decay. They have an irrational fear of growing old, they make pathetic concessions to youth, and society suffers by being frozen in adolescence.

As a writer, you have played the roles of a teacher, a social transformer, and even a revolutionary in Biafra. How did your insight as an imaginative writer help or inhibit you in carrying out these roles?

Well, I don't think that's a very easy question. I think I can sense what you are driving at. In a revolutionary situation, in a situation of great danger, in an institution and regime of violence, for instance, what does a creative artist do? This is a question which I will not presume to answer for everybody because a writer is a human being. He is not just a writer; he is also a person. He is also a member of society. Therefore, he must decide what role, besides that of writing, he can play. He must decide that himself. I decided that I could not stand aside from the problems and struggles of my people at that point in history. And if happened again, I would not behave differently.

But there are limitations, you know. For instance, in that kind of situation there is bound to be pressure to think alike. There is bound to be pressure, maybe, to surrender some of your cherished ideals. There may even be the danger (and this is not just talking about Biafra) of forgetting that art is not "brother" to violence. The writer has to keep reminding himself all the time that even where you think violence is inevitable, you still should realize what it is, you do not pretend that violence is good. It may be inevitable but it's not good. So when I see people talk about revolutionary violence, I think the artist has to be very careful. There is revolutionary violence, okay; but the artist would be endangering himself the moment he begins to write a poem which talks about the flowering of bullets. Bullets do not flower! It's tricky to get into that situation. I cannot say more than I have said, but I'll simply say again that an artist has to have his wits around him because he is stepping into a very dangerous domain. Fundamentally, art is on the side of life.

However much you may wish to deny it, people know and believe that you have a peculiar insight as a writer and that you occupy a very privileged position in society. That's the reason why they rely on you to help in a revolution, not only to preach against violence but also to probe the future and advise them.

Oh yes, I think that within your power you should do all that. I'm simply giving a kind of signal which I have noticed (not just out of the Biafran experience) about a total allegiance to a regime, for instance. Revolution will be prosecuted by people. And the artist who gives his total allegiance to a group of people is likely to be disappointed, is likely to find sooner or later (and more likely sooner) that the people are not all that he thought. So he should hold himself in some kind of reserve. This is all I'm saying. There may be an occasion for him to back out. And he should not destroy this possibility, this chance.

Kolawole Ogungbesan uses quotations from your public addresses, lectures and interviews to point out how much you have encouraged the African writer to play a meaningful role in his society: the writer as a teacher, a social transformer, a revolutionary, and an actor rather than a reactor – roles which he alleges you and Christopher Okigbo played in your native Biafra. He adds that while such crusading roles may not be wrong in themselves, they inhibit the production of long-lasting creative writing. Would you like to comment on this observation?

No, no, I think that's nonsense. Ogungbesan, unfortunately, is dead. He died last year. It's unfortunate, I think, that I should be dealing with that kind of thing in his absence. But it doesn't matter. The trouble is, he had a problem with Biafra, like many Nigerians who were on the federal side, and their problem was compounded by the fact they won the war. So they feel justified in whatever they thought and felt during that crisis, because it's very easy to imagine that right and victory are on the same side. So it's the problem Nigerians have with Biafra which is coming through in Ogungbesan's comment. He didn't think, for instance, that the poetry I wrote during the war is poetry. Perhaps he was right. Except that other people – those in Biafra with me, but especially those in neither Biafra nor Nigeria – think otherwise. (Two examples are Donatus Nwoga and Eldred Jones.) I received a letter from an Irish poet, a very good Irish poet, in which he said, after reading my poems, that he was full of envy. In his own situation, he wished that he or *any* of his countrymen in Ireland could write even a few lines as grave and moving about their problems. And he added, "This is not only your best work but also the best war poetry that has come out from anywhere in a long time." This is from someone I didn't even know. He may be overenthusiastic – this Irishman, and many others like him – I don't know. But put that beside Ogungbesan's view (and it's not just Ogungbesan; it's a whole group of people who were bitterly opposed to Biafra): "This is not poetry; this is nonsense; this is sentimental." So you realize then that you are perhaps not dealing with literary criticism; you may be dealing with political prejudice, ethnic prejudice, and that kind of thing.

In an interview at the University of Texas at Austin in 1969, you said, "I believe it's impossible to write anything in Africa without some kind of commitment, some kind of message, some kind of protest." Given the kind of political and literary strides that Africans have made, do you still believe African writing today should continue to be protest writing? If so, protest against whom and what?

Well, I think that I've already touched on that. The problem is the use of the word *protest*. It is too vague a word – too vague in one sense and too exact in another. Protest means from someone against another. But the way I prefer to see protest is that assumed mission, that natural condition of the artist to be protesting against what he is given. As an African, I have been given a certain role in the world, a certain place in the world, a certain history in the world; and I say, "No, I don't accept these roles, these histories – distorted, garbled accounts. I'm going to recreate myself." I'm protesting against the world. But if we are talking about a novel like *A Man of the People*, the protest is clearly more localized. I'm talking about the politics of the country after impendence. I'm protesting against the way we are ordering our lives. So I think protest will never end. The need for protesting will never end. I don't think it's a question of protest against Europe or simply protest against local conditions. It is protest against the way we are handling human society in view of the possibilities of greatness and the better alternatives which the artist sees.

Foreign commentators like David Carroll and Lloyd Brown appear to have got the message in your novels and this is why they have been able to write very brilliant essays juxtaposing your balanced view of Africa and the prejudiced view of Conrad's Africa, "the heart of darkness." If you were to write a novel today, what would its message be?

Well, that's a secret. I don't talk about something which hasn't been written because it inhibits the creative process.

But to take up what you were saying in the introductory part of the question – I mean, the people you mentioned – I feel at this point that the high standard of criticism from people like David Carroll and many others has raised the tone of our criticism immensely in the last several years and that we no longer see the kind of critical dilettantism we saw initially from people who were not really qualified either by temperament or training to get into it. They were doing it maybe because nobody else was. And now we have some very acute, some very sharp people. It's a challenge to the African to be up and doing instead of just sitting around and complaining about "all these people running around and writing about our authors." Many of these foreign critics are doing a lot of good work. Not so long ago an Indian magazine called *Literary Half-Yearly* devoted its pages to my work.[1] Contributors were from all over the world and most of them from the Commonwealth. Now, one of the things that struck me particularly was a piece by an Australian woman on *No Longer at Ease*. You know, that is a book that has not, in my view, received as good and perceptive attention as it deserves. And this Australian had somehow got into the relationship of blood between Obi and his mother (which is an important key to an understanding of the story) in such a way that I was absolutely astounded. This comes from taking literature seriously. Whoever she is, wherever she is, she took this book seriously and was able to uncover an important layer of its meaning. Maybe this is not the question that you're asking, but I thought I should mention this first as a tribute to what, at the level of criticism, some foreign critics and scholars are now giving to African literature and also as a challenge to our own people to get cracking. There are still areas where our people have an advantage, but that advantage will come to nothing if they do not read the books, if they don't take literature seriously, if they are consumed by prejudice, envy, whatever. Some of them, strangely enough, do not seem to believe that literature is important even when they make a living teaching it! Or are they? These things will have to change.

Many people regard you as a creative mentor. What advice do you offer to them that would help them start their creative writing careers?

Well, the advice that I always give is that they should start and they should strive to be themselves, to achieve honesty of tone, to achieve authenticity of tone, and not to pretend to be something that they are not; not to pretend to feel something that you know you don't feel just because you heard it is the right way to feel about something. Posturing is a disease which artists are very prone to. "What does an artist dress like? What does he wear? What kind of life does he live?" Things like that. "Then I will do that and become an artist." No. I think you should get to work with seriousness and not copy. No artist should copy another. We all probably start off imitating, but ultimately a good artist will soon find his own voice and will use it.

Your answer may have rendered my next question irrelevant, yet I think I should ask it. That is, you seem to have influenced directly or indirectly almost all the Nigerian novelists. Do you foresee a time when that influence will produce artistic monotony in the Nigerian novel?

No, it shouldn't. I think influence is not a bad thing. You can influence people in positive ways. I have dealt with certain things so the next person doesn't have to go over the same ground but that is not to say that the story of our past is finished, which is the way many people seem to take it. That is absolute nonsense. We haven't even started. We don't know who we are yet. So I think there are thousands of stories that can be written out of our past and our present and our future. The kind of influence which I would like to think that I have had is a positive one. We may say, "He has done this, okay. It is possible to do something even better." It is possible now that we know we can write. "He has used language in a particular way." It doesn't have to be Queen's English. It doesn't have to be pidgin. It is possible to do something else in the process of that recreation of ourselves that I was talking about. It is possible even to recreate the language that we are using. It's possible to go from there to push the English language to a limit or reject it. I mean we can say, "No, we've come to the end of that; I want to write in Igbo or something like that." All these things would be, in fact, a reaction to me as one of the first writers, and all this would be positive. But we should not sit down and say, "Achebe wrote about Ogidi; now I must write about Umuoji" and then repeat the same thing. No, that's not what I am saying.

Some of us aspire to make a career out of teaching your works. Do you have any advice for us?

No, I think you are doing a fine job and you should continue. I think the teaching of literature should go on and even increase because I think it is very important. When we talk about the confusion in our culture, about no morals, and so on, where do we get these things in the modern world if not from literature? I mean, we don't have the social institutions that we had in the past in which the values of the community were transmitted. How do we transmit a national culture to Nigerians if not through works of imagination? This is something that our people have not paid attention to. We are talking about modernization, industrialization, and so on, but we do not realize that we cannot even industrialize unless we have tackled the mind, the imagination, and thus the attitude of people to themselves, to their society, to work, and so on. How do you do these things if you cannot get to their minds, to their imagination? So literature is not a luxury for us. It is a life and death affair because we are fashioning a new man. The Nigerian is a new man. How do we get to his mind? Is it by preaching to him once in a while – by the leaders? No, I think it is something solid and permanent that we must put into his consciousness. That is what he reads, what he believes, and what he loves. We must dramatize his predicament so that he can see the choices and choose right.

Notes

* This interview took place on 11 April 1980 at the University of Florida at Gainesville, where Achebe was participating in the fifth annual conference of the African Literature Association.

1 *Literary Half-Yearly* 21 (January 1980). The journal is edited by Professor Anniah Gowda of the University of Mysore, and this special issue was guest edited by Professor Bruce King of New Zealand.

6 The Eagle on Iroko Critically Analyzes the Problem with Nigeria

Upon his return to Nigeria in August 1979, Chinua Achebe immediately resumed his writing career with the publication of short literary pieces, such as poems and short stories, and at the same time with taking part in the reformation of the structures of higher education in Nigeria. Moreover, he paid closer attention to some ongoing national issues, including the serious effort the General Obasanjo military regime was making in planning elections to return political power to civilian rulers. As we noted in a preceding argument, this was one of the issues that prompted Achebe to return home from his American expedition and make his contributions to reform some Nigerian situations. His interests in both educational and political issues led him to get seriously involved in activities he hoped would positively affect the unity and survival of Nigeria as one nation. Despite his hopes, however, he was aware that, historically, the former three prewar regions of Nigeria – the North, the East, and the West – had in the past built parochial and tribal political parties under leaders whose activities were antithetical to the creation of national unity. Achebe noticed with dismay that, even at this time when the military was about to lift their ban on political activities and hand over powers to elected civilian administration, the old political leaders were still making the same mistakes they made before that led to the waging of the civil war. For as the postwar military era was coming to an end, there were visible signs that the sociopolitical leaders were engaged in forming new political parties whose agenda and interests were not going to produce the peace, unity, and social justice they were preaching for everybody in the whole country. He discovered the potential shortcomings in the nation's body-politic after reading the campaign manifestos that the political parties published for the national election contested by Dr. Nnamdi Azikiwe of the Nigerian People's Party (NPP), whose membership was predominantly Easterners; Chief Obafemi Awolowo of the Unity Party of Nigeria (UPN), whose membership was predominantly Westerners; as well as Mallam Abubakar Waziri of the Greater Nigerian People's Party (GNPP), Mallam Shehu Shagari of the National Party of Nigeria (NPN) and Mallam Aminu Kano of the People's Redemption Party (PRP), whose respective memberships were predominantly Northerners.

On the surface, all the five registered political parties adopted names that purportedly implied that they were going to work for the common good of all

DOI: 10.4324/9781003184133-6

Nigerians, irrespective of their ethnic origins. But when their memberships, leaderships, and aims and objectives are critically analyzed, one finds that the unity, redemption, and coexistence of the citizens they campaigned on would not be realized to the benefit of everybody in all parts of the country. And all through their electioneering, it became obvious that the election contest was practically between Shagari from the North and Awolowo from the West. Although Azikiwe, an Igbo from the East, had served as President of Nigeria before the war, and was the most highly educated among the contestants, he was not elected. Which is why many of his Igbo ethnic people saw his non-election as the postwar president as part of the ongoing Igbo marginalization in Nigeria. In the end, the least educated of the contestants, Shehu Shagari, a Fulani from the North, was elected as the first post-military era civilian president of Nigeria. Some political analysts saw his election as continued retention of political power and leadership by Northerners since the civil war. However, his Igbo running mate from the East, Dr. Alex Ekwueme, became the Vice President, which was a nominal consolation prize the Northerners conceded to the Igbo people. And Chief Awolowo, a Yoruba from the West, became the leader of the opposition party in the federal government; he exercised political powers second to the Northerners. So, of the three dominant ethnic peoples of Nigeria, the Igbo were politically sidelined, even as their technocrats in the civil service continued to be used by every administration, from the post-military regimes to the current civilian administration of President Buhari. In this chapter, we learn from Achebe's analysis how the Igbo had been so unjustly treated.

To begin with, many of us Nigerians have often looked at the political problems of our country from ethnic viewpoints without thorough analysis, which is both naïve and simplistic in that we have not cared enough to look deeply into the root causes of the unpleasant events we often complain about. For instance, we have not made enough effort to fathom why Northerners have had a grip on national political powers to near exclusion of both Easterners and the Westerners, and why Easterners have had it worse. So, with impassioned critical analysis the Eagle on Iroko had to go beyond ethnic sentiments to offer some solutions to the problem.

As Chinua Achebe worked hard to effect some changes in the nation's divisive political situation, the powers that be noticed his achievements and thus decided in 1979 to reward him for his services to the nation with two national awards: Officer of the Federal Republic of Nigeria (OFR) and the first Nigerian National Merit Award (NNMA) for excellence. Like the Presidential Medal of Freedom in America, both accolades were the highest civilian honors that the outgoing Obasanjo military administration presented to Achebe for making especially meritorious and sustained contributions to the general effort of rebuilding Nigeria through his literary and cultural endeavors. The awards brought national and international recognition to him as a person, and visibility to Nigeria as a nation; thus, 1979 became a very remarkable year in his life. In addition, Achebe earned the awards for the roles he played in reforming and promoting cultural and civic education in Nigeria through his fiction and the oral and written speeches (including sociopolitical treatises) he made severally to inspire hope and unity in his fellow citizens. Furthermore, Achebe used the occasion of his reception of the two awards as an opportunity to do what he does best: to offer instructive criticism of some government actions so as to help its officials to find ways of making changes that could enhance the programs they create from time to time for the people. Although he eminently deserved both awards, there were some people who saw them as a means through which the government could make Achebe become less critical of their socioeconomic programs and activities. In reaction, Achebe made the following remark to allay the fears of those who felt he should not accept the awards because he did not need them:

> Now one of the weaknesses of Nigeria is failure to accept merit and quality, in various areas – in the sciences, in the arts, in everything. Politics is all that matters here. If you seek the political kingdom, everything else will be added unto you. . . . So when, in a fit of absent-mindedness, or whatever, the Nigerian nation says we recognize your achievements as a writer and we give you a medal, I don't see that I should reject it. Not that I need that medal. In fact, it was Femi Osofisan who said I didn't need it. Of course, I didn't need it and this was all the more reason why I thought I could take it because I really didn't need it. But for me, it meant that, for the first time, literature was being accorded a certain recognition. And while I was going to receive it, I was also writing a speech – this was before anybody else knew that this was going to happen – a speech in which I was going to say precisely this: that nobody is going to buy me with honors, and that I think that this will not be the end because we should have a situation in which national honors are given to writers, given to painters, given to sculptors, given to journalists. What we have here – if you go round this campus, you'll find that students' hostels are named after politicians that you cannot remember one year after they leave office. Statues are raised to politicians the first year they are in office; universities are named after living politicians. Now I think this kind of thing is wrong. And if we can change emphasis ever so little by bringing in scientists and writers, we will be encouraging other scientists, other writers.[1]

Furthermore, in his NNMA acceptance speech, titled "The Metaphor of the Rain and the Clock," Achebe gave the following assurance to the writers, critics, and citizens of Nigeria:

> Most writers are inveterate critics of their fellow men and of the society – a role imposed on them by their multiple vision, their natural skepticism and individualism. They are not good material for government information officers and public relations operatives. Show a writer the glittering skyline of your expanding metropolis and he will be looking down instead into your swollen, foul-smelling open drains. Point out to him the graceful sweep of your ultra-modern concrete and aluminium flyovers and he will spy out the

beggar living prehistorically under the rock shelter. That is the writer's nature and strength. To wish him to be otherwise is to wish impotence upon him and deny society the full vigor of his creativity. A writer who finds himself in perfect drill formation would almost be obliged by a natural cussedness, if you like, to shuffle and drag his feet. When he gets up to dance with his fellows he is apt to hear in his mind's ear the rhythms of a different drummer. In the words – frightening words – of Joyce Cary, "he is doomed to be free."

[. . .]

I think I am on safe ground if I say that Nigerian writers are not planning to send a delegation to President Shehu Shagari to pledge their unflinching support. Flinching support is more in their line of business. But I do hope that the military government's last-hour precedent of honoring writers at the highest level will be maintained by Shagari and succeeding regimes so that Nigeria may become an example of enlightenment to Africa and other parts of the world.[2]

Moreover, the acceptance speech demonstrated to the government authorities, his fellow writers, critics, and Nigerian citizens how fearless a committed writer should be in order to expose the true nature of the Nigerian situation – whether good or bad – in spite of the government's tendency to paint rosy pictures of their activities, which often worked to the detriment of the citizens. In other words, the assurance Achebe gave to both the government and the governed was that, as a writer, he would always write truth to power so he can make his readers understand the true state of the nation. Through that means, he inspired them to work together for the development of their native country. The speech also revealed the high hope he had for his *fatherland* Nigeria.

Between 1980 and 1983, Achebe traveled abroad numerous times to attend international conferences and to receive honorary doctorate degrees awarded by foreign universities in recognition of the work he had been doing to develop and promote African culture and civilization through its literature. For instance, in April 1980, he came to the United States while I was doing my doctoral studies and attended the ALA conference at the University of Florida at Gainesville. I met and had a formal interview with him on his writing career. Coincidentally, James Baldwin, the famous African American novelist, was also attending the conference. The two renowned novelists met for the first time, and shared in a joint interview their experiences as black writers who were busy expressing the black agony in two continents – racism in America and colonialism in Africa – and using their individual talents to protest the hydra-headed effects of both evil phenomena, while simultaneously articulating ways of overcoming them. The authors saw themselves as long-lost cousins who found each other after a century of separation. Those of us asking them questions on the issue from the audience did not want that session of the conference to end (Figure 6.1). And after a period of two decades, I found myself teaching the two authors' novels with commitment in my present institution, Southern Connecticut State University, New Haven, because of the interest they engendered in me at that Florida conference.

Figure 6.1 Chinua Achebe and James Baldwin hanging out in Florida discussing Africana issues

Source: Still from "I Heard It Through the Grapevine," Produced and Directed by Dick Fontaine and Pat Hartley, Living Archives Inc. (1982)

Prior to the April 1980 conference in Florida, Achebe traveled to Australia in March 1980, where he delivered at the Writers' Week in Adelaide an address as a guest in a forum on the theme of myth, symbol, and fable in African literature. After acknowledging Westerners' use of myth, symbol, and fable as separate ideas in writing literature, he went on to discuss how the three terms are holistically used in the art of storytelling in African literature. He made the distinction because of the problems he found arising from regional languages in Britain that are similar to those found in individual countries of the erstwhile British Commonwealth, including Nigeria. Achebe utilized the forum as an opportunity to answer some questions that readers of his novels had for him.

In 1982, he traveled to the University of Kent in the United Kingdom where he was invited to receive an honorary doctorate degree alongside the Archbishop of Canterbury, Dr. Robert Runcie. The university orator told the audience that "Achebe is now revered as a master by the younger generation of African writers and it is to him that they regularly turn for counsel and inspiration," which the orator regarded as a heavy responsibility. Thereafter, Achebe traveled to America, where he was made an honorary member of the distinguished American Academy of Arts and Letters.[3]

In the same year, Achebe also traveled to Ireland as a guest of the Irish government for the centenary of James Joyce. He was struck by the humble and dignified demeanor of the President of the Republic of Ireland, which inspired him to discuss the poor leadership qualities of Nigerian politicians in his forthcoming book, contrasting them to the Irish President's good example:

> Last year I was a guest of the Irish Government at the centenary of James Joyce. I sat with other guests and thousands of Dubliners in a huge municipal hall waiting for the President of the Irish Republic to arrive and inaugurate the event. Two minutes to go and I had still not seen any signs of his arrival. On the exact dot of five a tall fellow walked on to the stage followed by one man in uniform. The Chairman of the event (who incidentally was a writer and not the Irish Minister for Social Affairs, Sports, Children, Women, Trade Union and Culture) motioned the audience to stand. So that was the President! His ADC gave him his speech which he read and came down to sit in the audience to listen to a few tributes to Joyce.[4]

All told, Achebe's experiences during his foreign travels so deeply influenced his resolve to change both the literary and political landscape of his country that he firmly decided to become a practicing party politician in 1982, one year after he retired from service at the University of Nigeria, Nsukka, after teaching there and in American and Canadian universities for 10 years.

However, this was not the first time that Achebe contemplated the idea of becoming a practicing politician. For, after the military handed over power to the Shagari administration on October 1, 1979, he reviewed the general political situation in Nigeria and was convinced that if the civilian government was going to succeed this time around, its political culture had to be restructured – a task which entailed new people joining any of the five political parties to work to change the attitude of their leaders from within. As he wondered which party to join, Achebe was drawn to the PRP whose leader, Mallam Aminu Kano, was so highly impressed by his 1979 acceptance speech that he invited Achebe to his headquarters in Kano for discussions in which he sought to persuade Achebe to join his party. After the Kano visit, Achebe formally joined the party in late 1982. Ezenwa-Ohaeto describes how and why Achebe made this uneasy decision:

> [Thus] he took a decision to become active in politics and, after examining the five parties, accepted the invitation of Mallam Aminu Kano, one of the most selfless politicians that his country had ever produced, and joined the People's Redemption Party (PRP) in late 1982. Achebe preferred an interventionist role to that of a mere critic for he obviously believed that a political rupture was necessary. He attended meetings and engaged in several discussions about new structures since the general elections would be held the following year, 1983. His entry into politics did not lessen his contribution as president of the Association of Nigerian Authors – the official

nomenclature adopted at their annual conference at the University of Ife in November 1982 – or as editor of *Okike* with its associated activities.[5]

That Achebe, a revered and preeminent Igbo writer from Eastern Nigeria, was willing to join a political party whose leaders and predominant members were Hausa/Fulani of Northern Nigeria spoke volumes about the patriotic temperament of a man who indeed wanted to restructure Nigerian politics in words and deeds. Less patriotic Nigerians had expected him to join NPP whose members and leaders were primarily Easterners. Instead, Achebe decided to work from within PRP to effect changes across Nigerian ethnic boundaries. In appreciation of his vision and activities, PRP appointed him their deputy national Chair. As he traveled across the country recruiting members for the party, Achebe praised the personal qualities of the leader of their party and told why he wanted to oust President Shagari from office. He emphasized the fact that as a presidential candidate, Mallam Aminu Kano was exemplary in the way he conducted his affairs without pursuing enormous wealth at the expense of ordinary people. He also said that the leader urged Nigerians to cultivate a sense of pride in their agricultural development in order to meet the country's food requirements, suggesting the introduction of agricultural science in all post-primary and higher learning institutions in Nigeria.[6]

Achebe campaigned very hard to encourage all Nigerians, especially the Igbo of South East Nigeria, to join the PRP. As a result of his vigorous campaigning across the country, PRP found a foothold in NPP-dominated Igboland to the extent that within a short period of time notable Igbo men like his friend Arthur Nwankwo and Chief Sylvester Nwodo joined the party. Nwodo was soon appointed the deputy leader of PRP in Achebe's home state, Anambra, and they both helped to attract more Igbo people into the party. So it was ready to compete and win the 1983 national elections, especially the presidency. Moreover, Achebe used the information he gathered from the campaigns in some speeches he made on leadership qualities while diagnosing the Nigerian sociopolitical situation and as raw material for writing his book *The Trouble with Nigeria*,[7] which Arthur Nwankwo's press, Fourth Dimension Publishers, published in 1983. The release of the book was scheduled to coincide with the elections to tout further the qualities of their party leader. Unfortunately, however, Kano died suddenly before the book came off the press. Nevertheless, Achebe dedicated it to his memory and to that of an Igbo preeminent Nigerian jurist, Sir Louis Mbanefo, for both men lived virtuous lives while in office, and served the nation as honest, hard-working public servants and statesmen. In other words, Achebe memorialized their leadership qualities to inspire other Nigerian civil servants, politicians, and religious leaders to emulate both men, as they strove to build a better nation for all Nigerians and posterity. The blurb gives a sample of the trouble with Nigeria that Achebe discusses in the book as follows:

> Chinua Achebe, internationally acclaimed author, has now turned his considerable wit and wisdom to the problems of contemporary Nigeria.

This is a book that must be read by all Nigerians who care about their country, who feel they can no longer stand idly by and "wring their hands in anguish" while Nigeria is destroyed by bad leadership, corruption and inequality.

THE TROUBLE WITH NIGERIA is both a savage indictment of the current system and a message of hope for the future. The time for action is now. Read this book and join in the effort toward a new social and political order for Nigeria.

Through careful analysis, Achebe identified the trouble with Nigeria as deriving mainly from a failure of leadership, tribalism, a false image of ourselves, unacceptable Nigerian-style leadership, and a lack of patriotism. In addition, there was social injustice and a cult of mediocrity, indiscipline, corruption, as well as the *Igbo problem*. To solve these problems, Achebe offered the life and service of Aminu Kano as an example of how political leaders and public servants should live and behave while in office so they can competently tackle the society's problems.

Regarding the failure of leadership, Achebe asserted that there was nothing basically wrong with the Nigerian character, with the Nigerian land or climate or water or air or anything else. Instead, the problem was the unwillingness or inability of its leaders to rise to the responsibility of true leadership; that Nigeria could change with leaders who had the will, the ability, and the vision to lead in a manner that people will follow. Although such people are rare in any time or place, Achebe believed that "it is the duty of enlightened citizens to lead the way in their discovery and to create an atmosphere conducive to their emergence. If this conscious effort is not made, good leaders, like good money will be driven out by bad" (pp. 1–2). The enlightened citizens' failure to act was also part of failure of leadership Achebe is analyzing.

Furthermore, the citizens' ability to discover such leaders is hampered by their love of tribalism, which Achebe describes as "discrimination against a citizen because of his place of birth," instead of nationalism/patriotism, which is "the love of one's country." The problem is not new: during the war of independence, the founding fathers suppressed their tribalism and became "nationalists," but as soon as Nigeria gained political independence from Great Britain, tribalism reared its ugly head again because of the political leaders' insatiable greed and quest for power. They cleverly hid their personal ambitions and emphasized accumulating such power for the benefit of their gullible people.

Achebe illustrates how the ethnic power grab began with the rivalry of two Southern leaders, Dr. Nnamdi Azikiwe and Chief Obafemi Awolowo, in 1951, which introduced the practice of nepotism, incompetence, and corruption to the rest of Nigerian:

> In the life-time of many Nigerians who still enjoy an active public career, Nigeria was called "a mere geographical expression" not only by the British who had an interest in keeping it so, but even by our own "nationalists"

when it suited them to retreat into tribe to check their more successful rivals from other parts of the country. As a student in Ibadan I was an eye-witness to that momentous occasion when Chief Obafemi Awolowo "stole" the leadership of Western Nigeria from Dr. Nnamdi Azikiwe in broad daylight on the floor of the Western House of Assembly and sent the great Zik scampering back to the Niger "whence [he] came."

(p. 5)

By way of commentary on the event, Achebe adds:

Someday when we shall have outgrown tribal politics, or when our children shall have done so, sober historians of the Nigerian nation will see that event as the abortion of a pan-Nigerian vision which, however ineptly, the NCNC tried to have and to hold. No matter how anyone attempts to explain away that event in retrospect it was the death of a dream-Nigeria in which a citizen could live and work in a place of his choice anywhere, and pursue any legitimate goal open to his fellows; a Nigeria in which an Easterner might aspire to be premier in the West and a Northerner become Mayor of Enugu. The dream-Nigeria suffered a deathblow from Awolowo's "success" in the Western House of Assembly in 1951. Perhaps it was an unrealistic dream at the best of times, but some young, educated men and women of my generation did dream it.

(pp. 5–6)

Even though Azikiwe condemned what Awolowo did to him in 1951 because of tribalism, he went on to do the same thing to Professor Eyo Ita, an Efik serving in Enugu, without any qualms or prick of conscience, nor any consideration of its effects on the Igbo people, as long as it yielded him personal political power:

But when Chief Awolowo "stole" the government from him in broad daylight he abandoned his principle which dictated that he should stay in the Western House as Leader of the Opposition and give battle to Awolowo. Instead he conceded victory to reactionary ethnic politics, fled to the East where he compounded his betrayal of the principle by precipitating a major crisis which was unnecessary, selfish and severely damaging in its consequences.

Professor Eyo Ita, an urbane and detribalized humanist politician who had just assumed office as Leader of Government Business in Enugu saw no reason to vacate his post for a fugitive from Ibadan. Neither did most of his cabinet which in sheer brilliance surpassed by far anything Enugu has seen or is likely to see again in a long time.

Using his privately-owned newspapers and political muscle Azikiwe maligned and forced Eyo Ita and his team out of office. . . . And that was not all. Professor Eyo Ita was an Efik, and the brutally unfair treatment offered him in Enugu did not go unremarked in Calabar. It contributed in no small measure to the suspicion of the majority Igbo by their minority neighbors in Eastern Nigeria – a suspicion which far less attractive politicians than Eyo Ita fanned to red-hot virulence, and from which the Igbo have continued to reap enmity to this day.

(pp. 58–9)

Up until the publication of *The Trouble with Nigeria* in 1983, many of us Igbo people, who shared borders with our Efik neighbors in Eastern Nigeria, never fully understood why the so-called ethnic "minorities" abandoned us, the "majority," to fight the civil war with Nigeria, even though all Easterners agreed to wage the war as Biafrans against the Nigeria that forced them to secede from the country because of the mass killings of Easterners living outside of their region during the 1966/67 Northern Riots. Those of us who were Efik neighbors suffered more war casualties from their hands than from troops from other parts of Nigeria. Moreover, in the course of the war, Chief Obafemi Awolowo, who was the then-Nigerian Federal Commissioner for Finance, created a policy that led to the starvation of Biafrans, especially young children and women, arguing that starvation was a legitimate instrument of war. Because of the policy, more Biafrans died from hunger and starvation, and lack of medical supplies than those who died from guns and bombs. So, to end the bloody war, on January 15, 1970, the Biafran hierarchy surrendered to the federal military government on behalf of the people of Biafra. Consequently, in his capacity as Head of State, General Yakubu Gowon made an executive proclamation that there were "No victors, no vanquished" of the war as a way of bringing the ex-Biafrans back into the fold of their former compatriots. However, because the civil war gave Nigeria a perfect and legitimate excuse to cast the Igbo in the role of treasonable felon, a wrecker of the nation, Chief Awolowo, one of the hardliners, and the most powerful in Gowon's cabinet, used his position once again to punish the Igbo economically: "Under his guidance a banking policy was evolved which nullified any bank account which had been operated during the Civil War. This had the immediate result of pauperizing the Igbo middle class and earning a profit of £4 million for the Federal Government Treasury" (pp. 45–6).

In the end, the ego trip and insatiable greed for political power and financial benefits by the two Southern ethnic leaders, Dr. Nnamdi Azikiwe and Chief Obafemi Awolowo, became the ruination of the lives of many innocent Nigerians before, during, and after the civil war; for what they did beginning from 1951 that shaped and influenced the roles other Nigerian leaders like them have since been playing to tear the Nigerian nation apart resonates across all ethnic groups. But that is not to say that Achebe exculpated Northern leaders of comparable ethnic crimes of corruption and nepotism. For he condemned President Shagari especially for being insensitive to the problems of corruption emanating from his administration. Achebe focused on the Southerners who, out of a false image of themselves, claimed to be more enlightened and educated than the Northerners. Therefore, people expected that they should have been more nationalistic and less ethnic or tribalistic. Ironically, however, it was a Northern leader, Mallam

Aminu Kano, who became a nationalist because he lived a life of service worthy of emulation by other leaders. As a true Nigerian patriot himself, Achebe showed great courage in critically analyzing and exposing the greed, corruption, tribalism, and injustice he found in the leadership of Dr. Nnamdi Azikiwe, a fellow Igboman from his home state, Anambra.

Furthermore, like a bombshell, *The Trouble with Nigeria* exposed the unwholesome leadership styles of Dr. Nnamdi Azikiwe and Chief Obafemi Awolowo who were hitherto seen by many people as sacred cows, and their reputations as public servants deemed unassailable. Hence, it is hoped that if other renowned sociopolitical and literary analysts from other ethnic groups of Nigeria do what Chinua Achebe did, the unity, peace, and patriotism, which continue to elude Nigeria as a great country, maybe one day will become possible to realize for the good of the present and following generations of her citizens without regard to ethnicity, religious affiliation, political party, socioeconomic class, and gender. Maybe, a courageous leader will one day arise to take everybody there. That appears to be the hope of Achebe and every other detribalized Nigerian.

Following the sudden death of the presidential candidate of PRP, Mallam Aminu Kano, just before the general elections, there was a lot of confusion, hopelessness, and wrangling among the party hierarchy to the extent that people feared that the party would be incapable of fielding a new presidential candidate to replace Kano, considering especially that there were two factions within the party before his death – one formerly led by Aminu Kano and the other by Michael Imoudu. However, Chinua Achebe and other party faithfuls, who firmly believed in the vision and agenda the party developed under the leadership of Kano for the redemption of the country from its poor leadership, worked hard to reorganize and reunite the feuding party hierarchy. Their hard work paid off when they found two great party men, Hassan Yusuf and Alhaji Balarabe Musa, and presented them to the National Electoral Commission as their new party presidential and vice-presidential candidates respectively. Achebe served as the deputy party leader.

Finally, when the elections were conducted and the ballots counted, President Shehu Shagari's NPN won, and the other parties, UPN, GNPP, NPP, and the newly registered National Advance Party (NAP) lost because, according to them, the Shagari administration and his party rigged the elections. Resultantly, people staged massive violent protests in most parts of the country, especially in Eastern and Western Nigeria. Ostensibly, all the warning Achebe gave in *The Trouble with Nigeria* before the October 1983 elections against the rife sociopolitical and economic injustice, as well as the consequences of tribalism, nepotism, corruption, and clannishness, were so blatantly neglected by the political leaders and their followers that they created an environment of anarchy similar to that which readers saw in his fourth novel, *A Man of the People*, that led the narrator to crave "the Army to come to our rescue." That similarity inspired Mike Awoyinfa of the *Sunday Concord Magazine* to interview Achebe on the results of the general elections; he asked Achebe whether the Nigerian politicians had changed from the way he portrayed them in *A Man of the People*. In his response, which was published in that paper in October 1983, Achebe answered the question with candor and conviction because, as a deputy leader of another major political party, he had direct knowledge of the activities of the other political parties. He said that, if anything, the Nigerian politician had deteriorated; the corruption of Chief Nanga found in *A Man of the People* in the 1960s was on a minor scale compared with that of the postwar era, when Nigerians were talking about people stealing millions of naira compared to the thousands which were considered bad news during the time of Chief Nanga. The contemporary Ministers were in business where there are all kinds of corrupt scandals. Achebe's belief that the situation was really much worse was one of the reasons why he came out to say something that sounded really harsh to some people, but he felt that what he did was necessary. And when asked to comment specifically on the conduct of the 1983 presidential election, Achebe emphatically said:

> What has happened is a wholesale disregard of the rules – the rules of elections, the rules of fairness. If you don't have the attitude of fair play, then you cannot have a democratic system. There is no doubt that from the very beginning even before the actual elections, the people in power – I don't mean just the Federal government, I mean those in power all around – did not want anything that would upset them where they are in power. They wanted something that would upset somebody else. There is absolutely no doubt in my mind that there was widescale rigging of results. This is quite clear to me. It is left to those who can analyze it in the law court and all the other people to produce evidence. But [by] the evidence of my own eyes and my ears [it] appears that there was widespread rigging of the elections. And what this suggests is that we do not really care for democracy.[8]

Achebe's answers and comments in that interview reiterate the thesis of *The Trouble with Nigeria*, which is about the poor, corrupt leadership in all areas of the Nigerian lives. As long as the situation remained unchanged, Achebe was determined to call out bad leaders without any shred of fear.

Two ominous incidents cut short Chinua Achebe's political life in 1983: intra-party discrimination and deprivation against Igbo officials in PRP; and the December 31, 1983 military coup that brought back soldiers to the control seat of governance in Nigeria with effect from January 1, 1984.

Apart from losing the presidential election, PRP lost other national elections except the governorship of Kano State. The man who won it, Alhaji Bakin Zuwo, felt that because of his position as governor who controlled the government coffers, he had to control the party affairs as well with no regard for whatever ideas and opinions other party officials might express on issues affecting the survival of the party as a whole. Hence, he became what Igbo people call "*Eze onye agwala m*" [an incorrigible king]. His arrogance and disregard of other members' ideas, especially of those in the Kano chapter, became so blatant that many people challenged him openly about it. The most vocal critic of the governor's behavior was Dr. Junaid Mohammed, an academic who understood political issues more than the governor did. So when he pointed out the deficiencies in what the governor was doing, the governor retaliated by mounting a campaign for his expulsion from the party. But since he could not do it without the approval of other national officials, he was challenged by people like Comrade Uche Chukwumerije, an Igboman and secretary of the party. He refused to join the campaign for Mohammed's ouster, preferring instead that the party hierarchy give Mohammed an opportunity to defend himself against the governor's allegations. Reacting to that recommendation, the governor expressed his intention to expel Chukwumerije as well. So, at a national meeting, Achebe, in his capacity as national deputy leader of the party, asked Zuwo to rescind his decision on Mohammed's case, but the national President Hassan Yusuf, whom the governor sponsored financially, could not call him to order for fear of losing his sponsorship. The argument between Achebe and Zuwo was so serious that the governor angrily and unguardedly expressed how he felt all along about Achebe and other Igbo officials in the party when he said, "the Igbo are coming again," which was a reference to the leadership role Igbo people played in Biafra during the civil war. On hearing that, Achebe angrily left the meeting and the PRP for good; for the party officials from the North, such as Hassan Yusuf and Bakin Zuwo, had abandoned the personal qualities of Mallam Aminu Kano that drew him to the party in the first place. Besides, the national unity and peace that Achebe strove to achieve became unachievable under the leadership of the Northerners who saw PRP as their birthright, as it were.

The second reason why Achebe left party politics was that the military staged a coup on December 31, 1983, which was led by three Northern military officers – namely, Brigadier Sanni Abacha, General Muhammadu Buhari, and General Ibrahim Babangida. Before the coup, the general Nigerian masses had been complaining about the incompetence and endemic corruption of the Shehu Shagari administration. Chinua Achebe was enraged by it as well. Besides, he became critical of the way the administration incompetently managed their own over-advertised Green Revolution Program, which was full of waste and did not help feed the people as they intended it would. The army, which was keenly watching the activities of the new civilian administration after they handed power over to them, noticed with dismay that the very intolerable corruption, nepotism, and ethnic disharmony that characterized the First Republic still continued. That ostensibly caused them to return to the political scene by forcefully removing the incumbent President Shagari through a bloodless coup. As a result, on January 1, 1984, the army formally announced General Muhammadu Buhari as the new Head of State with General Tunde Idiagbon (a Yoruba) as his chief of staff, and General Ibrahim Babangida as chief of army staff. Once again, top Igbo military officers were excluded from the ruling army hierarchy even though many of them had been reintegrated into the Nigerian armed forces at the end of the war. Nevertheless, General Buhari posted military officers to replace all the civilian state governors and sacked their civilian administrations as well. Because of what the military did under the General, the Igbo people cynically coined a pun on his last name "Buhari," which means in Igbo language "to overturn" (a situation). By his actions, the strongman metaphorically became his name. Ironically, however, the military coup was initially welcomed by many people when they discovered that, unlike the erstwhile civilian administration, which was beleaguered by corruption, the new military administration was instilling visible discipline and fear in the minds of public servants and ordinary people in all walks of life. Thus, in a short while, much of the endemic corruption in government departments and agencies virtually disappeared. In no small measure, this was because Buhari and Idiagbon presented themselves to the public as no-nonsense generals whose commands must be obeyed, even by people in the highest echelon of government.

Following the dawn of another era of military rule in 1984, Achebe decided to devote more time to his writing and academic profession. First, he founded *Uwa Ndi Igbo*, a bilingual journal of Igbo life and culture, with the financial support of a German Africanist Ulli Beier, Alex Ekwueme the newly ousted Vice President alongside President Shehu Shagari, and Arthur Nwankwo, owner of Fourth Dimension Publishers and former Chair of the Anambra State Chapter of PRP. Achebe also applied for and received a substantial grant from the Ford Foundation in New York, which helped him greatly to found and edit the journal. Once the journal took off, it became a good opportunity for many Igbo writers in the Diaspora to express their thoughts on all aspects of Igbo world and culture in both Igbo and English languages. It also gave non-Igbo readers an opportunity to learn more about Igbo ways of life, thereby enhancing their understanding of some of the Igbo cultural issues, belief systems, and ethics contained in Achebe's novels, as well as those published by other well-established Igbo writers such as Buchi Emecheta, Flora Nwapa, Cyprian Ekwensi, Chukwuemeka Ike, Nkem Nwankwo, Onuora Nzekwu, Obi Egbuna, Eddie Iroh, John Munonye, Benjamin Okiri, Elechi Amadi, T. Obinkaram Echewa, and the younger but equally important novelists like Chimamandu Ngozi Adichie and Christopher Abani.

Second, Achebe received two appointments in the same year as Visiting Professor of English at the University of Guelph, Ontario, Canada, and Regents Professor of English at the University of California in Los Angeles. Both appointments took him away from Nigeria to North America, where he did some research and teaching, and resumed work on the third phase of his writing career, which he did not concentrate on during his brief stint with politics. He taught classes, conducted seminars, and delivered speeches on African literature and culture. Moreover, he worked closely with G. D. Killam on the African section of the University of Guelph journal, *World Literature Written in English* (WLWE), which Killam edited. At the end of his one-year appointment as visiting professor in 1985, and under the aegis of Killam, Achebe spent two more months working at Guelph as a Senior Commonwealth Practitioner and was honored by the university with an honorary doctorate (D.Litt.) on June 12, 1985. Furthermore, in that same year, Achebe was so motivated by the new award that he revived his interest in working on the unfinished manuscript of his fifth novel, *Anthills of the Savannah*. He reread it to see if he could finish writing it while he was still at the University of Guelph. At the time, another tragic incident took place in Nigeria, which he used as another incentive to finish the book. On August 27, 1985,

General Ibrahim Babangida, the erstwhile chief of army staff, overthrew his boss, General Muhammadu Buhari, through another military coup, and assumed the position of President and Commander-in-Chief of the Nigerian armed forces. By that unexpected act of betrayal to the army and the nation, the military admin-istration in Nigeria was unnecessarily prolonged once again. This incident in his homeland ostensibly caused Achebe to stay back longer than he may have hoped to work in North America, and he accepted an appointment as Fulbright Profes-sor of African Studies in the University of Massachusetts at Amherst from 1987 to 1988. He later published the novel in 1987. Killam took a photo of Achebe in Guelph during the informal launching of the novel, which was shortlisted for the 1987 Booker McConnell Prize.

Anthills of the Savannah, published 21 years after his fourth novel *A Man of the People*, was greeted by scholars and students of his fiction with great expectations. While some wondered whether the master storyteller still retained the ability to tell a complex story after so many years, others were confident that it would be as great as his earlier classics, *Things Fall Apart* and *Arrow of God*. The promotional statement on the book-jacket gave readers a summary of its salient themes:

> In one of the year's major publishing events, Chinua Achebe presents his long-awaited new work, *Anthills of the Savannah*.
>
> The author of such classics as *Things Fall Apart, Arrow of God*, and *A Man of the People* returns to his native Africa to tell a story of love and friendship; betrayal; and sudden, violent death. Using the conflict between the city and tribal villages, the ravages of the great African drought, and Third World poli-tics as a compelling backdrop, Achebe weaves a potent drama of modern Africa.
>
> Two years after the military coup that swept a brilliant young army officer to power, an uneasy calm reigns in the fictional African state of Kangan. The new leader's failure to be proclaimed President-for-Life has left him fearful and embittered, and now those who helped put him in power – his oldest and truest friends – suddenly find themselves helpless targets of his brutal rage.
>
> There is Chris Oriko, who knows his days are numbered as his former schoolmate degenerates into a ruthless dictator . . . Ikem Osodi, poet and editor of the local *National Gazette*, whose trusting heart struggles to believe that the truth of the printed word may yet influence his corrupted childhood companion . . . and Beatrice Okoh, Chris's lover, a strong, beautiful woman whose singular insight and wisdom may hold the key to surviving the cruel-ties of her troubled country.
>
> *Anthills of the Savannah* is a masterful story of contemporary Africa; angry, disenchanted, full of savage irony, yet, ultimately, filled with hope. And as Chinua Achebe lyrically explores the devastating political and emotional turmoil of his homeland, he offers a timeless contribution to contemporary literature.[9]

All the glowing sentiments expressed above have since been confirmed by readers and critics of the novel based on differing points of view. For instance, some

African female scholars and feminists praised the novel highly for the prominent roles Achebe assigned to two female characters, Beatrice and Elewa. In her own analysis of the novel, Chinyere Nwagbara concluded her article "'A Woman is Always Something': A Re-reading of Achebe's *Anthills of the Savannah*," with the following assertion:

> In *Anthills*, Achebe rejects limited and negative images of women prevalent in African literature especially by male writers. The women have broken the silence and are speaking out, defying shackles of convention in the male dominated societies. Beatrice, an example of the modern African woman, moves away from those processes that condemn women to oppression, suppression, and non-coexistence. That African women are voiceless is sometimes more of a myth than reality, because it is apparent that there are some classes of African women whose voices are heard, though they are not in the majority. Molara Ogundipe-Leslie confirms this as she notes:
>
> > Indigenous structures of political participation equivalent or parallel to those for me, existed for women, whereby women's voices were heard, their opinions consulted.
> >
> > (pp. 78–9)
>
> That a woman is always something is as old as creation itself. Achebe has successfully redefined and rewritten the African Woman in *Anthills of the Savannah*.[10]

For some feminist readers like Nwagbara, who felt that Achebe had not given enough credit to female characters before for the important roles they played in his previous novels, *Anthills of the Savannah* seemed to have redeemed him from what they saw as unequal treatment of women when compared to his treatment of their male counterparts. And yet, other female critics were not still satisfied, as Edith Ihekweazu, editor of *Eagle on Iroko: A Symposium for Chinua Achebe's 60th Birthday*, reported:

> With *Anthills of the Savannah*, Achebe has called up the feminist critics, who did not have him in their good books before. Most of them, like Catherine Bicknell, Rose Acholonu and Grace Okereke acknowledged an increasing personal and political awareness of Achebe's women, an artistic bias in their favor and a higher degree of assertiveness and independence. There is, however, also a dissenting voice. Obioma Nnaemeka is not satisfied with Beatrice and Elewa and sees them still excluded from language as the symbolic order. It may still be necessary to probe deeper into the role of women and their mythical dimensions.[11]

On the other hand, however, some male readers see the general theme of the novel as a quest for social change. But what the nature of that social change may not be clear to some readers, which is why Kez Okafor's analysis of the novel enabled him to write the article, "The Quest for Social Change: Reformation or Revolution," in which he opines:

> Until the publication of *Anthills of the Savannah*, the question did not arise as to whether the works of Chinua Achebe should be classified as revolutionary pieces or not. His earlier novels *Things Fall Apart, No Longer at Ease*, and *Arrow of God* which address the cultural nationalist issues of cultural validity and culture conflict clearly do not belong to the revolutionary tradition nor does *A Man of the People* in its concern with postcolonial delusions of self-sufficiency and political stability. However, *Anthills of Savannah* x-rays the present chaotic social context in the light of the ineptitude of African leaders and, at the same time, contemplates solutions to this despairing problem. To that end, it leads itself to an incisive analysis of its ideological leaning and, therefore, a re-clarification of the social outlook of the author himself. I shall in this paper attempt to determine the ideological leaning of *Anthills of the Savannah* through an analysis of the ideas, conflicts and tensions that affect the characters created by Achebe, and the peculiar situations in which he posits them.
> We take our cue from Ikem Osodi, the character that is obviously the voice of Achebe in the novel, when he states that:

> > Revolutions may be necessary for taking a society out of an intractable stretch of quagmire, but it does not confer freedom, and may hinder it. Bloody reformist? . . . Reform may be a dirty word now, but it begins to look more and more like the most promising route to success in the real world.
> >   (p. 99)

> These pronouncements denote Achebe's preference for "reformation" as against revolution.[12]

I agree with Okafor who accurately describes what Achebe does in the novel, which some cursory readers think is about revolution instead of reformation; and I think such a misreading may be due to the roles that the military characters play in it.

My own reading of *Anthills of the Savannah* is that the novel showcases the literary activism of Achebe the reformer and game-changer of the Nigerian postwar situation. As soon as the novel came off the press, Achebe sent me a review copy, aware that I would be interested in reading it and writing a critical response, which I would add as a supplement to the publications I had already done on all his previous novels. In the end, I was able to write and publish a book chapter on the novel, which is reproduced herein as the next chapter.

As a result of his hard work, Achebe published two books, *Hopes and Impediments* and *The University and the Leadership Factor in Nigerian Politics* in 1988, while he was still in America. He must have been working on the manuscripts of both books while he was still actively engaged in political activities in Nigeria. I believe that his long preoccupation with, and reflection on, how to solve the Nigerian leadership problem are what enabled him to publish *The Trouble with Nigeria*. However, while Achebe's focus in the book was solely on the problem of political leadership, *The University and the Leadership Factor in Nigerian Politics*,[13] written as its sequel, focuses on the university's failure to play useful leadership roles that would have saved people from the political predicament that caused them to look desperately for solutions. Achebe presented the message of the 22-page booklet as a contribution to a national forum, titled "Strategies for Nigerian Development," which the University of Nigeria, Nsukka, organized on September 23, 1986.

Achebe began his presentation by quoting Bernard Shaw who, upon arrival in New York harbor, said to awaiting journalists, "Don't ask me what you should do to be saved; the last time I was here I told you and you haven't done it!" He was telling the audience that he turned down previous invitations to participate in other forums because he had told readers how to solve the trouble with Nigeria in his 1983 book but they did not listen; but he accepted the current invitation because it came from his own backyard (the university), which deserved special attention. (p. 1). After that, he reiterated the essence of that book as follows:

> My little book *The Trouble with Nigeria* published three years ago on the eve of Shagari's second term opens [with] these words:
>
>> The trouble with Nigeria is simply and squarely a failure of leadership. There is nothing basically wrong with the Nigerian character. There is nothing wrong with the Nigerian land or climate or anything else. The Nigerian problem is the unwillingness or inability of its elders to rise to the responsibility, to the challenge of personal example which is the hallmark of true leadership.
>
> So the question of leadership was, and is, preeminent, in my view, among Nigeria's numerous problems. This little book does go on to identify others, such as tribalism, corruption, indiscipline, social injustice, a preference for mediocrity, etc. But my thesis is that without good leadership none of the other problems stands a chance of being tackled let alone solved.
>
> (pp. 2–3)

After stating his thesis, Achebe went on to say that people criticized his stand on the problem of leadership, alleging that his view of the Nigerian predicament was elitist because it emphasized the role of a crop of leaders rather than of the broad masses, and that his diagnosis identified individuals rather than an economic and political system as the source of the Nigerian problem (pp. 3–4). His answer to the two charges constituted the case he made during the forum against the failure of the university as citadel of knowledge that should have shown people the light for them to get out of their sociopolitical predicament. Instead, some of them allowed the politicians to influence them with their corrupt leadership styles.

Achebe's presentation was centered around three components to the equation for national development: systems, leaders, and followers. In an ideal world, he says, each would mesh nicely and efficiently with the others. But quite clearly, Nigerians were not in such a world, not even on the road to it, for they seemed, in fact, to be going in the opposite direction, toward a world of bad system, bad leadership, and bad followership. He then discussed where and how they should begin in order to have the best chance of success of changing the Nigerian system, the Nigerian leadership style, and the hearts of one hundred million Nigerians. In the end, he comes down heavily on the universities that have failed to provide the kind of leadership Nigeria needs to solve her problems:

> We must admit that the Nigerian university has not acquitted itself too brilliantly in this regard in the past. The university man who has sallied forth into national politics has had a rather dismal record. No one can point to any shining achievement in national politics which the nation can recognize as the peculiar contribution of university men. Rather, quite a few of them have been splashed with accusations of abuse of office and other forms of corruption.
>
>   Those who have remained in the ivory tower have hardly fared better. Many have cheapened themselves and eroded their prestige by trotting up and down between the campus and the waiting rooms of the powerful shamelessly vying for attention and running one another down for the entertainment of the politician. For this and other reasons the University has deservedly lost its luster, its mystique and squandered the credibility which it had had in such abundance at the time of Nigeria's independence.
>
> (pp. 18–19)

So we ask, "If such corrupt university people serve as leaders, what can the less educated masses do as followers to redeem the image of Nigeria as one of the world's most corrupt nations?" When all is said and done, Achebe's suggested strategies for revamping the poor leadership roles in Nigerian politics and university education can be trusted because he lived and practically experienced life in both worlds.

The second book that Achebe published in 1988 and later revised in 1989 while he was still serving at the University of Massachusetts, Amherst, entitled *Hopes and Impediments*, is a selection of essays he wrote for diverse occasions over a period of 23 years that represents his abiding concerns in literature and the arts, as well as his interest in wider social issues.[14] This revised edition contains a postscript on James Baldwin (1924–1987). The promotional review of the book outlines its content as follows:

> *Hopes and Impediments* draws on the best critical writings of this powerful writer over past twenty-five years, offering a new perspective on the human condition. These essays range from an analysis of Joseph Conrad that has

Figure 6.2 Chinua Achebe's 1988 reception at UMass
Source: UMass

infuriated many an English professor, to a moving tribute to James Baldwin. These are reflections on broad topics such as "The Truth of Fiction," "Thoughts on the African Novel," "Impediments to the Dialogue Between North and South," and on the present needs of his own society. Throughout these provocative works run the central themes of literature and art against the background of Europe and Africa and the black-white divide. Mr. Achebe brings to bear his unique creative energies in exposing the monster of racist habit.[15]

In the author's preface, Achebe expresses his elation at writing a book in which he compares how two writers, one white and the other black, treated the hydra-headed subject of racism in their works when he wrote, "To open the collection with a 1974 public lecture on Conrad's racism given at the University of Massachusetts, Amherst, and also close it at the same institution thirteen years later with a tribute to one of the most intrepid fighters [Baldwin] against racism, was, at the very least, a curious coincidence" (p. xiii) (Figure 6.2).

Readers who are familiar with the contents of most of the collected essays (which are about culture, literature, race, and art) would greatly appreciate the connection Achebe made in the book between what W. E. B. Du Bois and James Baldwin did during their times to fight the monster of racism in America, in contrast to what Joseph Conrad did in Europe to promote racism against Africans during his own time. As a consequence, his novella, *Heart of Darkness*, created a vicious image of Africa in the minds of Europeans that shaped their relationships with African countries through colonialism, neocolonialism, and imperialism – racist relationships that, for many centuries, European descendants have sustained with people of African descent in the Americas.

The essay I enjoyed reading the most from the collection is "The Igbo World and Its Art," because, as an Igboman, I am always eager to learn new information about our people, especially when it comes from the master storyteller, Chinua Achebe. He opens his discussion of the essay with the following assertion:

> The Igbo world is an arena for the interplay of forces. It is a dynamic world of movement and of flux. Igbo art, reflecting this worldview, is never tranquil but mobile and active, even aggressive.
>
> *Ike*, energy, is the essence of all things human, spiritual, animate and inanimate. Everything has its own unique energy which must be acknowledged and given its due. *Ike di na awaja na awaja* is a common formulation of this idea: "Power runs in many channels." Sometimes the saying is extended by an exemplifying coda about a mild and gentle bird, *obu*, which nonetheless possesses the power to destroy a snake. *Onye na nkie, onye na nkie* – literally, "everyone and his own" – is a social expression of the same notion often employed as a convenient formula for saluting *en masse* an assembly too large for individual greetings.
>
> In some cultures, a person may worship one of the gods or goddesses in the pantheon and pay scant attention to the rest. In Igbo religion such selectiveness is unthinkable. All the people must placate all the gods all the time! For there is a cautionary proverb which states that even when a person has satisfied the deity Udo completely, he may yet be killed by Ogwugwu. The degree of peril propounded by this proverb is only dimly apprehended until one realizes that Ogwugwu is not a stranger to Udo but his very consort![16]

As he continues the discussion, Achebe delineates a unique characteristic in Igbo life and art thus:

> It is the striving to come to terms with a multitude of forces and demands which gives Igbo life its tense and restless dynamism and its art an outward, social and kinetic quality. But it would be a mistake to take the extreme view that Igbo art has no room for contemplative privacy. In the first place, all extremism is abhorrent to the Igbo sensibility; but specifically, the Igbo word which is closest to the English word "art" is *nka*, and Igbo people do say: *Onye nakwa nka na-eme ka ona-adu iru*, which means that an artist at work is apt to wear an unfriendly face. In other words, he is excused from the normal demands of sociability![17]

Furthermore, Achebe argues that, despite the privacy the artist at work craves, his or her artistic product will ultimately emerge from privacy into the public domain. That means that there are no private collections among the Igbo beyond personal ritual objects like *Ikenga*. Indeed, the very concept of collections would be antithetical to the Igbo artistic intention. Collections by their very nature will impose rigid, artistic attitudes and conventions on creativity, which the Igbo sensibility goes out of its way to avoid. The purposeful neglect of the painstakingly and devoutly accomplished *Mbari* houses with all the art objects in them, as soon as the primary mandate of their creation has been served, provides a significant insight into the Igbo aesthetic value as process rather than product. Process is motion while product is rest.

The artistic theory that Achebe is enunciating in the essay explains the reason why in popular contemporary usage the Igbo formulate their view of the world as: "No condition is permanent." And in Igbo cosmology even gods could fall out of use; and new forces are liable to appear without warning in the temporal and metaphysical firmament. The practical purpose of art is to channel a spiritual force into an aesthetically satisfying physical form that can capture the presumed attributes of the force.[18] What an insight into Igbo life and art from Chinua Achebe!

To sum up, although Chinua Achebe ended *Hopes and Impediments* without a formal conclusion, the concluding paragraph of "Postscript: James Baldwin (1924–1987)" can be regarded as a conclusion befitting the entire book, for it captures the essence of his thoughts on racism and on the public service that a patriot renders to his people, race, and humanity, which James Baldwin, like him, made his lifetime mission:

> As long as injustice exists, whether it be within the American nation itself or between it and its neighbors; as long as a tiny cartel of rich, creditor nations can hold the rest in iron chains of usury; so long as one third or less of mankind eats well and often to excess while two thirds and more live perpetually with hunger; as long as white people who constitute a mere fraction of the human race consider it natural and even righteous to dominate the rainbow majority whenever and wherever they are thrown together; and – the oldest of them all – the discrimination by men against women, as long as it persists; the words of James Baldwin will be there to bear witness and to inspire and elevate the struggle for human freedom.[19]

As the Igbo say, "It takes a great man to recognize another great man." The tribute Achebe paid to Baldwin, a fellow renowned black writer in America, resonates in the Black World, and it may have indirectly served as an enduring tribute to Achebe himself because of the invaluable messages his publications and patriotic services convey to his fellow citizens and to humanity at large.

Notes

1   Biodun Jeyifo, "Literature and Conscientization: An Interview with Chinua Achebe," in Biodun Jeyifo, ed. *Contemporary Nigerian Literature: A Retrospective and Prospective Exploration.* Lagos, Nigeria: Nigeria Magazine, 1985: 19.

2 Chinua Achebe, "Writers Doomed to Be Free," *West Africa*, November 19, 1979: 2123.

3 Ezenwa-Ohaeto, *Chinua Achebe*, pp. 224–5.

4 Chinua Achebe, *The Trouble with Nigeria*. New York: Anchor Press/Doubleday, 1988: 34–5.

5 Ezenwa-Ohaeto, *Chinua Achebe*, p. 225.

6 *Ibid.*, p. 227.

7 Achebe, *The Trouble with Nigeria*, pp. 1–2.

8 Michael Awoyinfa, "Chinua Achebe, *Things Fall Apart* Was Nearly Stolen from Me," *Sunday Concord Magazine*, November 6, 1983: i, v, and xi.

9 Achebe, *Anthills of the Savannah*, from the book-jacket.

10 Chinyere Nwagbara, "'A Woman Is Always Something': A Re-Reading of Achebe's *Anthills of the Savannah*," in Ernest N. Emenyonu, ed. *Emerging Perspectives on Chinua Achebe, Volume 1: Omenka the Master Artist: Critical Perspectives on Achebe's Fiction.* Trenton, NJ: Africa World Press, 2004: 351.

11 Edith Ihekweazu, ed., *Eagle on the Iroko: Selected Papers from the Chinua Achebe International Symposium 1990.* Ibadan, Nigeria: Heinemann Educational Books (Nigeria) Plc., 1996: xvi–xvii.

12 Kez Okafor, "The Quest for Social Change: Reformation or Revolution?" in Ihekweazu, *Ibid.*, p. 225.

13 Chinua Achebe, *The University and the Leadership Factor in Nigerian Politics.* Enugu, Nigeria: ABIC Books & Equipment Ltd., 1988.

14 Chinua Achebe, *Hopes and Impediments.* New York: Doubleday, 1989: xiii.

15 *Ibid.*, the book's jacket.

16 *Ibid.*, pp. 62–3.

17 *Ibid.*, p. 63.

18 *Ibid.*, p. 64.

19 *Ibid.*, p. 176.

7   Of Governance, Revolutions, and Victims

Achebe and Literary Activism in *Anthills of the Savannah**

Chinua Achebe is one of the few African writers who truly play the role of keepers of the conscience of their people and defenders of the values of individual freedom and human rights. His writings portray him as a conscious artist in the traditional communal sense of the term; and in telling his stories, Achebe adopts a historical approach, which is to say that for anyone to understand the events of the present, he has to know the events of the past. The knowledge of both kinds of events, of course, should enable him to predict events of the future that ultimately are influenced and mediated by those of the past and the present. And because Achebe, as a writer, has this historical sense of events, he tends to use almost the same people and names as characters, the same West African geographical areas as setting; the same gods, goddesses, oracles, and rituals and ceremonies as an expression of the people's religion and cosmology; the same folk songs and tales as well as proverbs as the stylized verbal art of the people. All these folk and traditional elements form the basis of his thematic materials. The result is that Achebe's thematic concerns are predictable, and his social commitment easily appreciated.

In an article simply titled "Chinua Achebe," Michael J. C. Echeruo made the following ever-enduring assertion regarding Achebe's works:

> Behind his novels, short stories and poems there is this immense presence of a patrimony, a land, a people, a way of life. But while characterizing that land, detailing the history of its many crises, Achebe sees it as the one unchanging feature of the artistic and moral landscape, as the one permanent Being to which all efforts of the children of the land must be devoted. If we recognize this, we can then appreciate why Achebe is not the urban African, why his art is not the art of the metropolis. Rather Achebe is the artist in the communal sense of the term, the man of great wisdom, working within the limits and through the norms of his society as on the universality of his own personal vision.[1]

And in the concluding paragraph of the article, Echeruo predicts: "Given the pattern of Chinua Achebe's development as an artist and as a conscience for his people, it would indeed be surprising – it would be doubly disappointing – if his

DOI: 10.4324/9781003184133-7

next major work did not deal with that truly traumatic experience: The War." Reflecting on his earlier novels, Achebe once described his generation as "a very fortunate" one in the sense that the past was "still there," even if not "in the same force."[2]

Echeruo, Achebe's critic and fellow citizen, made these assertions out of the careful readings of Achebe's works and from his personal knowledge of Achebe the man. However, that "next major work," *Anthills of the Savannah*, was published in Britain in 1987 and in the United States in 1988,[3] more than 20 years after *A Man of the People*.[4] Although *Anthills of the Savannah* may not have dealt with "that truly traumatic experience: The War [the Nigerian Civil War]," all the same, it deals with another kind of war: bad governance of the Nigerian nation in particular, and by analogy, other African nations in general; ill-conceived revolutions; and social injustice. Whereas the Nigerian civil war was ostensibly over in 1970, this second kind of war that *Anthills of the Savannah* deals with is still against the people, suggesting ways of liberating them and freeing their land. The urgency and immediacy of his literary activism enable him to maintain the "immense presence of a patrimony, a land, a people, a way of life," while he plays the role of "an artist and as a conscience for his people" as he has done in his first four novels.

As a matter of fact, Achebe's failure to write about the Nigerian civil war specifically was a personal choice, neither because he was afraid to do so nor because he lacked the artistic capability. In fact, in an interview with Ann Bolsover, he says:

> It seemed to me that our history was beginning and since my writing, my fiction, is really my way of recreating history in the modern world I had to come to terms with this new history. I didn't want to write about Biafra. I still don't want to write a novel of the war. I may change my mind later on but I was doing things, all of them with the war, but from the side. Not confronting it properly. And this is something I can't do anything about.[5]

That new history began with the 1966 military coup, which became the start of military regimes in Nigeria. Achebe, like Ikem Osodi and Chris Oriko in *Anthills*, suffered untold hardships that shook his faith in his fatherland:

> It seemed to me that Nigeria really ceased to be what it was to me six years after Independence, and the excitement, and suddenly you had this bloodletting on a horrendous scale. Before that you had the experience of running away and hiding in your country, which was my own experience. Soldiers came to the radio station in Lagos where I worked to look for me. After all that, the country could not be the same. Africa couldn't be the same and I seemed to need some time, a lot of time to rethink things.[6]

The statement not only explains the long silence between the appearance of *A Man of the People* and *Anthills* but also frames the political nature and ambience of the latter novel. Like the fleeing Achebe (from Lagos to Igbo country), Chris

Oriko, fleeing (from Bassa to Abazon Province), meets personally the people who own the land, experiences their problems firsthand, and is, thus, disillusioned with the idea that Kangan was owned by the troika, Sam, Ikem, and Chris.

At the very beginning of *Anthills*, readers are introduced to the poor governance of Kangan. Instead of using an omniscient reporter or the I-narrator to tell his tale, Achebe uses witnesses who happen to be some of the major characters to do so. So we find on page 1 of the novel Christopher Oriko serving as First Witness. The political crime whose fallout the entire novel explores and dramatizes has already taken place. From time to time, though, allusions are made to that crime, and the suspected criminals, as it were, are called in as witnesses to say what they know about it. The effect of this technical device is that the characters, who are also members of the ruling class, are regarded by other members of His Excellency's cabinet as the saboteurs; and since the narrator's point of view appears to favor the suspects, the narrator assumes the status of a character before the narratee. The overall effect of the novel's shifting narrative voice on the reader of "conventional" novels is that he becomes confused in following the narrative thread. We will come to an examination of the narrative technique style later on.

If one may ask, what is the political crime that has been committed against His Excellency's government and Kangan? A coup, two years ago, gives power to a Sandhurst-trained soldier, Sam, and he becomes the Head of State of Kangan. From then on, Sam is known and addressed as His Excellency or H. E. for short. He chooses a cabinet of commissioners and senior government officials, including his boyhood friends, Chris and Ikem, to help run his government. Somewhere along the line, His Excellency wants to be President-for-Life. A national referendum is called to decide the issue; Abazon, Ikem's home province, says no to His Excellency's request, and Ikem is suspected by his colleagues in the cabinet to have had a hand in the Abazon provincial verdict. His Excellency "has already deteriorated into a paranoid despot surrounded by a sycophantic cabinet. Trying to protect his position any way he can, he has created a 'State Research Committee' which is really a secret police."[7] Chris watches His Excellency turning into a dictator, but his own role in the government portrays him as a pacifist. On the other hand, Ikem, the poet and journalist, writes bold editorials that he thinks can guide the government to take the right actions toward the downtrodden people of Kangan. Ironically, it is those crusading editorials and his meeting the delegation from Abazon that earn him the wrath of His Excellency. Ikem is fired as editor of the *National Gazette*.

In reaction to his dismissal, Ikem delivers a speech to the students of the University of Bassa. He is misquoted in a headline, EX-EDITOR ADVOCATES REGICIDE! Eventually, he is arrested and murdered by the grisly secret police. Chris fears for his life and goes into hiding. From that point of the novel on, His Excellency's role in the governance of Kangan is not very clear. What one reads about is the role of the State Research Council, whose activities plunge the nation into sporadic eruptions of bloody violence. With the help of the sought-after President of the Students Union, Emmanuel, the taxi drivers, and Beatrice, Chris becomes more militant. He dies as he attempts to save a student nurse, Adamma, from being raped by a drunken police sergeant in Abazon but not before His Excellency's death has been announced. Thus, the total over-throw of the triumvirate of Lord Lugard College alumni is completed. All told, His Excellency's government is a military regime. The people have no hand in its formation. The cabinet is made up of His Excellency's personal friends whose appointment is a nepotistic rather than a democratic act. So, those who are so favored as to be appointed as cabinet members must, of necessity, work to please His Excellency with the mistaken belief that worshiping a dictator assures one of more favor and a longer stay on the job. As a result, there is infighting in the cabinet: seeds of mistrust, suspicion, and betrayal are sown in His Excellency's mind against Chris and Ikem, who are considered as being closer, and therefore more favored, than others. There is a crack in the relationship of the three boy-hood friends. Things begin to fall apart because the apparently strong center of the cabinet cannot hold any longer. Ikem is disenchanted with the discharge of public affairs that has been shrouded in secrecy and so he questions its propriety:

> At some point he had assumed, quite naively, that public affairs so-called might provide the handle he needed. But his participation in these affairs had yielded him nothing but disenchantment and a final realization of the incongruity of the very term "public" as applied to those affairs shrouded as they are in the mist of unreality and floating above and away from the lives and concerns of ninety-nine percent of the population. Public affairs! They are nothing but the closed transactions of soldiers-turned-politicians, with their cohorts in business and the bureaucracy.[8]

However fatally flawed the government activities are, the functionaries always attempt to legitimize them by claiming that action was taken in the interest and for the wellbeing of the people, who are usually far away from government. As a political ideologue, Ikem meditates over the hypocritical relationship of the government to the people:

> 'Of course,' he admitted bitterly, 'we always take the precaution of invoking the people's name in whatever we do. But do we not at the same time make sure of the people's absence knowing that if they were to appear in person their scarecrow presence confronting our pious invocations would render our words too obscene even for sensibilities as robust as ours!'[9]

Indeed, any government that fails to involve the people in the governance of the country is bound to fail; and any government that pretends total commit-ment to the act of true governance stands condemned even by its own members when the truth is known. From the outset, one finds that the government of Kangan is flawed. The people know it and fake their loyalty to the government, and, even before its total downfall, Ikem knows that their government is a failure:

> The prime failure of this government began to take on a clearer meaning for him. It can't be the massive corruption though its scale and pervasiveness

are truly intolerable; it isn't the subservience to foreign manipulation, degrading as it is; it isn't even this second-class, hand-me-down capitalism, ludicrous and doomed; nor is it the damnable shooting of striking railway-workers and demonstrating students and the destruction and banning thereafter of independent unions and cooperatives. It is the failure of our rulers to re-establish vital inner links with the poor and dispossessed of this country, with the bruised heart that throbs painfully at the core of the nation's being.[10]

Here, Ikem sounds like Achebe in *The Trouble with Nigeria*.[11] All the socio-political ills that Achebe points out in that book of essays are recreated here in *Anthills*. They include massive corruption, subservience to foreign manipulations, hand-me-down capitalism, government use of force to elicit loyalty from workers and students, and government nonchalance toward the suffering of the masses. Those ills are rife in most West African governments, especially the current military regime in Achebe's home country, Nigeria. The theme of corruption is by now a familiar one in modern African and Nigerian fiction, and it is perfect material for Achebe's polished ironies and fine anger, especially as it touches on the exploration of failed leadership and misrule.

A government such as we have described so far inhibits the people's exercise of their personal and political liberties. It must be noted, however, that although the government may use all coercive agencies such as the State Research Council to oppress the people (with the mistaken belief that it can survive forever), there is bound to be some struggle by the oppressed for reform, change, or even outright bloody revolution against the oppressors. All the motivation that the people need in order to fight for their rights may just be the right leaders and ideas. In *Anthills*, those who come close to satisfying the yearnings and aspirations of the suffering masses in that direction are Ikem, Emmanuel, Beatrice, the white-bearded leader from Abazon, and Elewa's uncle. The first three represent the modern and urban force, and the last two represent the traditional and rural force. Both forces combine to examine the conditions of the grassroots people and attempt to protect them against the lies, corruption, and blatant abuse of power of the ruling class.

For his part, Ikem assumes, quite naively, that his editorial appointment, "public affairs so-called might provide the handle he needed" was to bring about peaceful changes in some of the government policies so as to ameliorate the people's lot. As that does not produce effectual results, he decides to use people and ideas to bring about the kinds of change he has in mind. The university, being a place for developing leadership and national ideologies, among other pursuits, is where Ikem goes for a hearing. He is warmly greeted, as he is introduced. He is cautious, as he attempts to deliver his message, making sure that his audience that propounds theories and ideas that eventuate in national ideology is itself well-educated in native and workable ideologies, not in parroting and disseminating foreign ones such as "the democratic dictatorship for the proletariat" (*Anthills* p. 155).

Ikem makes an immense speech that symbolizes the best in the old Africa and the new. Like his tribal elder, who speaks in metaphor and ambiguity of the injustice his people are suffering, Ikem addresses the students with subtle but modern irony.[12] It is a fiery lecture on the failures of revolutionary idealism. Carried away by the overwhelming response of the students, Ikem makes a statement that is interpreted by authorities as "fomenting revolt." He is so accused because, after the speech, the students are highly motivated to confront the ruling class; they take to the streets and mobilize the silent but powerful majority: the underclass.

One of those so thoroughly reeducated as a result of Ikem's propounded "new radicalism" is Emmanuel Obete, the President of the Students Union. He puts into practical use what he has learned from the speech, editorials, and practical lifestyle of his mentor, Ikem. His opportunity is the arrest and eventual mysterious death of Ikem. Reacting to that event, Emmanuel aids and abets the escape and activities of Chris, who is wanted by the secret police. In the process, Emmanuel learns how one dies nobly for one's beliefs and, sometimes, for one's country. It is he who gives Beatrice the details of the heroic death of Chris and consoles her over it. Emmanuel's role revives the downcast spirit of Beatrice: when the cycle of tyranny ends without necessarily bringing change for the better, "death settles the score, not only for Chris and Ikem [significantly, Emmanuel and Beatrice survive to represent youth and continuity, those hopes of the future] but also for His Excellency."[13] Indeed, Emmanuel and Beatrice remain to tell the story of the brushfire that they, the proverbial anthills of the savannah, have survived.

Beatrice's actual crusading role begins in chapter six of the novel, which is titled "Beatrice." In it, the narrator describes in detail her background, personality, education, relationship with the major characters, Sam, Chris, and Ikem, and her general political views. Her first act of rebellion against the government takes place at the Presidential Retreat in Abichi village, where she has been invited by the President to "come and meet Miss Cranford of the American United Press. Lou is in Bassa to see if all the bad news they hear about us in America is true," and to be paraded before Lou and the new power brokers around His Excellency as "the only person in the service, male or female, with a first-class honors in English. And not from a local university but from Queen Mary college, University of London" (pp. 74–5).

Beatrice notices Lou's impudent relationship with His Excellency and his cohorts and expresses disbelief:

> Her manner with His Excellency was becoming outrageously familiar and domineering. She would occasionally leave him hanging on a word she had just spoken while she turned to fling another at Major Ossai whom she now addressed only as Johnson. And wonder of wonders she even referred to the Chief of Staff, General Lango, as Ahmed on one occasion. And for these effronteries she got nothing but grins of satisfaction from the gentleman in question. Unbelievable!
>
> (p. 78)

In addition, Beatrice is shocked that Lou,

> without any kind of preamble, began reading His Excellency and his subjects a lecture on the need for the country to maintain its present [unpopular, needless to say] levels of foreign debt servicing currently running at slightly more than fifty-one percent of total national export earnings. Why? As a *quid pro quo* for increased American aid in surplus gains for our drought provinces!
>
> (p. 78)

When Beatrice challenges Lou's views on foreign debt servicing by referring her to Ikem's editorials in the *National Gazette*, Lou calls Ikem "a Marxist of sorts" who admires Castro of Cuba, who, no matter what he says, never defaults in his obligations to the international banking community, while he says, "Don't pay." Because His Excellency seems to be saying to Lou, "Go on; tell them. I have gone hoarse shouting the very same message to no avail" (p. 79), Beatrice is reminded of the incident of a girl who had remarked to her in England, "Your boys like us, ain't they? My girlfriend saiz it's the Desdemona complex." She is locked in combat again with Lou, a new Desdemona, "this time itinerant and, worse still, not over some useless black trash in England but the sacred symbol of my nation's pride, such as it was. Corny? So be it!" (p. 80).

What we see here is true nationalism. His Excellency and his high government officials are ridiculed by a foreign female journalist without knowing that they are! So Beatrice takes His Excellency boldly by the hand and leads him to the balcony railings with a breathtaking view of the dark lake from the pinnacle of the hill, where she tells him her story of Desdemona. Something possessed her as she told it, "If I went to America today, to Washington DC, would I, could I, walk into a White House private dinner and take the American President hostage. And his Defense Chief and his Director of CIA?" As if to emphasize her patriotic zeal and achievement, Beatrice remarks, "I did it shamelessly. I cheapened myself. God, I did it to your glory like the dancer in a Hindu temple. Like Esther, oh yes like Esther for my long-suffering people" (p. 81).

Generally, the trip to His Excellency's retreat offers Beatrice the opportunity to see firsthand all the ills of society that are brought about by poor leadership. For instance, she recollects the arguments Chris and Ikem had over the vast sums spent on the refurbishment of the Retreat – money, incidentally, which had not been passed through the normal Ministry of Financial Procedures (p. 73). Also, she studies at close quarters the behavior of the Director of SRC, Major Johnson Ossai, whom she describes as "reticent," "controversial," and "so excessively obsequious to His Excellency during the dinner," as well as the behavior of the Chief of Army Staff, General Ahmed Lange, whom she describes as a "more popularly known, more self-assured and more agreeable person altogether." What she learns about His Excellency and his men scares her, and she is apprehensive of the degenerating relationship of Sam, Chris, and Ikem, the "three green bottles standing on the wall." The final events of the novel confirm her fears and careful observations at the dinner. For it is the Director of SRC and the Chief of Army staff who planned and executed a countercoup in which His Excellency is killed. After His Excellency dies, General Lange promotes himself President and Head of State. To make his position secure, he gets rid of Major Ossai, who was himself promoted colonel for eliminating Ikem (pp. 76–7).

Beatrice's peculiar knowledge of people also gives Ikem an insight into the world of women. Ikem acknowledges that she charged him with assigning to women the role of a fire brigade after the house caught fire and had been virtually consumed. This forced him to sit down and contemplate the nature of oppression. He says:

> The women are, of course, the biggest single group of oppressed people in the world and, if we are to believe the Book of Genesis, the very oldest. But they are not the only ones. There are others – rural peasants in every land, the urban poor in industrialized countries, Black people everywhere including their own continent, ethnic and religious minorities and castes in all countries. The most obvious practical difficulty is the magnitude and heterogeneity of the problems. There is no universal conglomerate of the oppressed. Free people may be alike everywhere in their freedom but the oppressed inhabit each their own peculiar hell.
>
> (pp. 98–9)

While Beatrice inspires Ikem, he in turn inspires her. In fact, it is out of concern for the oppressed that she helps her boyfriend, Chris, to escape the SRC; dutifully keeps and nurses Elewa after Ikem dies; and when she gives birth to Amaechina, and names the child when Elewa's uncle fails to arrive in time for the naming ceremony. Generally, Beatrice's role is to provide service to her friends, Chris and Ikem; to her fellow women, including Elewa and Agatha; to her ethnic group (the Igbo speaking people of the novel); and to her country and her leaders who are ridiculed by the modern Desdemonas.

The white-bearded leader of the Abazon delegation plays a role that is important in two ways. First, when at the gathering in Harmoney Hotel, Ikem is accused of failing to join in his people's monthly meetings and other social gatherings, it is this leader, "tall, gaunt-looking and with a slight stoop of the shoulders," who comes to the defense of Ikem and his profession. To Ikem's accuser he says:

> Going to meetings and weddings and naming ceremonies of one's people is good. But don't forget that our wise men have said that a man who answers every summons by a town-crier will not plant corn in his fields. So my advice to you is this: Go on with your meetings and marriages and naming ceremonies because it is good to do so. But leave this young man alone to do what he is doing for Abazon and for the whole of Kangan; the cock that crows in the mornings belongs to one household, but his voice is the property of the neighborhood. You should be proud that this bright cockerel that wakes the whole village comes from your compound.
>
> (p. 122)

What Ikem is doing is he functioning as the editor of the *National Gazette*. He has chosen journalism as a means of carrying out "all the fight he has fought for poor people in this land," and the leader "would not like to hear that he has given up that fight because he wants to attend the naming ceremony of Okeke's son and Mgbafo's daughter" (p. 123).

There is a need for people to recognize individual talents – "To everyone his due? . . . To every man his own! To each his chosen title!" – and natural callings, such as the art of storytelling:

> To some of us the Owner of the World has apportioned the gift to tell their fellows that the time to get up has finally come. To others He gives the eagerness to rise when they hear the call; to rise with racing blood and put on their garbs of war and go to the boundary of their town to engage the invading enemy boldly in battle. And then there are those others whose part is to wait and when the struggle is ended, to take over and recount its story.
>
> The sounding of the battle-drum is important; the fierce waging of the war itself important; and telling of the story afterwards – each is important in its own way. I tell you there is not one of them we could do without. But if you ask me which of them takes the eagle-feather I will say boldly: the story.

> (p. 123)

This kind of role encourages Ikem to work harder for the people as he produces more editorials in the *National Gazette*. Indirectly, he has been made to regard his editorial appointment as the most important of the cabinet appointments, since that appointment involves "telling stories."

The second significance of the leader's role is embodied in the story "The Tortoise Who Was About to Die." The story is about the struggle of the underclass against the oppression by the ruling class. It teaches people how to fight for their liberation, which could result in either sociopolitical liberty or noble deaths: "*Because even after I am dead I would want anyone passing by this spot to say yes, a fellow and his match struggled here*" (p. 128). Abazon is oppressed by His Excellency's despotic government. Although the people suffer the worst drought in the history of Kangan and need some assistance from the government, they do not expect to receive any because they did not support His Excellency's ambition to become President-for-Life. Yet they have to send a delegation to His Excellency instead of standing still. In other words, the delegation is a form of struggle that may not result in practical solutions to their numerous problems, but it does give them some psychological satisfaction: so "that those who come after us will be able to say: *True, our fathers were defeated but they tried*" (p. 128).

Such a story as told by the leader (symbol of age and tradition) to Ikem and his people in Bassa (symbol of youth and inexperience), exhorts Ikem to literary activism. And when he is dismissed as editor of the *National Gazette*, he does not take it lying down. He goes to the university to make a speech, a move that is comparable to the tortoise's going "into strange action on the road, scratching with hands and feet and throwing sand on the road furiously in all directions." Ikem's message goes in the directions of Emmanuel, Chris, Beatrice, Captain Abdul, Medina, and the taxi drivers and changes their entire lives (p. 223). They all cooperate in their individual ways to fight the establishment and give hope to posterity.

In his own way, Elewa's uncle, who is another old man from the countryside, adds a new dimension to the type of education that the young men of Abazon in Bassa receive from the leader of the Abazon delegation. This second old man makes a speech at the naming ceremony of Amaechina, which touches on the survival of the people. One way of surviving the modern world is for one to adjust to changes that occur from time to time in the society. When he hears that the people have already done his work of naming the child, he does not grow angry, especially as he can still receive the rewards of the service that "All of Us" does for him. He does not fret just because people gather in this whiteman house and give the girl a boy's name (p. 227); for, that has been done by the people in the interest of the people. The overall import of the old man's speech as Beatrice perceives it is that "This world belongs to the people of the world not to any little caucus, no matter how talented." For she says,

> It is the same message Elewa's uncle was drumming out this afternoon, wasn't it? On his own crazy drum, of course. Chris, in spite of his brilliance, was just beginning to be vaguely aware of people like that old man. Remember his prayer? He had never been inside a whiteman house like this before, may it not be his last.
>
> (p. 232)

As he says prayers before breaking the kola nut, the old man refers to the root causes of national disunity: namely, religious bigotry and intolerance, poor and selfish national planning, and ethnic bickering. All those problems he prays against so that Kangan may once again enjoy peace, harmony, and security. As a matter of fact, before the old man joins in the naming ceremony, the effort toward national unity of all ethnic and religious groups for which the old man prays had already started. The group includes Igbo, Hausa, and Yoruba people who are also Christians, Moslems, and the "priestess of the unknown god" in ecumenical fraternization (p. 224). But what the old man's prayer does is to reinforce the importance of the ethnic and religious unity that should result in national unity, and to elicit from the up-and-coming leaders a pledge for its realization.

Achebe handles the theme of victimization from the very first page of *Anthills* through the last page. There are group victims, class victims, and individual victims. When the novel opens, readers hear His Excellency tell Chris, "You're wasting everybody's time, Mr. Commissioner for Information. I will not go to Abazon. Finish! *Kabisa!* Any other business?" (p. 1). Later on, readers are made to understand that Abazon is a province whose citizens are drought victims. Everybody suffers the effect of the worst drought in Kangan, and yet the government does not come to their aid. And when, eventually, a delegation of six Abazon leaders goes to Bassa in order to say yes to His Excellency's request, the leaders are put away in jail. They are accused of collaborating with Ikem, who is charged with the crime of advocating regicide. The leaders are neither released on bail pending trial nor are they given opportunity for legal defense. They are detained for the leaders' isolation and deprivation abroad, and hunger and death at home for all Abazon citizens.

The leaders are thus sacrificed because of the political "indiscretion" of their people and the inordinate political ambition of His Excellency the President. The Abazon leaders' imprisonment adds more tension for the President. The Abazon leaders' imprisonment adds more tension to the already tense society that faces starvation and extermination. Men, women, and children all suffer from the consequences of a political decision that they may not have taken part in. It seems as if their suffering is group karma.

The leader is a storyteller. He tells tales of survival techniques, in the face of formidable adversity. His story does not give prescriptions for their suffering; instead, it gives more headaches! That is why Ikem will in future decide to make a speech that does not augur well for the survival of the oppressive ruling class. Ordinarily, anyone seeing what has happened to the leaders of Abazon in Bassa would think enemies of the government would be cowed into fear, as the government is rapidly turning Bassa into a police state. Instead, the people gain strength through the suffering of the great storyteller, and there is a greater degree of suspicion and distrust of the government.

The underclass of Kangan are class victims. The author's first graphic description of this category of victims occurs in chapter four in which the Second Witness – Ikem Osodi – discusses the barbarism of the public execution of armed robbers, which is becoming mass entertainment on the beach. Ikem is opposed to it and writes powerful editorials attacking all forms of capital punishment. On the other hand, his colleague Chris charges that Ikem is a romantic, "that the ordinary people of Kangan believed firmly in an eye for an eye and that from all accounts they enjoyed the spectacle that so turned my stomach" (p. 39).

While Chris misreads the apparent enjoyment of the oppressed class, Ikem expresses anger over the ease with which the ruling class has adopted attitudes of the white colonialists when he rhetorically asks:

> How does the poor man retain his calm in the face of such provocation? From what bottomless wells of patience does he draw? His great humor must explain it. This sense of humor turned sometimes against himself, must be what saves him from total dejection. He had learnt to squeeze every drop of enjoyment he can out of his stony luck. And the fool who oppresses him will make a particular point of that enjoyment: *You see, they are not in the least like ourselves. They don't need and can't use the luxuries that you and I must have. They have the animal capacity to endure the pain or, shall we say, domestication.* The words the white master had said in his time about the black race as a whole. Now we say them about the poor.
>
> (p. 40)

Here Achebe, through Ikem, is commenting on the victimization complex of the poor; that is the poor accepting their suffering as if it were the natural order. But behind that apparent animal capacity to endure pain is the poor men's quiet but cynical rebuff of the ruling class's inhumanity to them. That is why toward the end of the novel Chris's companion can counsel a policeman on a checkpoint – an agent of oppression – who laments that he has no motorcycle:

> Make you no mind. No condition is permanent. You go get. Meself as I de talk so, you think say I get machine? Even common bicycle I no get. But my mind strong that one day I go jump bicycle, jump machine and land inside motor car! And somebody go come open door for me and say *yes sir!* And I go carry my belle like woman we de begin to pregnant small and come sitdon for owner-corner, take cigarette put for mouth, no more kolanut, and say to driver *common move!* I get strong mind for dat. Make you get strong mind too, everything go be all right.
>
> (p. 193)

And to Chris, the Commissioner for Information – another government agent – whom he teaches how to escape arrest by the police: "Ehe! Talkam like that. No shaky-shaky mouth again. But oga you see now, to be big man no hard but to be poor man no be small thing. Na proper wahala. No be so?" Chris, having undergone some transformation mentally and physically, concurs with his companion's views when he says, "Na so I see-o. I no know before today to pass for small man you need to go special college" (p. 194) – an opportunity that his trip north to Abazon province offers to him.

The brutalization of Kangan society by its government officials turns every individual, low or high, into a victim. Sam, His Excellency the President, for example, is a victim of his own inordinate political ambition. Up until the time he becomes Head of State, he is described as a man who insists that things be done right; but he is so distant from the dispossessed of the country – "The crippled kindred in the wild savannah" – and from his cabinet members that he is unable to ensure that things are, indeed, done right. Even in his dealings with his government officials, he is seen to be paranoid but certainly not depraved. In fact, he exhibits qualities that prove that he is at the helm of his government affairs from time to time; but he is also credulous to a point of being fooled into mistrusting and hating his close friends. His lusty credulity, therefore, makes him rely more and more on the secret police for the day-to-day running of his government, and that brings about his total undoing.

Chris is as distant from the masses as His Excellency. However, from Beatrice's account, he is a very intelligent and debonair person. His inability to hurt a person prevents him from seeing and challenging the inhumane treatment of the masses by the government as quickly and as clearly as Ikem does. Hence, he calls the more militant Ikem a "romantic." It is the same pacific attitude toward people, especially His Excellency, that prevents him from resigning from His Excellency's cabinet, despite Ikem's prodding. He does not obey His Excellency's order to fire Ikem from his editorial appointment. It is only when Ikem has been abducted and murdered that he gets near the people and becomes militant. Even at that, his militancy is short-lived; but his act of defending and dying for the weak and young is a mark of heroism that is so powerful in encouraging the young men and women who are the future of Kangan.

Ikem, the moral embodiment of the novel and keeper of the conscience of the society, is the one character who initiates much of the political action of the novel that the Head of State considers subversive; therefore, Ikem must be punished for it. In a way, Ikem suffers a kind of monomania in the sense that he knows how dangerous the role that he is playing can be, and still he stubbornly continues with it. John Gross remarks, "A real-life Ikem would surely have been more deeply compromised by his role as editor of a semi-official paper; and though the fictional Ikem has his inner doubts, his reflections tend to be impossibly abstract and wordy."[14] That may be true but readers do not forget that "Ikem is also Achebe's alter ego," who believes that "a genuine artist, no matter what he says he believes, must feel in his blood the ultimate enmity between art and orthodoxy." Ikem longs for union "with earth and earth's people." His love of truth and people transcend political ideology, and he becomes a popular hero among students after Sam dismisses him from the *Gazette*.[15]

Ikem dies because, according to Lee Leseaze, "Mr. Achebe also puts his faith for a better future in an old tradition: storytelling." Stories are what make us different from cattle, he tells us. What's more: "Storytellers are a threat. They threaten all champions of control, they frighten usurpers of the right-to-freedom of the human spirit – in state, in church or mosque, in party congress, in the university or wherever."[16] Indeed, Ikem falls victim, but his allegiance to truth changes the world of men and ideas, and after he dies, Kangan is never its old self again. That is why his death is a precursor to the deaths of Chris and Sam.

All three men rose to power together, and all three die at the end of the revolution, thereby falling from power together. Commenting on the demise, Neal Ascherson observes that "in their very different ways, the three boys from Lord Lugard College have all expiated the sin that two of them recognized but one did not": that failure to re-establish vital inner links with the poor and dispossessed." The three murders, useless as they are, represent the departure of a generation that compromised its own enlightenment for the sake of power – "even the bold opposition enjoyed by Ikem Osodi."[17] However, the other characters such as Beatrice, Elewa, Agatha, Emmanuel, and Abdul, who attempt to re-establish vital inner links with not just the poor and dispossessed but also the aged and the storytellers, are scourged but not murdered.

In addition to the three men, there are other individual victims in the novel: Beatrice, who loses her friends and intellectual companions, Chris and Ikem; Elewa, who loses her common-law husband, Ikem; Emmanuel, who loses his political mentor and revolutionary comrade, Ikem and Chris, respectively; and Amaechina, born posthumously to Ikem, are all victims of bad governance and misrule. Their unbearable pains are vividly described by the narrator and through the interior monologues of the victims themselves:

She looked at each in turn with a strained smile on her countenance. "Truth is beauty, isn't it? It must be, you know to make someone dying in that pain, to make him . . . smile. He sees it and it is. . . . How can I say it? It is unbearably, yes *unbearably* beautiful. That's it! Like Kunene's Emperor Shaka, the spears of his assailants raining down on him. But he realized the truth at that moment, we're told, and died smiling. Oh my Chris!

Two lines of tears coursed down under her eyes but she did not bother to wipe them.

(*Anthills*, p. 233)

Any writer who thinks and writes the way Chinua Achebe has in *Anthills of the Savannah* is bound to offend some of his readers and, therefore, must suffer criticism. And since there are clear indications in the novel that Achebe's sympathy is for Ikem Osodi, critics may tend to regard Ikem as Achebe's spokesman. Therefore, whatever views Ikem expresses about Kangan (which some readers think resembles Achebe's native Nigeria), must also be Achebe's personal views on that government. Hence, Achebe should, and ought to, expect the kind of treatment that Ikem suffers, and also some criticism from those who do not understand, or deliberately fail to appreciate, the true role and burden of a committed third world writer like Achebe.

That is why, despite the generally favorable critical comments on Achebe's achievements in *Anthills*,[18] one can still read unfavorable comments on the novel such as the following:

Achebe's doubtlessly heart-felt message also gets in the way of *Anthills'* success as fiction. For the most part, he speaks with the diction and verve of a first-rate novelist; at other times, he's far too earnestly didactic, given to rhetorical comment on the nature of tyranny, the plight of the poor and dispossessed. The trouble with this kind of language is that it may reverse priorities, making editorializing more important than the thrust of the narrative.[19]

Indeed, what Ken Adachi calls a reversal of priorities is only a fault from a *purist's* point of view; yet, judged from Achebe's overall aim and technique in *Anthills*, it is rather an innovation. Achebe does not allow an omniscient reporter to tell the tales of the novel. Instead, he wants participants to tell their own tales as they play the roles of witnesses. It is a conscious choice that Achebe the artist has made, which means that to him editorializing becomes an important weapon for bringing the testimonies of the participants in the poor governance (which is a shared experience) together. That is also why the narrative shifts from time to time, making the authenticity of the tales depend on the candor of the characters themselves and not on the assumed authority of the author.

By "editorializing" rather than "dramatizing" the events of the novel, Achebe adds a new dimension to the art of novel writing. That is why he declared to a *Daily*

Texan reporter, "Basically I have come to the conclusion that the novel, the form, can carry more than we have tended to give it. Perhaps we have not been bold enough in assigning tasks to the novel."[20] Nevertheless, the type of task he assigns to the novel makes novel writing a highly political art, but he practices it with courage, despite the danger he has endured in the past. He knows that "it is more dangerous to be a writer in Africa than in America," and illustrates that assertion by recounting how he had "predicted" the first Nigerian military coup in *A Man of the People*, and six months later, when a countercoup took place, some of those who suffered from the first coup figured that if he was able to predict the takeover, he must have been part of it. So armed soldiers went to the radio studios where he worked looking for him, but he was at home. Staff members telephoned him immediately. "They said that there were two drunken armed soldiers there who wanted to know if my pen was as strong as their guns," Achebe recalls.[21]

Achebe's victimization includes being denied some honors that he highly deserves. For example, in January 1988, Achebe left the University of Massachusetts and returned to Nigeria, flown there by Lagos State University, which was to award him an honorary degree at an academic convocation. A day before the ceremony, the government ordered the university to cancel it. The university was never given a reason for the cancellation. "The newspapers speculated that I was too controversial and that that was the reason for the cancellation," Achebe says. "I think the newspaper speculation is accurate."[22]

While that deprivation was going on in Achebe's home country, a knowledgeable foreign critic who had just read *Anthills* was making a passionate case abroad for an international award for Achebe. In an article, "Africa and the Nobel Prize," Bernth Lindfors wrote:

> Chinua Achebe thus appears to be the only viable candidate from black Africa remaining [without the award], but many feel that he is easily the best and most deserving of high literary honors. Indeed, he suspects he would have won the Nobel Prize years before Soyinka did, had he continued writing at the pace at which he started. However, the Nigerian Civil War threw him off his stride, turning him away from long fiction to poetry, essays, short stories, and children's books. Because he had made his initial impression with the novel some critics ignored these briefer works (even though several of them won major prizes) and persuaded themselves and others that he had stopped writing altogether. Anyone doubting his present creative vitality should take a look at *Anthills of the Savannah*, a powerful new novel he published a few months ago. Nominated immediately for England's Booker Prize, it may well become the definitive treatment in fiction for military rule in Africa. Such evidence of undiminished literary prowess may also soon put Achebe, Africa's premier novelist, back into contention for the Nobel Prize. He certainly merits the most serious consideration.[23]

Anthills is an important novel in a lot of ways. "Considered in terms of Achebe's body of works it replays familiar scenarios. There seems, however, to have been a maturing of Achebe's perceptions about politics and the human condition."[24] Indeed, it is a maturing that derives from the author's meeting firsthand with the suffering masses during the Nigerian civil war, and from the practical experience he gained during the brief period he served as a party official of the PRP. Both types of experience and his almost natural sympathy for the poor and dispossessed all combine to deepen his natural creative sensibility. The result is that Achebe is enabled to articulate a mature view of governance, revolutions, and victimization.

Hence, in *Anthills*, he emphasizes that the strength of the human race is its unpredictability: "man's stubborn antibody called surprise. Man will surprise by his capacity for mobility as well as for villainy." For that reason, all that can be done is to understand what cannot be done, that all total solutions fail and that therefore "we may accept a limitation on our actions but never, under no circumstances, must we accept restrictions on our thinking" (p. 223).

Playing his usual self-imposed role of the novelist as teacher, Achebe has used *Anthills of the Savannah* as a forum to discuss the issue of bad governance and misrule in most West African countries and how it has destroyed many rulers, crippled their national economy, inhibited their citizens' political liberty, and turned both the ruler and the ruled into victims. In the end, Achebe does not prescribe revolution as the solution to the hydra-headed problems of the nations; for he says through Ikem:

> Experience and intelligence warn us that man's progress in freedom will be piecemeal, slow and undramatic. Revolution may be unnecessary for taking a society out of an intractable stretch of quagmire but it does not confer freedom, and may indeed hinder it.

> (p. 99)

Through the discussions and conversations of the characters and the commentaries of the narrator, Achebe has told us where the rain started to beat us. Now that we know, we ought to get to our destination quicker.

Notes

* Culled from Kalu Ogbaa, ed., *The Gong and the Flute: African Literary Development and Celebration*. Westport, CT: Greenwood Press, 1994: 129–47.
1 Bruce King and Kolawole Ogungbesan, eds., *A Celebration of Black and African Writing*. Zaria, Nigeria: Ahmadu Bello University Press, 1978: 151.
2 *Ibid.*, p. 162.
3 Chinua Achebe, *Anthills of the Savannah*. London: Heinemann Educational Books Ltd., 1987; New York: Anchor Press/Doubleday, 1988. The edition that we have adopted in this discussion and out of which we have quoted passages is the Heinemann Educational Books Ltd., The African Writers Series, 1988.
4 Chinua Achebe, *A Man of the People*. London: Heinemann Educational Books Ltd., 1966.
5 *Africa Events*, Vol. 3, No. 11 (November 1978): 76.
6 *Ibid.*

7 *Washington Times*, February 15, 1988, p. E8.
8 Achebe, *Anthills of the Savannah*, p. 141.
9 *Ibid.*
10 *Ibid.*
11 Achebe, *The Trouble with Nigeria.*
12 *Sunday Times* (London), September 20, 1987, p. 56.
13 *Ibid.*
14 *New York Times*, February 16, 1988.
15 Charles Johnson expresses this view in the *Washington Post*, February 7, 1988, p. 10.
16 *New York Times*, February 16, 1988.
17 *New York Review of Books*, March 3, 1988, p. 4.
18 Details of the favorable critical views can be seen in the blurbs of the three editions of the novel.
19 See Ken Adachi's comments in *The Sunday Star*, January 21, 1988, p. A21.
20 *Daily Texan*, Friday, February 19, 1988, p. 11.
21 For details, see the *Hartford Courant*, Monday, May 16, 1988, pp. C1 and C8.
22 *Ibid.*, p. C8.
23 For the full comment, see *World Literature Today*, Vol. 62 (Spring 1988): 222–4.
24 See Charles Johnson's review of *Anthills* in the *Washington Post*, February 7, 1988, p. 10.

8 Year 1990 and After
A New Life and Phase IV of Achebe's Writing Career

Chinua Achebe ended Phase III of his writing career in 1989 with great accomplishments, such as publishing the American edition of *Hopes and Impediments: Selected Essays*; serving as Visiting Distinguished Professor of English at City College of the City University of New York, during which time the Borough of Manhattan proclaimed May 25 Chinua Achebe Day; founding *African Commentary*, a magazine for people of African descent; being elected first President of the Nigerian chapter of PEN and reelected President of Ogidi Town Union; being appointed by the Indian Government to an International Jury to award the annual Gandhi Prize for Peace, Disarmament and Development (1989–1992); being awarded honorary doctorates (D.H.L.) by Westfield College, Massachusetts, (D.Litt.) by Open University, Great Britain, and (D.Litt.) by University of Ibadan, Nigeria, respectively; and, receiving the Callaloo Award.[1] These accomplishments inspired him to work on his scheduled assignments for the coming year with greater determination.

He began Phase IV of his writing career in 1990 with the hope of achieving more goals in his life as well: First of all, he was looking forward to celebrating his 60th birthday in November, and to enjoying the celebrations of an international symposium that his fellow scholars in the arts and humanities, as well as Nigerian authors, planned in his honor, titled "Eagle on Iroko: Achebe at 60," to be held in February at the University of Nigeria, Nsukka, as part of his birthday celebration. Before then, he began traveling to give public lectures and conduct seminars on African literature, art, and culture in some places in North America, Europe, Asia, and Africa, as an important aspect of Phase IV of his writing career. Achebe also served in two other American colleges: Dartmouth College in New Hampshire and Bard College in New York, and he received many awards in recognition of his publications and for the academic work he was doing as a distinguished professor in many institutions of higher learning. But the most unforgettable incident, which took place in his life in 1990, was his involvement in a near-death automobile accident on March 22 that partially paralyzed him and changed his life forever!

All the incidents mentioned above took place immediately after the end of his service at the City College of the City University of New York in December 1989, which was followed by his three-month appointment (from January to

DOI: 10.4324/9781003184133-8

March 1990) as Montgomery Fellow and Visiting Professor of English at Dartmouth College. From there, Achebe embarked on foreign travels to carry out his previously scheduled speaking engagements in many parts of the world. According to Phanuel Akubueze Egejuru, what followed thereafter became a turning point in his life:

> From Dartmouth, he travelled to other places for various assignments. In January, he appeared in London Weekend Television's South Bank Show. As an introduction to his own lecture, he talked of his recent participation in Ireland's celebration of one thousand years of the founding of the city of Dublin. The program he appeared on was titled, "Literature as Celebration." He found that title very applicable to his own lecture: "African Literature as Celebration." He then used the Mbari tradition of Owerri Igbos to explain the significance of the title of his lecture. Achebe found the Mbari phenomenon a very useful metaphor in his attempt to help the West understand not only the Igbo concept of art but also the black man's generosity of spirit. Because, through Mbari, the people celebrate every presence in their society. And celebration in the context of Mbari does not mean only praise and approval of good happenings but also of bad and unfortunate happenings in society. Soon after this lecture, he flew back to Nigeria in February for the symposium held at the University of Nigeria, Nsukka, to celebrate his 60th birthday. . . . Participants in various disciplines of the Humanities came from different parts of the world. There were also diplomats representing countries from Europe, the United States, Canada, Britain and some other countries within the Commonwealth.[2]

The symposium was a spectacular display of academic paper presentations by literary scholars from many parts of the world and Igbo cultural exhibitions rolled into one Nigerian national festival, which looked like the funeral celebration of the revered Igbo elder, Ogbuefi Ezeudu, in *Things Fall Apart* (p. 112). There was a lot of singing and dancing to the sounds and rhythms of talking drums and flutes performed by hired professionals. Igbo masqueraders dexterously displayed their warrior skills, all in praise of their renowned native son and writer, Chinua Achebe, whose pen had proved to be mightier than the sword, as he metaphorically fought the cultural war that Western writers and colonial administrators had been waging for more than a century against Africans, especially against the cultures of his native Igbo and other ethnic peoples of Nigeria. And yet, there were many foreign scholars and writers who came to pay their respect to an author whose literary works were a source for their own critical works on African literature. To underscore the international import and milieu of the celebration, Ezenwa-Ohaeto wrote:

> Many scholars from all parts of the world interested in African literature assembled at Nsukka. They came from all continents. The distinguished Michael Thelwell came from America with Bernth Lindfors and John Povey;

G. D. Killam from Canada, Denise Coussy from France, Alastair Niven and C. L. Innis from Britain, Gareth Griffiths from Australia, Raoul Granqvist from Sweden, Wolfgang Zach from Austria, and A. L. Imfeld and Ulla Schild from Germany. It was a magnificent gathering. The voices of countless writers and critics, the books they had authored and the ebullience of their greetings as they paced backwards and forwards sent smiles into every heart. For the first time in living Nigerian memory, over one hundred and fifty papers were delivered on a single writer in a conference in Nigeria when the literary world went to Nsukka.[3]

All the personalities mentioned above had not only written critical works on African literature but also had included Achebe's works of fiction in their curricular offerings in such courses as "Commonwealth literature," "third world literatures," and, lately, "African literature" in the English departments of their universities, as a means of learning about African cultures and civilization through its literature.

Indeed, the symposium was a grand occasion in which Achebe's fellow scholars and writers presented papers expressing their individual appreciations of the great work he had been doing as an African writer and cultural promoter. For instance, in his own contribution at the occasion, titled "Achebe's Vision of a New Africa," Donatus I. Nwoga, a fellow Igbo/Nigerian literary scholar, asserted that

> We know from these that Achebe has always seen the writer as one of the main guides and activators in the national consciousness formulation and even in the provocation of action for the salvation of the nation. This mental and psychological influence should extend over the liberation of the mind from the inferiority complex of believing that the past of Africa was one dark night of savagery with nothing to offer the present, a darkness from which the colonizing white man rescued us. At the same time this liberation should also encompass a freedom from a victim stasis which sees the situation in which Africa finds itself today as a product of the viciousness of our past colonial existence.
>
> In more recent times, Achebe has expressed a social vision less dominated by reaction to the reality of colonialism, a vision that exercises itself with the situation in which the peoples and nations of Africa are living in Africa itself and in Africa's interaction with the peoples and nations of the world. His statement of this vision is in terms that are less political than humane, less nationalistic than human, so that he is enunciating a vision of society that would be applicable in any situation where human beings live and interact. I am careful to add that this is because Achebe is both a Nigerian and a citizen of the world, not because he has left the problems that identify the trouble with Nigeria to look for the problems of a "universalist" world.[4]

Nwoga's articulation of "Achebe's Vision of a New Africa" was important in the sense that some readers, who appreciated Achebe's early brave and fiery pronouncements on the colonizer-colonized relationship between the Western world and African countries, later thought that the tone of voice in his writings and lectures was becoming a little mellow, ostensibly because he was living and doing some of his writing in the United States at the time. On the contrary, however, some Africans who lived in America and attended the lectures and seminars Achebe delivered there, knew that he still condemned what Western colonization of continental Africa did to her peoples; but he also chose to acknowledge some of the benefits of those colonial systems such as Africans acquiring the colonizers' languages that enabled their writers and politicians to communicate with the outside world as they fought against colonialism and imperialism. It is, in fact, the acquisition of British education (including their history, religion, and culture), which was taught in English, that empowered Achebe to fight, through his writings, the cultural war with the West. Without such education, it would have been impossible for Achebe or any other African writer to fight against any foreign powers whose languages they did not understand. Moreover, Achebe always promoted the brotherhood of mankind in his writings, as long as the West and the South showed mutual respect for each other. That is the notion of otherness in his writings; and that is one of the main points of emphasis in his lecture, titled "African Literature as Celebration," which he delivered in London in January 1990. It is the same promotion of mutual understanding and respect among Nigerian ethnic peoples that he stressed in his book *The Trouble with Nigeria*, which we examined in our earlier discussion. For in their dealings with one another, the ethnic peoples of Nigeria placed the primacy of ethnicity over and above the superiority of patriotism and national service. In other words, "Achebe's Vision of a New Africa" included the same vision for a new Nigeria, which he advocated for in 1970, immediately after the civil war. If, in their national debates, Nigerians had taken into consideration his prescriptions for dealing with the hydra-headed trouble with their country, who knows whether things would have stopped falling apart for all the citizens, regardless of their ethnic, religious, and sociopolitical backgrounds?

I applaud the paper presenters for their high praises of Achebe because of what he achieved over the years in his writings, each emphasizing what was important in his texts. For sometimes one finds nuggets of valuable information even in their postscripts, such as "As We Saw Him" by John Munonye, and "Chinua Achebe: A Personal View" by Alan Hill, – the two essays comprising "Section H: Postscriptum" of *Eagle on Iroko: Selected Papers from the Chinua Achebe International Symposium 1990*. What one learns here may open more doors to future scholarship and understanding about Achebe. For instance, in his postscript, Munonye, who was Achebe's coeval both at Government College, Umuahia, and at the University College, Ibadan, praised Achebe for his literary inspiration in both institutions. Munonye joked about how some literary critics had referred to him as the son of Achebe, but he went on to refer to Achebe as his inspirer instead of an elder Nigerian novelist, Cyprian Ekwensi, whom some people refer to as the Nigerian Defoe. In conclusion, Munonye stressed the role of Achebe as a world-renowned writer:

Let me again round up. All eyes once again on the iroko and the eagle mounted on top: the height, power and excellence which our nation, and the entire African continent, indeed the entire black race has achieved on the world literary landscape through our brother and friend. And that universal voice is such that from its great height it falls distinct and clear, lacking obscurities, affectation, or prevarication. It is one thing to sing from a mountain top and another to be heard well, and still another to be listened to with such great absorption and great delight no matter that the strain might suggest gloom at times.[5]

Munonye was speaking not only on behalf of his classmates at the two institutions they attended, but also for the Association of Nigerian Authors (ANA), which had chosen Achebe as its first president.

From Alan Hill, acquisitions editor in Heinemann Educational Books Ltd., London, we learn about the great role Chinua Achebe played in the development of its African Writers Series: *Things Fall Apart* was the first African novel to be published in that series, and later on, the company appointed Achebe Editor of the Series. Hill began his personal view of Chinua Achebe as follows:

I first met Chinua Achebe 30 years ago. We had just published his novel *Things Fall Apart* in a modest edition of 2000 copies, which had been well received in Britain, but was dismissed in USA by the New York *Herald Tribune* as "an authentic native document, guileless and unsophisticated." In Nigeria, however, nobody seemed to have heard of it at all. In the University of Ibadan, they didn't take me seriously when I told them that one of their own alumni had written a great novel. "What, Chinua Achebe write a novel! How ridiculous . . .!"

I was making my first trip to Nigeria. It was a sentimental journey, my mother having been born in Cameroon. I was eagerly looking forward to meeting Chinua, who was living then in Ikoyi. I was greeted in front of a handsome residence by a slim young man in a sharp suit and dark glasses, who had just got out of his Jaguar: the very model of a modern "yuppie," so it seemed to me. *To my surprise this turned out to be Chinua Achebe himself. However, behind the outward appearance, I at once felt the strength of a most unusual personality.*[6]

(emphasis added)

Hill gave further details of his meeting with Achebe, saying that he invited Achebe to edit a series of works of African writing that they were planning in London, and Achebe readily agreed to do it. "He belied the 'yuppie' image by taking on what turned out to be an onerous but crucial job, without seeking any reward other than his service to the new-born literature of the African continent." But the most important fact I learned from Hill's postscript was that "One of Chinua's greatest coups was when, on a visit to Makerere, he picked up a student's half-finished MS, and strongly recommended it to us. We published the novel in 1964 under the title of *Weep Not, Child,* by James Ngugi (as Ngugi wa Thiong'o was then called)."[7]

Until Hill's revelation that it was Chinua Achebe who recommended Ngugi wa Thiong'o's unfinished manuscript to Heinemann for publication, people did not know what Achebe privately did to promote the writing career of a fellow African writer, since both men eventually became renowned authors who unrelentingly strived to develop modern African literature as a means of fighting sociocultural and political wars against British colonialism and imperialism in East African and West African sub-regions about the same time. At any rate, Alan Hill's postscript credits Achebe as being the founder of modern African fiction and promoter of African literature generally at both the continental and international levels. In that sense, the 1990 international symposium held in celebration of Chinua Achebe's 60th birthday unquestionably helped to immortalize him as the guru of African literature.

As soon as the euphoric birthday celebrations were over, Achebe rushed back to the United States to finish his short-term appointment at Dartmouth. He had only two weeks to rest before going to California to assume his next appointment at Stanford University. While returning, Achebe was asked to come back to Ogidi to settle a serious dispute involving the crucial issue of changing the Igweship of the town by rotation in order to end the monopoly of the office by one specific family or kindred. Since he had already spent some time with his people during the birthday celebrations in February, he needed time to prepare for some academic work before going to Stanford, but he felt compelled to go deal with the situation immediately in Nigeria as a part of his role as President-General of Ogidi Town Union, a position for which he was reelected in 1989:

> [It] was thus crucial for him to rush home from the United States and confront a disgruntled Ndichie over the sensitive issue of Igweship. He knew how important his presence was for the success of any meeting, because "every time he wasn't there, the meeting will have no head." Therefore, it was a veritable act of courage and devotion to his people that made Chinua risk a journey from the United States back to Nigeria, barely a month after the celebrations of Eagle-on-Iroko.
>
> He successfully presided over the meeting during which the heated topic of rotating the Igweship was reopened. Tempers flew as the Ndichie vigorously defended their proscribed traditional role of kingmakers. They were quite vociferous in demonstrating their disappointment in the President whom they had virtually begged to take over that office. All progressive elements of Ogidi were horrified even frightened by the unexpected reaction of the Ndichie. It was quite a revelation because people from Ogidi and beyond assumed that everybody in Ogidi loved Chinua. In fact, his friend, old man Johnson Okudo spoke of him in terms of *Olisa e nwee ilo* – God has no enemy. As for Achebe, it was just a meeting like all other meetings where people disagreed and shouted at one another. So, he left Ogidi for Nsukka from whence he would return to the United States.[8]

Achebe planned to leave the country on March 22, 1990 on his way back to the United States, but things did not go according to plan. What happened to him as he and his older son Ikechukwu left Nsukka for Enugu Airport, where they would catch a plane to Lagos and from there return to the United States, is narrated as follows by Egejuru, who interviewed him and some family members:

> [The ride] was quite smooth and soon Chinua dozed off. As soon as they passed the Awka campus of Anambra State University of Technology, at a spot uninhabited by people, it happened! The axle broke into two. The car somersaulted several times before it landed on Chinua who had been ejected during the somersaults. Meanwhile, his son who was trapped in the car, realized what happened. He started calling and looking for his father in the car; he didn't find him. There was so much dust and heavy smell of petrol that Ikechukwu got frightened. He continued frantically calling his father. He recalled:
>
>> I was thinking the car would burst into flames. I kept calling him. Then I realized he was not in the car. I managed to get out of the car, then I saw him under the car.
>
> Several motorists stopped to help lift the car. One of those who stopped was a lecturer at Awka College of Education. It was the lecturer's station wagon they used to carry Chinua from one clinic to another, in Awka. The longer they searched for doctors, the worse his condition became. There was no choice but to go straight to the University Teaching Hospital Enugu. As soon as they moved, the car broke down. Everybody came out to push the car. While they were struggling to get the car moving again, message was sent to the Teaching hospital to alert them about the patient on the way.
>
> As fate would have it, one of the orthopaedic doctors at the hospital was Dr. J. U. Achebe, son of Chinua's brother John. He was contacted and informed that a relative of his was in a car accident. They didn't tell him who it was. When he came and saw who it was, he was devastated.[9]

After initially being treated locally in Nigeria to stabilize him, Achebe was flown to the Paddocks Hospital in London for full treatment of a spinal cord injury that partially paralyzed him. Following many months of intensive treatment and care there, Achebe miraculously recovered both physically and emotionally from the accident, but he was confined to wheelchair, which he was taught to drive for mobility at home and in the classrooms, and wherever he gave talks and conducted seminars after the accident.

When he was discharged from the hospital, he returned neither to Ogidi nor Stanford University. Instead, he went to Bard College in Annandale-on-Hudson, New York, where he was provided with the type of privacy he needed for undisturbed physical and spiritual recuperation. Explaining to Egejuru the reason why he made the choice of going to Bard, Achebe said:

> It came to me as a surprise. Well, I get invitations. This time, I was still in the hospital. I wasn't yet thinking of where we were going to go from the

hospital. Stanley Diamond, a distinguished anthropologist, was a friend from Biafra days. He wrote me to ask how I was doing. Then he said whenever I was ready to leave, I should consider Bard because they were very keen. He knew I was going to spend a term at Stanford before the accident. And Stanford had sent someone just to say they would reschedule my visit whenever I was ready. But Bard was something else. I didn't know where it was. I may have heard the name. I didn't know anything about them, but Stanley was very eager. He was sure they would match whatever any other school would offer, including the top Ivy League schools. So I said fine. But this kept coming up and eventually we said we would look at it more closely. In the end, the Vice President of Bard came to England on a conference and he telephoned me.[10]

Egejuru further reports that it was during the telephone conversation that Achebe was told that Dr. Leo Botstein, the President of Bard, had listened to him speak during an international conference of writers and artists held in Budapest two years earlier. It wasn't until his arrival at Bard that he finally met Dr. Botstein. . . . It was at this dinner that the President retold the story of how he first met Achebe.[11]

Ostensibly, everything done to save Achebe from dying from the accident, from the time he was dragged out from underneath the car and sent to the University Teaching Hospital at Enugu and subsequently through the Paddocks Hospital in London, and then to Bard College in New York, was done according to God's plan, plus that of his spirit double *Chi*. However, one cannot overlook the second part of his saving grace; that is the personal role Achebe played directly and indirectly for his survival, comprising his capacity and determination to endure excruciating pains throughout the period that began from the moment the accident happened and ending with his treatment and healing abroad. In addition, he had help from the many people he met in Igboland in Nigeria, as well as those in continental Africa, and in many parts of the world, places he visited while serving as Ambassador Extraordinaire pleading the Biafran cause when his Igbo ethnic people and other Biafrans were fighting to ward off their total annihilation and the brutality of three nations – Nigeria, Great Britain, and the USSR. In other words, his selfless services to his Igbo people in particular and Africans in general were being rewarded then by the efforts of those who contributed to the work of saving the life of a godly man. This included the help of a friend he met in Biafra, Stanley Diamond, who worked with President Botstein to bring him to Bard, where he lived and served for eight years. Achebe's life at that time became a living proof of the Igbo apothegm, *"Onye kwe, Chi ya ekwe"* – If one agrees, his spirit double agrees (to his survival). In truth, because Achebe was determined to live despite all the odds against him, those people his services touched for good at one time or another became his guardian angels in his time of need. Thus, he became his name Chinualumogu Anichebe – God hears and fights for me – which he abbreviated to Chinua Achebe!

Figure 8.1 Chinua Achebe at Bard College

Source: Bard College

Even though the accident made 1990 a bad year for Achebe initially, good things also happened to him in that year. Apart from being honored in the international symposium, Achebe received a citation from the USSR Academy of Sciences and a Triple Eminence Award from ANA. Also, he was awarded an honorary doctorate (D.Litt.) by Georgetown University, USA, was appointed Charles P. Stevenson, Jr. Chair of Literature at Bard College, New York, 1990–1998, and had a major street in the university town of Nsukka renamed "Chinua Achebe Road" in his honor.

In 1991, while continuing to convalesce and work at Bard College, Achebe received more awards for his accomplishments: the Langston Hughes Award from Lincoln University, USA., and honorary doctorates (D.Litt.) by Skidmore College, USA, (D.Litt.) by The New School for Social Research, USA, (D.H.L.) by Hobart and William Smith Colleges, USA, (D.H.L.) by Marymount Manhattan College, USA, and (LL.D.) by University of Port Harcourt, Nigeria, respectively. Moreover, he was listed in *1000 Makers of the Twentieth Century* by the *Sunday Times* of London.

In 1992, two more American universities awarded Achebe honorary doctorates (D.Litt.) by City College, City University of New York, and (D.Litt.) by Westfield State University, Massachusetts. He also showed scholars in the field of African literature that he was still actively practicing his craft when he edited (with C. L. Innes) *The Heinemann Book of Contemporary African Short Stories* in the same year. The promotional statement about the book reads as follows:

> Capturing the diversity of African writing across the continent, this important new anthology draws together well-established authors and the best of new writers.
>
> From the harsh realities of South Africa, elegantly described by Nobel Prize winner Nadine Gordimer, to the fantastic world of Booker Prize winner Ben Okri, from the magical realism of Mozambican Mia Couto to the surreal world of Ghanaian Kojo Laing, the editors have distilled the essence of contemporary African writing.
>
> Blending the supernatural and the secular, the marketplace and the shrine, this anthology gives the reader a taste of the full range of African literary styles.[12]

The distillation of the essence of contemporary African writing that Achebe (with Innes) achieved in this anthology of contemporary African short stories, just as he did when he served as Editor of African Writers Series of the Heinemann Educational Books Inc., gave visibility to the best of the new African writers and added to the fame of the already established ones. Moreover, before the publication of this anthology, readers of African literature were used to reading mostly works by writers from West Africa, East Africa, and Southern Africa; but here, Achebe and Innes covered writers from rarely mentioned areas of the continent: Central Africa and Northern Africa. Their inclusion attests to the varied experiences Achebe acquired through his wide travels that led him to understand the need for a continental unity of Africans who had been fractured by colonialism, imperialism and, above all, religion. And as many scholars of African studies know, when Nigerian literature is mentioned, people rarely pay attention to works by Northern Nigerian writers because of their Islamic background, and when it comes to the study of continental African literature, writers from Northern Africa are neglected for the same reason. One surmises that this inclusive help may have been one of the reasons why *Sunday Times* of London honored him as one of the *1000 Makers of the Twentieth Century*, and why his fame continued to resonate for the rest of his life and beyond.

Honors and accolades continued to accumulate. In 1993, Achebe was appointed Visiting Fellow and Ashby Lecturer, Clare Hall, Cambridge University, and was awarded an honorary doctorate (D.H.L.) by Colgate University, USA. And from 1994 through 1997 he received more honorary doctorate awards and Medals of Honor from American Ivy League Schools and State Universities. Without resting on his laurels, Achebe edited (with Robert Lyons) *Another Africa* in 1998 and was appointed as an Honorary Vice President of the Royal African Society, London.

1999 was a remarkable year in Achebe's personal and professional life; for it was the first time that he and his family members in America visited his hometown of Ogidi and other towns of Nigeria, nine years after his accident. His son Ikechukwu, who was living in London, went home ahead of them to make arrangements that would make Achebe feel comfortable during their brief visit. Upon arrival in Ogidi, Achebe was accorded a number of welcome receptions, including Thanksgiving service attended by his extended family members, friends, villagers, church members, Igbo sociocultural dignitaries, and political leaders like the governor of his home state of Anambra and the then Nigerian President, Olusegun Obasanjo. Throughout this visit, from August 23 to September 27, 1999, Achebe and his family members were treated as celebrities, which he saw as a triumphal return to his people and country (Figure 8.2).

In addition, Achebe delivered an important lecture in Igbo language to the Igbo people, titled "*Echi di Ime: Taa bu Gboo*"[13] [Tomorrow is Pregnant, Today is yet Early] as the fourth in the Annual Odenigbo Lecture Series, to honor the invitation of its founder, the very Reverend Anthony Obinna, Catholic Archbishop of Owerri Archdiocese in Nigeria. Obinna had given Achebe the title, "*Echi di Ime*" but he added "*Taa bu Gboo*" to it so he could express fully his thoughts on the issues he was about to discuss. He used the lecture as a good opportunity to do two things: (a) to comment on Igbo political leadership in Nigerian geopolitics, and (b) to promote the writing of Igbo literature in writers' native dialects until such a time in future that Igbo people who are raised in the language are able to develop a form of the language acceptable to them, so that they don't have to continue depending on the "Union Igbo" that foreigners *engineered* for them without adequate knowledge of the complexity of Igbo language situations; for Union Igbo divided instead of uniting the Igbo people.

On the first point, Achebe was critical of the Igbo political leaders and practitioners at both state and federal levels, for not working honestly and democratically

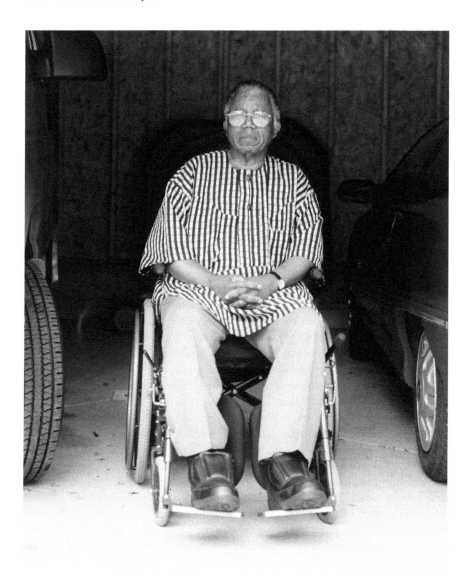

Figure 8.2 Chinua Achebe bounced back to a happy, active life after his life-threatening
        motor accident

Source: Getty Images

in the interest of the people who elected them as their representatives. He also
condemned them for exhibiting servile, cowardly, and malleable attitudes in their
relationships with the federal government officials, especially corrupt presidents,
which caused ordinary Igbo persons to feel as if they were second-class citizens

in their own country since the end of the civil war. As he contrasted their bad behaviors to those of the prewar Igbo leaders that characterized the Igbo as a preeminent ethnic group in Nigeria, Achebe also eulogized a contemporary Igbo leader, Dr. Alex Ekwueme, the former Vice President of Nigeria during the Shehu Shagari administration, hailing him as a man of high principle and integrity who served Nigeria democratically and honorably. Ekwueme exemplified the dignity and pride of an Igboman while in office, character traits that some of his coevals compromised in their quest for personal enrichment and aggrandizement.

As to the second point, Achebe delivered his lecture in his native Ogidi dialect to demonstrate to other Igbo writers that they too could do it if they cared enough about the Igbo culture and civilization to express it in their dialects. To many in the audience, it was a fascinating proposal, for before giving the lecture, Achebe had been doing most of his writing in English, and they did not believe he could also write so well in Igbo, albeit in Ogidi dialect. As he made this important language development proposal, he restated an argument he had made numerous times before that the British imposition of English as a lingua franca on Nigerians divided the communities culturally into those who could speak the language of the colonizer, and those who could not speak it. He traced the origin of the written Igbo language problem back to the Missionary Era of the 1840s, when white missionaries introduced Christianity in Igboland and began translating the English Bible into Igbo. Moreover, Achebe gave in the lecture a summary of the Christian evangelical movement in Igboland and how the process of translating the Bible did incalculable harm to Igbo society by adversely affecting their culture and unity, and stultifying the process of developing their own written literature.

Specifically, he critically discussed how Archdeacon T. J. Dennis worked with some Igbo clergymen and scholars to create a language for the church and missionary education they dubbed "Union Igbo." That language was made up of words arbitrarily drawn from some areas of Igboland, such as Onitsha, Isuama, Unwana, Awka and Owerri, and was adopted as a compulsory language for use primarily in Catholic masses and schools. And the division that developed among the missionaries during the process of translating the Bible affected the way the adherents of the Christian denominations behaved: the relationships between the Catholics and the Protestants, and between the Protestant denominations – the Presbyterians, the Scottish, the Methodists, and Anglicans – were so grave that the non-Igbo people wondered whether the good news of Jesus Christ that the church was preaching was true. So they hesitated to join the church. To date, the church denominations' hunt for members, which created the division among them, led the Igbo people to call all Christians "Ndi Uka" – quarrelsome people. And such quarrels that affected the people religiously, politically, and culturally, then and now, are succinctly described in Achebe's trilogy, *Things Fall Apart, No Longer at Ease,* and *Arrow of God.*

In the end, Achebe exhorted people not to despair because of their past mistakes and failings, for they still had enough time "today" to correct them for a better but uncertain "tomorrow." He cited the name of a historic Igboman,

Olaudah Equiano (Ekweano), who was captured in his hometown in Orlu area by slave raiders during the eighteenth century and sold into slavery in Barbados in the Caribbean. By sheer dint of hard work, he taught himself to read and write, and bought his sovereignty back from his owners. Thereafter, he emigrated to London a free man. Achebe emphasized that Equiano did not lament his past life in slavery; instead, he turned his adversity into an opportunity to write and become the first to use his writing skills to reveal the Igbo culture and civilization to international readers, which became a blessing in disguise for him personally and the Igbo race in general.

There were other Igbo folk stories and apothegms that Achebe told in the lecture to drive home the points he was making on Igbo ethos and worldview to the audience.

Apparently, the proposal for Igbo language development that Achebe made in the lecture was well received by other notable Igbo scholars who, in their own way, had made similar proposals on the same burning issue of language development for the Igbo people. Professor Donatus I. Nwoga, for instance, made his proposal in a book chapter, titled "From Dialectal Dichotomy to Igbo Standard Development," but the proposal went from the development of dialects to the development of an Igbo standard. As an introduction to the chapter, Nwoga wrote:

> What I intend to do in this chapter is to give expression to some of the ideas which I personally consider important in the now critical assignment which is to give Igbo language studies definition and direction. I want, in this presentation, to go beyond the perennial question of what dialect should constitute the core of standard Igbo to the urgent question of how to make the present standard capable of fulfilling its role in the busy world of Nigerian language policy discussions.[14]

After that, he discussed the context of the language policy that necessitated the development of a standard for the Igbo language, stressing the need for such a standard. Like Achebe, he gave the genesis of the development of the written form of the Igbo language. However, he gave more detail about the history of its development: Isuama Igbo, c. 1841–1872; Union Igbo, 1905–1939; Central Igbo, 1939–1972, and Standard Modern Igbo, 1973 and after. He then discussed the development of the standard, the choice of dialect, graphization, and the need for an Igbo language board to enforce some rules of exclusion and inclusion of certain aspects of the language in the process of developing the envisioned standard. To conclude, Nwoga wrote:

> [Finally,] the import of this chapter centers on the Igbo changing their orientation from internal conflict to uniting to confront external situations. Nigeria has recognized the Igbo language as one of the major languages in Nigeria, mainly because the Igbo constitute the second largest language group in Nigeria. While we waste our emotional and creative energies in

internal conflict over whose dialect is to be selected, we cannot achieve the requisite level of development, sophistication, and creativity which will give Igbo language the status of competing for national use and interest. Let us, therefore, accept a standard received by the Society for Promoting Igbo Language and Culture, develop it with the full resources of the Igbo language and creative imagination of individual Igbo artists, establish an Igbo Language Board, and produce an Igbo dictionary. The identity and dynamism of the Igbo will then be matched by the identity, wealth, and expressiveness of their language.[15]

Overall, Chinua Achebe's effort to deal with both issues of Igbo sociopolitical leadership problem and the dearth of literature written in Igbo dialects is quite laudable. However, because the lecture was difficult for some Igbo people to read either in its original Ogidi dialect or the Igbo-Izugbe dialect version, which Dr. P. A. Ezikeojiaku translated for the Odenigbo Committee, one is happy to learn that people like Onwubiko Agozino, an Igbo scholar and professor of sociology at Virginia Tech, USA,[16] are translating the lecture from Igbo to English for easy reading and full understanding of the issues and points raised by Achebe in it. It is hoped that the proposal will continue to inspire more writers to produce Igbo literary works in their dialects, just as they should also take part in the ongoing process of developing a standard Igbo language. Chinua Achebe ended the year and millennium with awards of honorary doctorates (D.Litt.) by Ohio Wesleyan University, Delaware, Ohio, and (D.Litt.) by Trinity College, Hartford, Connecticut.

Year 2000 was the beginning of the twenty-first century and the final phase of Chinua Achebe's writing career that ended in 2013. He published *Home and Exile*,[17] which is comprised of three lectures that he delivered as the 1998 McMillan-Steward Lectures at Harvard University on December 9, 10, and 11, 1998. The titles of the three lectures are: "My Home Under Imperial Fire," "The Empire Fights Back," and "Today, the Balance of Stories," all of which are connected by the overarching central theme of European dispossession of continental Africa and her peoples, which took in the forms of slave trade, colonialism, and imperialism. However, Achebe's narration of events began with his odyssey from Awka, where his father served as a catechist and teacher for the Anglican Mission that began in 1904, to his hometown of Ogidi, where his father began his retirement from service in 1935. He recalls one of his childhood memories of his first homecoming, which he describes as being extraordinary even for such recollections. He was five years old and riding in a motor vehicle for the first time. The paradox of his homecoming was that he had looked forward very much to that experience, but it was not working out right for him.[18] That initial paradox in his narrative would ultimately characterize the nature of his youthful experience all through his stay at Ogidi, just like the paradox in his professional life as a world-renowned writer living as an exile in various places in Nigeria and North America, away from home, which he passionately missed because of what his home meant to him. Even as a child, Achebe felt the sense of dispossession or loss of his cultural roots when he eventually returned from Awka to his hometown of Ogidi and embraced their culture fully. Eventually, the childhood stories he was told there became the raw material he appropriated to develop some of the incidents in his novels, short stories, and in articles on Igbo worldview and culture. At that point, Achebe's personal story sounded like a "portrait of the artist as a young man." An appreciation of the book begins with the promotional statement about the book, which previews its content and the boldness of Achebe as a storyteller:

> His fiction and poetry burn with a passionate commitment to political jus-tice, bringing to life not only Africa's troubled encounters with Europe but also the dark side of contemporary African political life. Now, in *Home and Exile*, Achebe reveals the man behind his powerful work.
>
> Here is an extended exploration of the European impact on African cul-ture, viewed through the most vivid experience available to the author – his own life. It is an evocative snapshot of a major writer's childhood, illuminat-ing his roots as an artist. Achebe discusses his English education and the relationship between colonial writers and the European literary tradition. He argues that if colonial writers try to imitate and, indeed, go one better than the Empire, they run the danger of undervaluing their homeland and their own people. Achebe contends that to redress the inequities of global oppression, writers must focus on where they come from, insisting that their value systems are as legitimate as any other. Stories are a real source of power in the world, he concludes, and to imitate the literature of another culture is to give that power away.[19]

Upon arrival in Ogidi, Achebe was immediately thrust into the process of acquiring some important informal education, including a lesson in *otherness* as it relates to religious faiths. He did so by observing the way his non-Christian uncle was accommodated in his catechist father's home, how the Christian and non-Christian members of his extended family and the town's people managed to coexist in spite of their disagreements on many issues and, above all, how the stories (part history and part mythology) he heard from them enriched his knowledge of Igbo history and culture. He would, eventually, appropriate the stories to write his fiction in the future. Here is an example of how he did it in *Home and Exile*:

> Both my parents were strong and even sometimes uncompromising in their Christian beliefs, but they were not fanatical. Their lives were ruled, I think, as much by reason as by faith; as much by common sense and compassion as by doctrine. My father's half-brother was not the only heathen in our extended family; if anything, he was among a majority. Our home was open to them all, and my father received his peers and relatives – Christian or not – with kola nut and palm-wine in the piazza, just as my mother received her visitors in the parlor. It was from the conversations and disagreements in these rooms, especially the piazza, that I learned much of what I know and have come to value about my history and culture. Many a time what I heard

in those days, just hanging around my father and his peers, only became clear to me years and even decades later.[20]

Achebe recounted the story of how one of Ogidi's neighboring towns migrated into its present location a long time ago and made a request to Ogidi to settle there. Ogidi people granted them their request because they had plenty of land to spare. But when the neighbors made a second and more serious request regarding religious worship, Ogidi people gave them a stiff condition which the neighbors also accepted to live by, because they were desperate. Explaining the significance of this story, which touches on local intra-Igbo religious imperialism, Achebe said:

> For many years this fragment of local lore meant no more to me than one more story of internal migration in Igboland, probably part history and part mythology, the kind of story one might hear invoked or manipulated in a court of law today in boundary litigations between towns. But its profound significance dawned on me later – the reluctance of an Igbo town to foist its religious beliefs and practices on a neighbor across the road, even when it was invited to do so. Surely such a people cannot have had any notion of the psychology of religious imperialism. And that innocence would have placed them at a great disadvantage later when they came to deal with European evangelism. Perhaps the sheer audacity of some stranger wandering thousands of miles from his home to tell them they were worshipping false gods may have left them open-mouthed in amazement – and actually aided their rapid conversion! If so, they were stunned into conversion only, but luckily not all the way to the self-righteousness and zealotry that went with the stranger's audacity. The levelheadedness of my parents would seem to be a result of that good fortune.[21]

Achebe cited the fable of a negligent chicken and the assembly of his fellow animals, whom he thought must be serious democrats, to assert that in the worldview of the Igbo, the individual is unique, and the town is also unique. But they are able to bring the two competing claims together in a popular assembly where everybody is free to express their opinions freely without fear of reprisals. So in all probability, the Igbo would not wish to live under the rule of a king. And that is why sometimes one of them would actually name his son Ezebuilo: "A-King-Is-An-Enemy." Moreover, his use of the fable of the chicken as a metaphor further explains the Igbo people's belief in the uniqueness and primary necessity for individual freedom, which extends to the freedom and autonomy of each of the hundreds of their villages and towns. And because the Igbo were so deeply suspicious of political amalgamation, they were stretched to the limit whenever they faced an enemy who was able to wield the resources of a centralized military power, acting directly or through local surrogates. However, they always found their fortification in their histories and creation myths. Achebe is stressing here the importance of storytellers and myth creators as keepers of the essential Igbo cultural worldview, which emphasizes their sense of freedom and independence, no matter the circumstance in their history they find themselves in.

The rest of the discussion in the first lecture is centered on how the Igbo storytelling habits and sense of individual freedom Achebe learned at home enabled him to publish *Things Fall Apart*, which he intended to challenge and correct the untrue image of Nigeria and Nigerians that Joyce Cary created in his novel, *Mister Johnson*. As some of his readers know, Achebe was inspired to write his protest novel while still in college because he and his fellow Nigerian students at the University College, Ibadan, were compelled by their English professors to read not only Cary's novel but also other "African" novels by British authors, including Joseph Conrad's *Heart of Darkness*. Despite such protest, *Time* magazine of October 20, 1952, did a cover story on Cary that described *Mister Johnson* as "the best novel ever written about Africa" (p. 22). After reviewing the history of British colonial writings on Africa and illustrating the fictional images of sub-Saharan Africans with quoted passages from *Mister Johnson*, Achebe came to the conclusion that "There is such a thing as absolute power over narrative. Those who secure this privilege for themselves can arrange stories about others pretty much where, and as, they like. Just as in corrupt, totalitarian regimes, those who exercise power over others can do anything" (p. 24).

It is that imperial power the European colonialist writers, as storytellers, exercised over Africans that Achebe attempted to challenge in his second lecture, "The Empire Fights Back." Even though he admits that his experience of classroom rebellion over *Mr. Johnson* may have played a role in his decision to become a writer, he could not have made the decision without having compelling reasons to write:

> For me there are three reasons for becoming a writer. The first is that you have an overpowering urge to tell a story. The second, that you have intimations of a unique story waiting to come out. And the third, which you learn in the process of becoming, is that you consider the whole project worth the considerable trouble – I have sometimes called it terms of imprisonment – you will have to endure to bring it to fruition. For me those three factors were present and would have been present had Joyce Cary never been born or set foot in Nigeria. History, however, had contrived a crossing of our paths, and such crossings may sometimes leave their footmarks, faint or loud, on memory. And if they do, they should be acknowledged.
>
> (pp. 38–9)

After saying that, he went on to assert that there was no way that Cary would have written a Nigerian novel that Nigerian students could have accepted as their story, not because he was European but rather because he was a product of a tradition of presenting Africa that he had absorbed at school and Sunday school, in magazines and in British society in general, at the end of the nineteenth century. In theory, a good writer might outgrow these influences, but Cary did not (p. 39).

In the rest of the lecture, Achebe discussed how Western critics continued to praise the literary works by European writers on Nigeria (and other African countries), which so conditioned the imagination of their African readers that they began to look down upon the works of their own writers, like Amos Tutuola's pioneering novel *The Palm-Wine Drinkard*, which is a true Nigerian story told by a Nigerian storyteller. He cited the case of two Nigerian students in London in 1952 who felt so ashamed and embarrassed by Tutuola's story of their homeland, written as they saw it, in incorrect English, that some of them went up in arms without reading the book! (pp. 69–70) And even some established writers like Buchi Emecheta, a Nigerian novelist who lives and writes in London, revealed in an interview she granted to Adeola James in 1986, that what Nigerian authors write in their country "sounds quite stilted," and she seemed to be making every effort to minimize her "Africanness" so that her books could sell in British bookstores (pp. 71, 81). What a shame!

Finally, in the third lecture, "Today, the Balance of Stories," Achebe discussed the beginning of the reclamation of the African story that her writers were making in their literary works that constitute postcolonial literature. He emphasized how Jomo Kenyatta of Kenya, for an example, used the metaphor of a conversation between humans and the animals in his essay, "The Gentleman of the Jungle," to not only reclaim the Kenyan story but also to spearhead their war of independence against British colonialism. After describing how African writers and political leaders fought hard and won political independence for their countries, he also remarked, "The twentieth century for all its many faults did witness a significant beginning, in Africa and elsewhere in the so-called third world of the process of 're-storying' peoples who had been knocked silent by the trauma of all kinds of dispossession" (p. 79). This he followed with a warning:

> After a short period of dormancy and a little self-doubt about its erstwhile imperial mission, the West may be ready to resume its old domineering monologue in the world. Certainly, there is no lack of zealots urging it to do so. They call it "taking a hard look" at things. The result is a hardening of views on such issues as the African slave trade and the European colonization of Africa, with the result, generally, of absolving Europe from much of the blame and placing it squarely on African shoulders.
>
> (p. 83)

In my analysis, I randomly selected many passages from all three lectures to emphasize the many memorable lessons I found in *Home and Exile*, which I felt general readers, especially Nigerians and Africans, should learn about the dispossession of their countries and continent. And those valuable lessons are about European, especially British, colonial, and imperial history and its effects on African culture and literature. The lectures (especially the first) offer Igbo readers in particular a great opportunity to learn more about their unique culture and worldview that stresses the notion of individuality, emphasizing one person's freedom and autonomy over the collective freedoms and independence of a whole people. It is a notion that continues to set the Igbo apart from other Nigerian eth-nic nationalities; but their republican streak comes with a cost, as they learned from experience during the Nigeria-Biafra War. Additionally, Achebe taught any aspiring writers three *sine qua non* they must consider before deciding to become professional writers.

In the end, one can argue that the three lectures Achebe delivered at Harvard reveal his eminent qualifications and capability to play the role of "the novelist as teacher" – a role he called on other African writers to play so they could make serious efforts to reclaim the African story of the colonial and postcolonial era from European writers. Finally, the impact of what Achebe achieved in *Home and Exile* is summarized by Sherri Barnes as follows:

> Reading Achebe is to know Africa in a way that few are able to tell. Achebe weaves anecdotes from his childhood, schooling, and writing life with Afri-can proverbs and literary and political theory to contribute beautifully to the "process" of "re-story-telling" peoples who had been knocked silent by the trauma of all kinds of dispossession. His passion and truth are sensuous and contagious, warming one's soul (the blurb).

All things considered, the book was a good "New Century" present from Chinua Achebe to all those who wanted to know him better as a writer and as a truthful teller of the African story that European writers had distorted to give Africa and Africans a bad image on the world stage.

In 2005, Achebe published *Collected Poems*.[22] According to the publishers, the book draws on his three books of poetry, and includes seven previously unpub-lished poems. It reveals a lifetime of poetic engagement with politics, war and culture, inherited wisdom, and new futures. Achebe's poems are ironic, generous, and tender, drawing deep on Igbo traditions, confronting his continent's harsh realities of violence and exploitation.[23]

The arrangement of the poems into the following groupings – "Prologue," "Poems About War," "Poems not About War," "Gods, Men and Others," and "Epilogue" – represents Achebe's reminiscences on major issues of politics, war, and culture in Nigeria, and their devastating and tragic effects, especially on his native Igbo people, beginning from 1966 through 1999. The first poem "1966," which appears in the Prologue grouping is a description of the apathy and failure of the Nigerian political leaders to deal with bloody political conflicts in certain parts of the country until they boiled over to cause the first bloody coup in Nige-ria on January 15, 1966. The poem set the scene for all the other poems in the "Poems About War".

Before the coup, there were bloody political conflicts in the western region and the middle belt of Nigeria, but the federal government was apathetic and negligent in finding any immediate and adequate solutions to them, because of the blatant corrupt actions of political leaders. And the entire country waited for salvation from the sociopolitical malaise without any relief coming from the national insecurity organizations. That is why, in the poem, the poet speaker says, "absentminded/ our thoughtless days/ sat at dire controls/ and played indolently" (ll. 1–4). The hatred that brewed between political parties later turned into a deadly conflict between the northern and southern regions until it came to a boiling point: "slowly downward in remote/ subterranean shift/ a diamond-tipped/ drill point crept closer/ to residual chaos to/ rare artesian hatred/ that once squirted warm/ blood in God's face/ confirming His first/ disappointment in Eden" (ll. 5–14).

The metaphor Achebe uses to describe the spilling of blood in lines 12–14 is a pungent biblical allusion to the story of Cain murdering his brother Abel, which is comparable to the Northern Nigerians murdering in cold blood their fellow Nigerians, especially the Igbo people, during the Northern riots that followed that first bloody coup, and the subsequent coups that took place on May 29, July 29, and September 29, 1966 against Eastern Nigerians.[23] The 1966 coups led to a full-blown 30-month Nigeria-Biafra War in 1967–1970.

Achebe describes another scene in the Prologue of a powerful and violent collision between two "road users" that leads to the death of the powerless and the survival of the powerful in the poem, "Benin Road." The encounter is between a motorist and a butterfly, both plying one road. The first three lines of the poem, "Speed is violence/ Power is violence/ Weight is violence," sets the scene of violence that underscores the advantage that the motorist driving speedily in a heavy car has over the butterfly. "The butterfly seeks safety in lightness/ in weightless, undulating flight" (ll. 5–6). That flight could not save it when it collides with the motorist: "But at a crossroads where mottled light/ From old trees falls on a brash new highway/ Our separate errands collide" (ll. 6–8). Although they had separate reasons for using the road, destiny brought them together in a deadly encounter. In the concluding stanza, the motorist arrogantly and without any remorse for killing the *gentle* butterfly says, "I come power-packed for two/ And the gentle butterfly offers/ Itself in bright yellow sacrifice/ Upon my hard silicon shield" (ll. 9–12). Oh yes, in conflicts the powerful always blame victims for their demise or misery!

On the surface, some of the other poems in the Prologue may appear to be unrelated to physical wars; and yet they do when they are closely read and analyzed. Take for instance the poem "Agostinho Neto" which is a tribute to the former Angolan politician and poet. He served as the first President of Angola, having led a popular movement for the liberation of Angola in the war for independence. Children sing his praise as the "middle one favored by fortune" for he followed the example of Kwame Nkrumah, the first African leader to wage a war of independence against British colonizers of his country and to have won: "Kwame/ Striding ahead to accost/ Demons" (ll. 3–5). But Neto paid stiffer penalties for his daring change of the Portuguese in his native land: "No! Your secure strides/ Were hard earned /Your feet/ Learned their fierce balance/ In violent slopes of humiliation;/ Your delicate hands, presently/ Groomed for finest incisions,/ Were commandeered brusquely to kill,/ Your melodious voice to battle cry," (ll. 7–14).

Here we see a well-trained surgeon and poet whose work gave healing to his suffering people being forced to bear arms to fight in the battlefields for their liberation – a patriotic act that showed his public persona as grim, but "Perhaps your family and friends/ Knew a merry flash cracking the gloom/ We see in pictures" (ll. 15–17). He could have chosen an easier life like "Africa's idiot-kings/ Who oversee in obscene palaces of gold/ The butchery of their own people" (ll. 23–25). Achebe's tearful eulogy for President Neto of Angola, a worthy son of Africa and poet, concludes:

> Neto, I sing your passing, I,
> Timid requisitioner of your vast
> Armory's most congenial supply.
> What shall I sing? A dirge answering
> The gloom? No, I will sing tearful songs
> Of joy; I will celebrate
> The Man who rode a trinity
> Of awesome fates to the cause
> Of our trampled race!
> Thou Healer, Soldier, and Poet!
>   (ll. 26–31)

Achebe's eulogy on the death of Agostinho Neto is similar to the one he gave in *Hopes and Impediments* for James Baldwin, a fellow black writer who fought for racial justice and equality in America.

Achebe opens the section, Poems About War, with a befitting poem, "The First Shot," which describes the first salvo that Nigeria fired against the young Republic of Biafra, after its president, Major General Yakubu Gowon, promised the whole world that he was only using police action against the seceding former Eastern Nigeria to force them back to the Nigerian federation: "The lone riffle-shot anonymous/ in the dark striding chest-high/ through a nervous suburb at the break/ of our season of thunders will yet/ steep its flights and lodge/ more firmly than the greater noises/ ahead in the forehead of memory" (ll. 1–7). As it turned out, that initial frightening act of war presaged the course of greater destruction and vandalism Nigeria meted against Biafrans that began from the first coup of January 1966, and continued through the Northern riots, to the subsequent coups and noisy protests of the same year, which are referred to as "our season of thunders" that eventuated in full-blown war.

We see examples of the effects of the war on people, especially children, as described in the poems, "A Mother in a Refugee Camp", "Christmas in Biafra (1969)", and "Air Raid". In the refugee camps, mothers who had been dislocated from their homes were forced to take care of their sick and malnourished children until some of them died of kwashiorkor or edema, or bullets from Nigerian air raid shots.

All the children in the refugee camps faced lurking death to the extent that while "Other mothers there/ Had long ceased to care, but not this one:/She held a ghost-smile between her teeth,/ And in her eyes and memory/ Of a mother's pride . . ., she had bathed him/ And rubbed him with bare palms/ . . . "In their former life this was perhaps/ A little daily act of no consequence/ Before his breakfast and school; now *she did it/ Like putting flowers on a tiny grave*." [emphasis added] The unceasing mother's love and care for her dying child, and the preparation of his body for burial, as if he was going to school, attest to the deep unbreakable bond of love between mother and child!

We see the same bond of love between mother and child in "Christmas in Biafra (1969)." In the first stanza, Achebe paints the same sad tableau of hunger, sickness, and imminent lurking death: "This sunken-eyed moment wobbling/ down the rocky steepness on broken/ bones slowly fearfully to hideous/ concourse of gathering sorrows in the valley/ will yet become in another year a lost/ Christmas irretrievable in the heights/ its exploding inferno transmuted/ by cosmic distances to the peacefulness/ of a cool twinkling star."

What follows the lost joyous Christmas is: "To death-cells/ of the moment came far away sounds of other/ men's carols floating on crackling waves/ mocking us. With regret? Hope? Longing? None of/ these, strangely, not even despair rather/ distilling pure transcendental hate." Yet, despite her unfathomable agony, the mother puts "Her/ infant son flat like a dead lizard/ on her shoulder his arms and legs/ cauterized by famine was a miracle/ of its kind. /Large sunken eyes/ stricken past boredom to a flat/ unrecognizing glueyness moped faraway/ motionless across her shoulder."

In the end, instead of the Christmas service being a celebration of joy and hope, we can visualize the palpable agony of a Biafran mother and her malnourished and sick child sorrowfully departing the Christmas scene:

> Now her adoration over
> she turned him around and pointed
> at those pretty figures of God
> and angels and men and beasts –
> a spectacle to stir the heart
> of a child. But all he vouchsafed
> was one slow deadpan look of total
> unrecognition and he began again
> to swivel his enormous head away
> to mope as before at his empty distance . . . .
> she shrugged her shoulders, crossed
> herself again and took him away.

She takes him away to a certain misery and imminent death and eternal separation.

The next poem "Air Raid" is a lurid description of how Nigeria was using Soviet-made fighter planes to bomb Biafran towns and villages indiscriminately, slaughtering civilians in broad daylight, without any challenges from a Biafran airforce that deployed their few planes to fight the enemy in the battlefields: "It comes quickly/ the bird of death/ from evil forests of Soviet technology/ A man crossing the road to greet a friend/ is much too slow./ His friend cut in halves/ has other worries now/ than a friendly handshake/ at noon." This depicts a scene of destruction by an air raid that was a common occurrence everywhere in Biafra. The Nigerian and Soviet pilots who flew the planes did not care to avoid the refugee camps boldly marked with Red Cross banners. When all was said and done, more civilians died of starvation and hunger, and diseases than those who were killed in the battlegrounds. In my book, *General Ojukwu: The Legend of Biafra*,[24] I outlined the role the Soviets played (which Achebe referred to in the poem) in the massacre of Biafrans, especially children, women, and the old and the infirm, throughout the war:

> In addition to Nigeria and Great Britain obstructing relief supplies to Biafra, the Soviets had been giving the Nigerian Army fighter aircrafts to bomb Biafran civilians in marketplaces and soldiers in the warfronts. Also, they gave Nigerian troops some communication equipment for use to win the battles in the fields, and electronic gadgets to jam Radio Biafra – "the ruler of the airwaves" which Nigeria called "the rebels' pirate radio" – to win the propaganda warfare. The Soviets gave Nigeria the latter aid to prevent international organizations and governments from getting accurate information on the Biafran cause and problems they needed to formulate policies on sending adequate humanitarian supplies to Biafra. The Soviets' argument was that if Biafra was killed quickly because of their heavy military assistance to Nigeria, then they would have found a foothold in Nigeria at this time of Communist expansionism in Africa and Asia. But Radio Biafra worked hard to subvert the planned Nigeria-Soviet détente; and the foxy Britons outsmarted the Soviets, who never gained a foothold in Nigeria during or after the war.

> (p. 151)

So far, I have cited and analyzed a few poems from Achebe's *Collected Poems* to exemplify his frame of mind as he brooded, in 2005, on the permanent damage the Nigeria-Biafra War inflicted on Nigerian citizens of Eastern origin, especially the Igbo people, whom General Gowon and Northern soldiers targeted for extermination. Achebe expresses soulful regrets over the human loss in such poems as "The Explorer" on pages 8–9, which he dedicated to an unknown person whose unburied remains are discovered in the forest after the war. "Biafra, 1969" describes the destruction of the prewar Eastern Nigerians' metaphoric Jerusalem. "An 'If' of History" asks people to imagine the dire consequences of World War II if Hitler had won it, which is an indirect indictment of the world body for doing nothing to save Biafrans from the brutality of Nigeria, Great Britain, and the USSR during the war. "Remembrance Day" expresses memories of the war victims who died without any true reconciliation of all parts of the country. "A Wake for Okigbo" is a literary rendition of an Igbo ritual for his friend, college classmate, and fellow writer, Christopher Okigbo, who died while fighting the war in the frontlines on the Biafran side. And "After a War" describes what has happened to people after the bloody war. Achebe expresses his final thought on the war thus:

After years
of pressing death
and dizzy last-hour reprieves
we're glad to dump our fears
and our perilous gains together
in one shallow grave and flee
the same rueful way we came
straight home to haunted revelry.
                    (Christmas 1971)

In conclusion, most of the poems in the other sections of *Collected Poems*, including those about love and relationships between gods and human beings, also contain some sadness and sorrow, as well as a little bit of hope and skepticism, emanating from the impact of the civil war on the Igbo people, who are still suffering from it socially, politically, and economically, ostensibly because of the part they played in it. Hence, in his publications and speeches, Achebe made it his self-appointed responsibility to fight against the marginalization, ethnic discrimination, deprivation, and injustice meted out against the Igbo people since the end of the civil war. We can also see these themes discussed on a grander scale in Achebe's last published work, *There Was a Country* (2012). He brooded deeply on the economic, emotional, physical, and psychological consequences experienced by the Igbo people as victims of the war and found out that their wounds were still too fresh to be ignored or left unhealed. His writings on the war have continued to generate national debates, which, in a way, have furthered the process of healing he intended them to provoke within and outside of Nigeria.

In 2009, Chinua Achebe published *The Education of a British-Protected Child*,[25] which is a collection of 17 interrelated essays, some of which had been previously published elsewhere in different versions. For instance, "The University and the Leadership Factor in Nigerian Politics" was published in 1989 as a booklet in Nigeria by ABIC Books & Equipment Ltd. The recurrent themes of occupation, dispossession, and humiliation of Africa and African peoples by European powers, which began with Slave Trade and Partition of Africa and eventuated in European colonialism and imperialism, form the bulk of the topics Achebe passionately dealt with in this book. The thrust of his narration of events is now more on continental African issues, but it spills over onto African American issues as they relate to Africa. As usual, readers get a preview of contents of the book from its jacket announcement, as follows:

Chinua Achebe's characteristically measured and nuanced voice is everywhere present in these seventeen beautifully written pieces. In a preface, he discusses his historic visit to his Nigerian homeland on the occasion of the fiftieth anniversary of the publication of *Things Fall Apart*, the story of his tragic car accident nearly twenty years ago, and the potent symbolism of President Obama's election. In "The Education of a British-Protected Child," Achebe gives us a vivid portrait of growing up in colonial Nigeria

Figure 8.3 Chinua Achebe reading from his book *The Education of a British-Protected Child* at Brown University, Providence, Rhode Island

Source: Brown University

and inhabiting its "middle ground," recalling both his happy memories of reading novels in secondary school and the harsher truths of colonial rule. In "Spelling Our Proper Name," Achebe considers the African American diaspora, meeting and reading Langston Hughes and James Baldwin, and learning what it means not to know "from whence he came." The complex politics and history of Africa figure in "What Is Nigeria to Me?" "Africa's Tarnished Name," and "Politics and Politicians of Language in African Literature." And Achebe's extraordinary family life cones into view in "My Dad and Me" and "My Daughters," where we observe the effect of Christian missionaries on his father and witness the culture shock of raising "brown" children in America.

The wise decision Achebe made to assemble in one volume all the essays he wrote and presented to international audiences from 1988 through 2009 during his world travels makes it easy for readers to follow the range of his experiences during the period. He made the same wise decision when he published 15 essays he wrote and presented to similar international audiences from 1961 through 1974 in *Morning Yet on Creation Day* in 1976. And it seems to me prophetic that Achebe referred to his first book of essays as "morning yet on creation day," for the depth, breadth, and amplitude of his discussion of issues in *The Education of a*

British-Protected Child evince unmistakably the maturity, experience, and wisdom of the world-renowned author that Achebe eventually became.

If one read only the title of the book before reading all the issues discussed in it, one might expect to learn solely about how Achebe was educated under the British educational system, which is the subject of only the first essay. However, the other essays persuaded me that Achebe was instead educating his readers on the damning evidence that Europe refused to acknowledge African peoples' presence, cultures, and humanity in the world. For he succinctly traces the root causes of such refusal to the dark era of the Atlantic slave trade and the partition of Africa that prompted European colonization and imperialism in the continent. His deep study of the twin subject of colonialism and imperialism, coupled with his superior knowledge of African culture through its literatures, made him an erudite and bold debater on such subjects. The successes he achieved in correcting what he called "poisonous writing, in full consonance with the tenets of the slave trade-inspired tradition of European portrayal of Africa"[26] can be measured by the number of accolades, especially honorary doctorates many world universities and colleges awarded to him.

Moreover, the points he made in the essays about Dr. Martin Luther King, James Baldwin, and Langston Hughes are so enlightening that it is hoped that they could change the minds of some African Americans who may still hold grudges against Africans in their midst because of their mistaken understanding of slave history. It was especially enlightening to read about Achebe explaining to Baldwin how white men cleverly used slavery in the Americas and colonialism in Africa to divide the black race. And his discussions of his personal relationships with his dad, two daughters, and his homeland contain valuable lessons for both black Americans and Africans who can learn to survive some of the pangs and pains of living in America as a minority group.

In the end, one is struck by critics' acclaim for the value of the book and its author's rare artistry and wisdom: "Charmingly personal, intellectually disciplined, and steadfastly wise, *The Education of a British-Protected Child* is an indispensable addition to the remarkable Achebe oeuvre"; and "African literature is incomplete and unthinkable without the work of Chinua Achebe. For passion, intellect and crystalline prose, he is unsurpassed."[27] Such high praises coming from scholars as well as a fellow renowned writer like Toni Morrison affirm some of the qualities that caused his native Igbo people to give Achebe the honorific name the Eagle on Iroko!

In 2012, Achebe published his final monumental book, *There Was a Country: A Personal History of Biafra*. At his behest, his publishers sent me a review copy in advance. My review of the book is reproduced as the next chapter of this biography, which is followed by another chapter in which I examine the critical opinions of other reviewers of the book. Both chapters serve as an overview of the last stories that this celebrated Nigerian storyteller told. The reviewers' divergent critical evaluations and the author's expressed hopes for postwar Nigeria are regarded as important contributions toward an overall understanding of the life and times of Chinua Achebe, a Nigerian patriot.

Figure 8.4 Chinua Achebe and wife at Brown University campus

Source: Brown University

Notes

1 The Achebe Family, *Celebrating the Life of Chinua Achebe: A Life of Purpose.* New York: Doubleday/Anchor Press, 2013.
2 Phanuel Akubueze Egejuru, *Chinua Achebe: Pure and Simple: An Oral Biography.* Ikeja, Nigeria: Malthouse Press Ltd, 2001: 74.
3 Ezenwa-Ohaeto, "Celebration for Chinua Achebe," *ALA Bulletin,* Vol. 16, No. 2 (1990).
4 Donatus I. Nwoga, "Achebe's Vision in a New Africa," in Edith Ihekweazu, ed. *Eagle on Iroko: Selected Papers from the Chinua Achebe International Symposium 1990.* Ibadan, Nigeria: Heinemann Educational Books (Nigeria) Plc, 1996: 152–3.
5 John Munonye, "As We Saw Him," in *Ibid.,* p. 547.
6 Alan Hill, "Chinua Achebe: A Personal View," in *Ibid.,* p. 548.
7 *Ibid.,* p. 549.

8 Egejuru, *Chinua Achebe*, p. 76.

9 *Ibid.*, p. 77; see also chapters 8 and 9 for a full narration of the story of the accident.

10 *Ibid.*, p. 88.

11 *Ibid.*

12 Chinua Achebe and C. L. Innes, eds., *The Heinemann Book of Contemporary African Short Stories*. Oxford, UK: Heinemann Educational Books Ltd., 1992: Blurb.

13 I read the document in its English translated version.

14 Donatus I. Nwoga, "From Dialectal Dichotomy to Igbo Standard Development," in Kalu Ogbaa, ed. *The Gong and the Flute: African Literary Development and Celebration.* Westport, CT: Greenwood Press, 1994: 103.

15 *Ibid.*, pp. 115–16.

16 I used Professor Agozino's English translation of Achebe's lecture for my analysis.

17 Chinua Achebe, *Home and Exile*. New York: Oxford University Press, 2000.

18 *Ibid.*, p. 1.

19 *Ibid.*, See the book's jacket.

20 *Ibid.*, pp. 10–11.

21 *Ibid.*, pp. 12–13.

22 Chinua Achebe, *Collected Poems*. Manchester, England: Carcanet Press Ltd., 2005.

23 *Ibid.*, see the blurb.

24 Ogbaa, *General Ojukwu*, p. 151.

25 Chinua Achebe, *The Education of a British-Protected Child: Essays*. New York: Alfred A. Knopf, 2009.

26 *Ibid.*, pp. 87–8.

27 *Ibid.*, see the book's jacket and blurb.

9 My Review of Chinua Achebe's *There Was a Country: A Personal History of Biafra**

In an article published in 1978, titled "Chinua Achebe," Michael Echeruo pre-dicted that "Given the pattern of Chinua Achebe's development as an artist and as a conscience for his people, it would indeed be surprising – it would be doubly disappointing – if his next major work did not deal with that truly traumatic experience: The War." Reflecting on his earlier novels, Achebe once described his generation as "a very fortunate" one in the sense that the past was "still there," even if not "in the same force."[1] Although Achebe's next major work was a novel, *Anthills of the Savannah* (1987), which does not deal with the Nigeria-Biafra War, the one which does, titled *There Was a Country: A Personal History of Biafra*, was just published in 2012, 34 years after Echeruo's prediction. As a Nigerian first and a Biafran during the war, Achebe wrote it as a man who was involved virtually in all aspects of the war, from its promising beginning (for the newborn Republic of Biafra) to its regrettable tragic end. This fact, in a way, makes the book an authoritative insider's story. If closely read, one can find ample evidence to prove that Achebe still maintains his usual pattern of development "as an artist and as conscience for his people" – the Nigerian people as a whole – which is a patri-otic role that Echeruo spoke of in his article. However, given Achebe's thorough and detailed critical analysis of the war in his book, it is neither "surprising" nor "doubly disappointing" that it took him many years of thoughtful deliberations and thorough research before he finally published it. Besides, that Achebe took his time to do such a good job of it is not surprising to an Achebephile like me, for it is his nature to exercise great patience and caution in whatever he does as a writer – a work ethic that a character in *Things Fall Apart* expressed proverbially thus: "If the penis does not die young it will eat bearded meat." And in *Morning Yet on Creation Day*, Achebe expressed the same idea directly when he wrote: "Fools rush in where angels fear to tread" (61–64). Evidence of the thorough research he did to support his facts and claims in his story can be verified from the 53 pages of notes cited in the book (pp. 267–319).

There Was a Country is divided into four parts, each containing important seg-ments that Achebe could have easily developed into separate books or book chap-ters if he so chose. The Introduction glimpses the issues discussed in the whole book and frames the argument around the main topic of the Nigeria-Biafra War (1967–1970). He foregrounds the overriding theme of the book with a profound

DOI: 10.4324/9781003184133-9

Igbo proverb – the hallmark of his masterful Igbo storytelling habit that one finds in most of his writings – to underscore the great importance and tenor of the story he is about to tell: "An Igbo proverb tells us that a man who does not know where the rain began to beat him cannot say where he dried his body" (p. 1).

Contextually, the metaphoric rain that beat Nigerians and eventuated in the civil war began four to five hundred years ago, from the "discovery" of Africa by Europe, through its partition into colonies that were given to various European powers to control and then rule with absolute power. During that ominous exercise, Great Britain was handed the area of West Africa, which would later become Nigeria, and the European powers did so without any African consultation or representation (p. 1). After summarizing the precolonial and postcolonial history of Nigeria, including the remote and immediate causes of the war, Achebe declares: "It is for the sake of the future of Nigeria, for our children and grandchildren, that I feel it is important to tell Nigeria's story, Biafra's story, our story, [and] my story" (p. 1). From the introduction, one gets the sense that Achebe feels compelled as a writer by the desire – even the destiny – of a patriot to write the story of his homeland with commitment, integrity, and purpose, in the hope that his fellow Nigerians would listen to him and thereby learn to dry their metaphoric drenched bodies quicker. In a word, the introduction, which traces the root causes of the war to the foundations of the Nigerian national history, surpasses what others have written on the subject, and presages why Great Britain was hell-bent to aid Nigeria to by all means destroy the Republic of Biafra.

In Part 1 of the book, Achebe introduces the reader to the colonial ambiance of his hometown, his nuclear and extended families, and his upbringing – in a mixture of native and foreign cultural milieu – during a period of time he fondly refers to as "magic years." He describes with fondness his happy background and life in his village before his primary exposure to the outside world, as he leaves home to acquire Western education in a high school at Umuahia and a university college at Ibadan. Before then, the roles his parents played in spreading Christianity and Western education in Igboland, his personal development in those foreign institutions, as well as the experiences of his coevals are so succinctly delineated that they read like a short history of British colonial government and missionary activities in Nigeria – a history that is familiar to Igbo people of my generation that is one or two below Achebe's. Clearly, some of us could identify with the author's colonial and postcolonial experiences, which he narrates with exuberant pride and joy as a young Nigerian of Igbo extraction. Furthermore, the narration of the events evokes in the reader a nostalgic yearning for life in the Igbo country of the time, especially where he describes the effective British colonial educational systems, Igbo cultural ceremonies (unlike what they are today), his meeting with his prospective wife Christie and her family, as well as what inspired him to write his first novel, *Things Fall Apart*, and why he characterizes his generation of Nigerians as a lucky one. Ironically, however, all these events are narrated to emphasize the loss of the happy times in Nigeria, and to foreshadow the future traumatic events of the civil war, which become the thrust of the entire book. As he painstakingly recalls and narrates the events photographically, Achebe subliminally prods his readers to vicariously feel the overarching traumas of the war, brood over them, and vow to themselves, "Never again, Nigeria!" This seems to me the essence of this war story.

The joyful and optimistic feeling Achebe had as a young Nigerian continued up to Nigerians' march to national political independence. But this brief period of brightness in their history quickly turned into a cloud of uncertainty, which began to form during the early years of post-independence, when there was a decline in the nationalistic spirit. The decline worsened when the army staged the first bloody coup in Nigeria on January 15, 1966, which resulted in a series of other deadly events, such as stressful ethnic tensions and resentments, a split in the army itself, countercoups and assassinations, and the pogroms that Northerners committed against Easterners, especially the Igbo people. The series of attempts by political leaders to resolve the bloody conflicts between Easterners and other Nigerians woefully failed to produce the desired peaceful resolution to the conflicts. The last of the peace efforts, which resulted in the Aburi Accord, was neither respected nor implemented by the federal government when the two delegations to the peace talks in Ghana returned home to Nigeria. In the end, the nightmarish cloud of political uncertainty, which had hovered over the nation for a long time, turned into a bloody civil war that no one on either side of the conflict could stop.

In Part 2, Achebe carefully lays out the divergent Biafran and Nigerian positions on the civil war, and the attempts by the OAU to bring peace between the warring parties, as well as the roles Western countries played in the war, which he dubbed "the triangle game: The UK, France, and the United States." His analysis of events reveals why these efforts failed to help stop the war, given the motivations of the countries supporting Nigeria diplomatically and militarily. Of course, they all wanted the oil found in large quantities on Biafra land.

In the segment titled "The Writers and Intellectuals," Achebe quotes foreign journalists who asserted that some of the leading international thinkers of the era were so appalled by the Biafran tragedy that they took it upon themselves to pay the breakaway republic a visit and get a firsthand look at the suffering, the destitution, and the starvation there (105). He does so to validate and buttress his claims of what evils Nigerians did to Biafrans, which were unknown to the outside word until the journalists published their reports about them based on direct experience.

In the next segment, "The War and the Nigerian Intellectual," Achebe narrates the laudable roles Nigerian intellectuals played not just in the rapid development of Nigerian literature in English but also in their involvement in nationalistic efforts before and after independence, when they sought ways to bring Nigerian ethnic peoples together to stop the imminent war. He also narrates how Ojukwu appointed some of the intellectuals, including Achebe himself, as roving ambassadors to plead the cause of Biafra in international forums. The role Achebe played in that capacity should cause readers of his works to revere him even more as a world-renowned author and statesperson.

Achebe's deliberation of the differences in the backgrounds of the major Nigerian actors in the conflicts, Ojukwu and Gowon, adds some clarity to the understanding of how they conducted the war and why it was difficult for people to bring them to the table for peace making. The nuanced differences between them are seen also in the eerie description of the gory incident of "The Asaba Massacre," for there was blood, blood, blood everywhere, seeping through every page.

Beyond the description of bloody incidents in the Igbo territories of Asaba and Biafra, Achebe narrates how Ojukwu appointed a group of Igbo intellectuals called the National Guidance Committee, charging them to write a constitution for Biafra establishing the fundamental principles upon which the government and people of Biafra would operate. The final work of the committee became the Ahiara Declaration. Since after the war, some Nigerians have been consulting it as a road map, which helps them to serve the government competently. Achebe should be applauded for appointing and leading the other members of the committee, even though he does not (out of his natural humility) claim responsibility for the huge success of their work. Until revealing his role in the committee here in this book, most Biafrans (except in the inner circle of government at the time) believed that the Ahiara Declaration was the brainchild of Ojukwu, the Oxford-trained General of the Biafran People's Army.

Another dimension to Achebe's services to the Biafran nation, which touched on the literacy of its citizens, was his stint at establishing a publishing company, the Citadel Press, which enabled him and his collaborator, John Iroaganachi, to publish wartime children's books. Although the press was bombed by the Nigerian Air Force, the concept of establishing it never died, for his friends, Arthur Nwankwo and Samuel Ifejika, established another publishing company, Nwabuife Books, on the original spot of the stillborn press after the war. It thus became a foundation press, which has been publishing many books for the nation.

In Part 3, Achebe discusses General Gowon's three-pronged attack on the Republic of Biafra that led to an economic blockade and starvation of its citizens in what Achebe calls "the fight to the finish." Gowon had succeeded in cutting Biafra off from the sea, robbing its inhabitants of shipping ports to receive military and humanitarian supplies. Achebe asserts:

> The afflictions marasmus and kwashiorkor began to spread farther, with the absence of protein in the diet, and they were compounded by outbreaks of other disease epidemics and diarrhea. The landscape was filled by an increasing number of those avian prognosticators of death as famine worsened and the death toll mounted: *udene*, the vultures. . . . Some estimates are that over a thousand Biafrans a day were perishing by this time, and at the height of Gowon's economic blockade and "starve them into submission" policy, upwards of fifty thousand Biafran civilians, most of them babies, children, and women, were dying every single month.
>
> (p. 210)

And yet, the UN remained silent and did nothing to save innocent Biafrans from the genocide and brutality perpetrated by Nigerians, who were aided and abetted by Great Britain and the USSR.

From that point of the war onwards, Biafra started losing the war diplomatically (as Azikiwe withdrew his support for Biafra) and militarily (as Nigerian troops recaptured Owerri), in spite of the fact that Biafran troops took an oil rig from Nigeria in the Kwale incident, which should have empowered them to fight harder. In the end, by January 1970, there was sunset in Biafra, Land of the Rising Sun.

After the detailed description of the fall of Biafra, Achebe devotes the rest of Part 3 to raising questions about the genocide that Nigeria meted against the peoples of Biafra:

> My aim is not to provide all the answers but to raise questions, and perhaps to cause a few headaches in the process. Almost thirty years before Rwanda, before Darfur, over two million – mothers, children, babies, civilians – lost their lives as a result of the blatantly callous and unnecessary policies enacted by the leaders of the federal government of Nigeria.
>
> In the case of the Nigeria-Biafra War there is precious little relevant literature that helps answer these questions: Did the federal government of Nigeria engage in the genocide of its Igbo citizens through their punitive policies, the most notorious being "starvation as a legitimate weapon of war?" Is the information blockade around the war a cause of calculated historical suppression? Why has the war not been discussed, or taught to the young, over forty years after its end? Are we perpetually doomed to repeat the mistakes of the past because we are too stubborn to learn from them?
>
> (p. 228)

After asking these questions, whose answers are yet to be given by both the Nigerian leaders and the Western countries involved in the war against Biafra, Achebe goes on to present the arguments Igbo people, international journalists, and nongovernmental organizations (NGOs) made against Nigeria's commission of genocide against his people and backs them up with several documented sources. He follows up with a presentation of the case against the Nigerian government. On page 233 of the book, Achebe opens a Pandora's Box when he cites a callous statement credited to the revered Yoruba leader, Chief Obafemi Awolowo and echoed by his cohorts: "All is fair in war, and starvation is one of the weapons of war. I don't see why we should feed our enemies fat in order for them to fight harder." Then Achebe adds: "It is my impression that Chief Obafemi Awolowo was driven by an overriding ambition for power, for himself in particular and for the advancement of his people in general." He then goes on to trace the source of Awolowo's ambition.

Even though what Achebe accuses Awolowo of saying is validated from documented sources, the Yoruba people are justifiably outraged by the way Achebe presented it, especially when no one can prove that Awolowo's personal ambition was also the ambition of his entire ethnic people. On the other hand, the Igbo people are also offended by it, because they now know the source of the government policy that led to the deaths of over two million of their kith and kin. All told, the argument over that controversial statement has prevented many Nigerians from reading the book carefully to understand fully Achebe's total message. What I think personally about the controversy is that Gowon should be the one held accountable for the deadly policy he implemented, no matter who devised it, because he was the head of the military government at the time. Nevertheless, as a fair-minded person, Achebe did not fail to include General Gowon's answer to the case of genocide against his government (pp. 236–9). Readers should judge his defense for themselves.

Achebe devotes Part 4 of the book to conducting a postmortem examination of the death of the old Nigeria and the stillborn Republic of Biafra. Writing under the title "Nigeria's Painful Transitions: A Reappraisal," he argues:

> The post Nigeria-Biafra civil war era saw a "unified" Nigeria saddled with a greater and more insidious reality. We were plagued by homegrown enemy: the political ineptitude, mediocrity, indiscipline, ethnic bigotry, and corruption of the ruling class. Compounding the situation was the fact that Nigeria was now awash in oil-boom petrodollars, and to make matters even worse, the country's young, affable, military head of state, General Yakubu Gowon, ever so cocksure following his victory, proclaimed to the entire planet that Nigeria had more money than it knew what to do with. A new era of great decadence and decline was born. It continues to the day.
>
> (p. 243)

Readers should note well that before publishing this book, Achebe had outlined most of the same sociopolitical ills, which have been plaguing Nigeria, in another book, *The Trouble with Nigeria* (Fourth Dimension Publishers, 1983), during the time he campaigned for a political party with Mallam Aminu Kano, all in the spirit of playing his role as conscience for his Nigerian (indeed, Igbo) people. The question then is: when shall we Nigerians learn to listen to the voice of the sage and be wiser in our ways? Or shall we continue to behave like the deaf and the dumb?

In the final segment of the book, "Postscript: The Example of Nelson Mandela," Achebe lionizes President Nelson Mandela of South Africa for being the embodiment of a man whose sacrifices and selfless leadership brought unity and progress to all ethnic and racial groups in his country. Thus, he recommends Mandela's leadership qualities for emulation by Nigerian leaders. Achebe also draws their attention to the evil effects of the governance of wickedly corrupt African leaders on the citizens of their countries, which in some ways resemble what Nigerians experienced under their military rulers. Achebe ends his war memoir on that note, still playing his role as the conscience for his people.

In conclusion, Achebe interlaces his narration of incidents in the war with many poems, which sound partly like dirges and partly like the blues, which conforms with the Igbo way of telling war stories. As an Igbo raconteur, he tells part of the story in prose and part in esoteric proverbial language to lament the loss of life – *akwa ariri onwu* – in honor of the dead, and thereafter continues with the story line. We see Achebe doing so when he discusses the death of his dear friend Christopher Okigbo, and those of the nameless Biafran soldiers and civilians, especially the malnourished and starved babies in refugee camps, whom he and his young family met as fellow refugees. By creating this new genre of literature in *There Was a Country: A Personal History of Biafra*, Achebe has once again boldly demonstrated that a memoir, which is a Western literary creation, can be modified into a hybrid genre to serve his Igbo (indeed, African) creative purpose, just as he did in his first novel, *Things Fall Apart*. Now the world watches to see what other writers might do with the example he has set for them to follow.

Notes

* Culled from *Journal of the African Literature Association (JALA)*, Vol. 7, No. 2 (Winter 2012/Spring 2013): 173–80.

1 Kalu Ogbaa, ed., *The Gong and the Flute: African Literary Development and Celebration.* Westport, CT: Greenwood Press, 1994: 130.

10 Other Critics' Reviews of *There Was a Country: A Personal History of Biafra*

In 2012, Chinua Achebe published his final book, *There Was a Country: A Personal History of Biafra*, amid a series of sociopolitical and religious crises ravaging Nigeria, which mirrored some of the deadly incidents he critically discussed in this book. For example, an Islamic terrorist group called Boko Haram was roaming the northeastern part of Nigeria, torturing and killing their victims, including kidnapping and raping over 200 female high school students; the Niger-Delta region was agitating for more compensations for the oil Nigeria was mining from their territory; the indigenous peoples of Biafra were agitating for the actualization of their defunct Biafra; the Igbo of the southeastern political zone were demanding that the federal government create one additional state for them, to equalize the number of states allotted to each zone in the country; and, people from all parts of the country were protesting the general insecurity and rampant kidnapping of people for money, all of which were problems that stultified the economic situation of the masses. Besides, the general corruption of the ruling class and their naked misuse of the oil revenues – the main source of the national economy – were visible evidence that the country was gravitating toward another civil war or total collapse. Bang! Here comes *There Was a Country*, a book that discusses amid so many controversial national subjects of the tragedy of Nigeria-Biafra War, which some people reacted to with varying degrees of prejudice. Why? Because its author, Chinua Achebe of Igbo ethnic extraction, dared to support his personal opinions with stubborn facts on the causes, the course, and the prosecution of that war as he saw them. And some readers saw the book as an attack on particular Nigerian political leaders. Predictably, the initial responses to the book by Nigerian critics were as divergent as the critics' ethnic backgrounds.

So, it was not a surprise that, in an ethnically diverse society like Nigeria, readers and critics of *There Was a Country* would write their reviews of it with one form of prejudice or another. Ethnic sentiments usually affect the way people view issues in our Nigerian society, which, sometimes, are as dangerous as the racist attitudes of people in a multiracial society like the United States. However, what was very surprising to me is the level of animosity and hatred that some of our learned critics expressed in their reviews, attacking Achebe personally for daring to discuss the massacres of Igbo people during the Northern riots,

DOI: 10.4324/9781003184133-10

and the genocide fellow Nigerians committed against Biafrans during the con-
sequent civil war. In addition, the critics also denied that such crimes ever took
place. That is why some Igbo readers and critics, who either experienced the war
directly or learned of it from their parents, would write different reviews of the
book. Foreign readers also expressed various opinions in their reviews based on
specific issues that Achebe articulated. One way or another, people's reactions to
the book have been political and divisive.

For instance, Andrew Rosenbaum began his analysis with a comment on
Achebe's narrative technique, saying it was "almost cinematic in its ability to go
from an intimate scene to a great sweeping take of an army marching – without
skipping a beat."[1] He followed with another statement supporting Achebe's critical analysis of Nigeria's failing economy:

> The country of Nigeria is a basket case and has been for most of its indepen-
> dence. *In this book, Chinua Achebe tries to explain why.*
>
> (emphasis added)

> Ranked 14th for the past ten years on the Failed States Index (published
> by the Fund for Peace), Nigeria is racked by corruption, crime, and local
> rebellion. This is despite the fact that it is the eighth largest oil exporter in
> the world, and, incidentally, the fifth-largest exporter to the U.S., supplying
> nearly a tenth of our oil. . . . In the 2011 Transparency International Corrup-
> tion Perception Index, which measures perceived levels of public corruption,
> Nigeria was ranked 143 out of 183 countries.[2]

One can easily see that Rosenbaum, a foreign reader and critic, was able to
recognize what some of our own erudite Nigerian critics refused to acknowledge
in their reviews. He concludes his analysis as follow:

> Chinua Achebe's book was written to show how governance in Nigeria ran
> off the rails, largely through the civil war with Biafra. He wrote it in his old
> age, though he had written obliquely about Biafran experience in poems
> earlier in his life. But now he feels the plain tale must be told: "It is for the
> sake of the future of Nigeria, for our children and grandchildren, that I feel it
> is important to tell Nigeria's story, Biafra's story, our story, my story."
> [. . .]
> Chinua Achebe brings much more to the story than just the stark history.
> He brings in poetry, Igbo myths and religion, anecdotes of the artists and
> writers he grew up with in the country, and much discussion of the role of
> the writer in society.
> *The whole makes for a remarkable type of history, at once personal and objec-*
> *tive. If one is at all interested in Africa, this book should not be missed.*[3]
>
> (emphasis added)

Another foreign critic, Rob Spillman, wrote for the *Los Angeles Times* while he was living and teaching in Lagos, Nigeria. His cavalier tone of voice and cursory treatment suggest that he really did not understood Achebe's point of view. He began with the statement, "Chinua Achebe, the Nigerian author of the ground-breaking 1958 novel 'Things Fall Apart' is widely considered the most influential African writer of the 20th century. A staple in school curricula worldwide and with more than 10 million copies in print, Achebe's novel is an African story told in an African manner by an African – remarkable for colonial times."[4] Thereafter, without any transition, he went on to say in the next paragraph:

> While Achebe identifies himself as a Nigerian author, he is also Igbo, one of the three dominant tribes in the vast country of more than 200 million people. It was the Igbo who led the cessation from Nigeria in 1967, forming the Republic of Biafra, resulting in a nearly 3-year-long civil war that killed more than 3 million people, mostly Biafran, who were starved to death by Nigerian government's food blockade. While recently teaching in Lagos, I could still feel the reverberations from the international disaster, including lingering ethnic tensions and reports of the Boko Haram, the violent northern jihadist separatist group, spreading terror nationwide with what many see as governmental support.[5]

Spillman went on to assert that Achebe did not openly identify himself as Igbo. But how can that be true when, in fact, Achebe began Part 1 of the book with his personal history, which clearly includes the pride he always felt whenever and wherever he discussed his cultural education and life in Igboland?

After his belated response to Achebe's discussion of the Igbo massacres in the North, Spillman expressed complete doubt on Achebe's objective narration and analysis of the war incidents. He also cast doubt on Achebe's objectivity because of the active roles he played in defense of his new country Biafra:

> Considering that Achebe was deeply involved with the government of the breakaway republic *and fled Nigeria in 1972 for the U.S., where he has lived on and off ever since*, this objective stance is strained at best.[6]
>
> (emphasis added)

Oh, how little Spillman knows about Achebe's behavior to make such an outlandish conjecture! People who knew Chinua Achebe personally can tell that he was not a coward like many other Nigerians who fled the country. Going to live in America was a choice he made freely so he could teach and continue his professional writing where he had better resources and opportunities. Moreover, Spillman's bias continues in his conclusion:

> Unfortunately, his argument is muddled by exhaustive, somewhat stultifying sections about the makeup of the Biafran government, committee deliberations over creation of Utopian laws, and the derivation of the national flag

and anthem. Much of the prose here is flat and uninspired (and seemingly unedited). To whit: "Food was short, meat was very short, and drugs were short." It is a slog through this messy yet heartfelt hybrid memoir-history for anyone not completely versed in Nigerian history.

The ruthless and reckless decisions that fueled the Biafran conflict, mostly swept under the historical rug, are well worth documenting, and Achebe's book is an imperfect attempt at revealing the truth. Just as "Things Fall Apart" blazed the path for more African writers to write their own stories, hopefully "There Was a Country" will bring about more rigorous, soul-searching calls for historical reckoning, a necessary step toward true African democracy.[7]

I cannot see how anyone can accept Spillman's review as fair and balanced, considering the weaknesses one finds in it.

Overall, his bias demonstrates why Achebe forewarned his African and world audiences numerous times in his public lectures, essays, and books to beware of getting their information from foreign writers on African issues with questionable motives. For, like Joseph Conrad, who visited Congo in Central Africa and wrote *Heart of Darkness* for European audiences, and Joyce Cary, who lived in Nigeria as a colonial officer and wrote *Mr. Johnson* for British audiences, Roy Spillman, who lived and taught briefly in Nigeria, was feeding his foreign audience bad information about Achebe's new book. They could believe what he says in his review because living and teaching in Nigeria automatically *qualified* him as an *authority* on Nigerian history. Hopefully, the weaknesses we have pointed out may inspire more people to read Achebe's book and discover for themselves the accurate facts it contains.

Ike Anya, an Igbo writer, reviewed *There Was a Country* for *African Arguments* on Facebook.[8] Going through it, one can see that he was more receptive to Achebe's anguished narration of the incidents that took place in Nigeria before, during, and after the Nigeria-Biafra War. As the son of Igbo parents who lived in Biafra, he learned a lot about the war from them and from the records they kept as memorabilia:

> In our house in Nsukka, the small university in eastern Nigeria where I grew up, my parents' bedroom harbored a cupboard, reached only by standing on a stepladder. In that cupboard lay a battered brown leather satchel, filled with memorabilia from Biafra. I remember Biafran stamps, currency notes and coins, photographs, receipts, letters, and a small green hard backed pamphlet: *The Ahiara Declaration.*
>
> From time to time, under conditions of great secrecy, the satchel would be brought down and my brothers and I would be allowed to rummage through it as my parents told us stories of their harrowing experiences during the war. We would look at photographs of friends and family "lost" in the conflict, or during the massacres of Igbos that preceded it. We would marvel at the lightness of the Biafran coins. I don't remember my parents explicitly saying

it, but somehow it was communicated to us that the satchel and its contents were not to be discussed outside the family home.

In Nigeria in the 1970s when I grew up, Biafra was only talked about in hushed tones, in an atmosphere of an unspoken fear that talking about it could bring reprisals.

And . . . I found myself hugging him instead and felt to my embarrassment, tears running down my cheeks. As I apologized, avoiding the bemused stares from some of the staff at the venue, I explained to Biyi that I had felt such a powerful reaction because the story he was telling us was *the story of my family – of my parents and grandparents.*

(emphasis added)

That evening, as [I was] on the phone I described my feelings watching the Biafran refugees fleeing the university town of Nsukka to my mother, who had herself fled the town with my father and elder brother in 1967, she said, "I am glad that our story is going to be told, that the world will remember."[9]

I quoted this long passage from Anya's review to show how emotional all the Igbo people who lived in Biafra and their immediate descendants, feel about the agony of their defeat, which includes a recollection of mass massacres in Northern Nigeria and genocide in Biafra. If the scenes of Biafran refugees in a movie about the war was capable of evoking such powerful emotions from Anya, the question becomes, why is it that other critics are incapable of imagining the anguish and deep-seated emotional wound Achebe felt while writing his story – our story – of Biafra, which we Igbo people feel whenever we remember our people's genocide, just as Jewish people do whenever the story of their Holocaust is told? And why do some reviewers exhibit such emotional detachment in their analysis of the book?

After foregrounding his review with such powerful emotions, Ike Anya asserts that "Chinua Achebe's new book *There Was a Country: A Personal History of Biafra* emerges into this landscape of memory and remembrance, 40 years after the war ended. In the book Achebe, a few weeks before his 82nd birthday, finally sets out to tell the story of his Biafra." But although Ike also concedes that Achebe makes some concessions to alternate points of view, especially in relation to the legacy of colonialism and the moral imperative on writers to produce committed literature, he is less conciliatory on the question of whether the actions of the Federal Government of Nigeria during the war constituted war crimes and, possibly, genocide. "[Achebe] scrupulously names the officers and individuals responsible, and provides their viewpoints, based on news and other reports."[10]

In sum, Ike Anya tried his best to write a balanced review, especially because he felt some degree of empathy for the suffering Igbo people Achebe described. However, calling the book "Achebe's Biafran memoir" is not quite an accurate depiction of its genre. Nonetheless, this is one of the few reviews that emphasize the Igbo massacres in the North and the Biafran genocide that other critics have conveniently ignored.

Ernest N. Emenyonu, a renowned professor of English and Africana Studies, published his review in *African Literature Today*.[11] He began with a quotation he believes defines Achebe's mission as Africa's leading creative writer and philosophical thinker dating from the mid-twentieth century.

> It was the driving force that led to Achebe's classic novel, Things Fall Apart (1958), now over 12 million copies in sales and in translations more than 65 world languages. With it, Achebe not only challenged and effectively repudiated the European telling of the African story from 'the insider's' vision of Africa, but also established for the literary world, the African art of storytelling in modern setting.

Still framing the argument of his review, Emenyonu asserts:

> Chinua Achebe described *Things Fall Apart* as Africa's response to decades of European distortions of African realities and the African story. Some European readers hated the publication of the book, some called Achebe names, and others despised his guts as an African audaciously casting aspersions on European images of precolonial and colonial Africa.
>
> Now, early in the 21st century, Achebe is taking issues with the telling of the story of the Nigerian Civil War, forty-five years after the event. The wording of this new book is very carefully crafted to establish for critics and readers that this is Chinua Achebe's vision of the Nigerian Civil War, 1967–1970. However one reacts to it, no one should lose sight of the fact that it is the author's own story and he leaves the door open for anyone else to tell his or her own story, for after all, the answer to a "bad" book is a "better" book. Achebe has told his, so can anyone else.
>
> (p. 187)

He then calls out some Nigerian scholars who, in April 2011, before Chinua Achebe had finished writing his new book, and before his literary agents found him a publisher, had begun second-guessing in online exchanges, the theme of the book and preparing weapons of attack if Achebe did not write what they had in mind or how they wanted it said. The point Emenyonu makes here is that no matter how well the book turned out, such scholars and the general readers were preemptively going to read it with jaundiced eyes. He defends his criticism of such scholars claiming that their cynical reactions and implicit innuendos were triggered by what Achebe said in a keynote address he delivered on October 9, 2008 at the Nigerian Institute of International Affairs (NIIA), Victoria Island, Lagos to mark the Silver Jubilee of *The Guardian Newspaper*: "I would be a Nigerian in my next life." Those who the statement offended included some Igbo scholars who uncompromisingly still held on to Biafra and the values it promised and symbolized. But non-Igbo scholars were not offended by it because they erroneously thought that Achebe had totally forgotten the idea of Biafra and embraced Nigeria as it was after the war. So, Emenyonu used his review as a platform to clarify what Achebe meant by that statement and illustrated it with Achebe's succinct elaboration:

> Being a Nigerian is abysmally frustrating and unbelievably exciting. I have said somewhere that in my next reincarnation I want to be a Nigerian again; but I have also, in a rather angry book called *The Trouble with Nigeria*, dismissed Nigerian travel advertisements with the suggestion that only a tourist with a kinky addiction to self-flagellation would pick Nigeria for a holiday. And I mean both.
>
> Nigeria needs help; Nigerians have their work cut out for them – to coax this unruly child along the path of useful creative development. We are the *parents* of Nigeria, not vice versa. A generation will come, if we do our work patiently and well – and given luck – a generation that will call Nigeria father or mother. But not yet.[12]

What Achebe said further crystalizes his reason for publishing his book at the time he did. Which is not to say that he so blindly loved Nigeria that he would not protest what Nigeria was doing wrong. And Emenyonu added, "And to authenticate his unequivocal protest, Achebe has refused to accept Nigeria's highest national honor (Commander of the Federal Republic) twice awarded him in the recent past."[13] Emenyonu's primary task was to correct the misrepresentations of what Achebe said in other writers' reviews. He made those corrections throughout his response.

Commenting on the structure of the book, Emenyonu tells his audience that each of its four parts has something to offer by linking the sociopolitical history of Nigeria to both the Nigerian writer and Nigerian literature. Hence, *There Was a Country* is as much a personal history of Biafra as it is Chinua Achebe's partial autobiography. He quoted the book copiously to show Achebe's careful narration of the history of failed Nigerian political leadership, beginning from the time Great Britain imposed Abubakar Tafawa Balewa as Prime Minister, who thus became a conduit through which Britain would maintain control after Nigeria's attainment of political independence in 1960. Achebe also discussed the leadership role of Chief Obafemi Awolowo, Nigeria's wartime finance minister, who created inimical policies that led to the starvation and death of millions of Biafrans and their economic strangulation at the end of the war. These facts were based on verifiable information from published and unpublished sources of the war. Yet, some reviewers would not condemn, as Achebe did, the roles that Balewa, Gowon, and Awolowo played that led to the downfall of Nigeria's first republic. Instead, they characterized his work as having been fueled by ethnic animosity against those leaders because they were not Igbo. In doing so, they purposefully overlooked how Achebe earlier had boldly condemned the role of Dr. Nnamdi Azikiwe (an Igbo leader) in *The Trouble with Nigeria*, which Achebe also recalled in *There Was a Country*.

Emenyonu opined that "People may hate *There Was a Country* or its author for reasons personal to them, but they cannot wish away its impregnable veracity or the purity of Achebe's analytical insights into complex and complicated issues of humanity and nationhood. Someone had the guts to finally tell it like it is to Nigerians!" To synthesize some ideas Achebe expressed in the new book he asked rhetorically:

> Who else has told Nigerians with impunity that both General Yakubu Gowon and General Odumegwu Ojukwu allowed the Nigeria-Biafra War to drag on as long and disastrous as it did for reasons of selfish ego and personal aggrandizement? . . . Who else can look erstwhile Biafrans in the face and tell them that there were other options equally as honorable and dignified as secession in the face of insurmountable odds?
>
> (p. 124)

And then he stressed his point further with a direct quote from the book:

> I think that around March 1968, when we were in a position to achieve a confederation, we should have accepted the chance or opportunity. When we were insisting that Biafran sovereignty was not negotiable, as the govern-ment thought at the time, we ought to have considered the tragedy of the situation, because this country would have been much better if we had a confederation of four to six states, other than what we have now. Around the time of the Kampala talks there were definite signs that a confederation could be achieved. The Biafran side was adamant on the fact of sovereignty being nonnegotiable.
>
> (p. 126)

As one who lived in Biafra, I agree with the sentiments expressed here except that there was no way Biafrans could have known that the Nigerian military authorities would implement the negotiated confederation if they accepted it, bearing in mind that there was a similar agreement reached between Nigeria and Biafra in Aburi, Ghana in 1967, known as the Aburi Accord. When the representatives of both parties returned home, Nigeria had reneged on the implementation of the whole agreement. That is why the Biafrans were not just adamant about negotiating their sovereignty during the Kampala talks, they were also afraid that the Nigerian side might once again break the deal as they did after the Aburi Accord. So they needed more concrete evidence of trust from Nigeria before renouncing their sovereignty at that time in the war.[14]

Emenyonu concluded his review by saying that

> All in all, *There Was a Country* is a book no Nigerian can afford not to read. Readers all over the world familiar with his previous works will expect noth-ing but creative excellence and integrity from Chinua Achebe. So, saying that *There Was a Country* is an excellent book may sound like stating the obvious, but indeed in this book, Chinua Achebe surpasses himself in both artistry and thematic relevance in an unprecedented way as he fuses and merges into one work the quintessence of fictional art and the eternity of

facts. The poems that precede some topics in the book give the reader a clue of the narrative to follow and Achebe's ability to communicate serious themes as well in one genre as in another with equal impact. Achebe was never more animated and nostalgic in the entire book than in the sections on the poet, Christopher Okigbo. No work on Nigerian history or political development can be considered complete or valid without reference to *There Was a Country*.

(p. 198)

Emenyonu's powerful endorsement could have been used as a blurb to promote the book. But he also pointed out errors that should be corrected in a future edition.

Before publication of *There Was a Country*, there were already many published nonfictional works, including biographies, memoirs, personal accounts, and essays on the causes, course, and execution of the Nigeria-Biafra War. But none of them generated as much critical scrutiny as Achebe's personal history of Biafra. The reactions of scholars and general readers to the issues that Achebe raised and succinctly discussed inspired Nigerian and foreign scholars to reread existing literature on the civil war. So, four years later, the renowned Nigerian professor of history at the University of Texas at Austin, Dr. Toyin Falola, co-edited with Ogechukwu Ezekwem a very important book titled *Writing the Nigeria-Biafra War*,[15] containing chapters written by Nigerian and foreign scholars. The promotional blurb reads:

> The contributors examine writers' and protagonists' use of contemporary published texts as a means of continued resistance and justification of the war, the problems of objectivity encountered in memoirs and how authors' backgrounds and sources determine the kinds of biases that influenced their interpretations, including the gendered divisions in Nigeria-Biafra War scholarship. By initiating a dialogue on the civil war, this volume engages in a much-needed discourse on the problems confronting a culturally diverse post-war Nigeria.

The blurb inspired a distinguished Nigerian professor of sociology at Virginia Tech University, Dr. Onwubiko Agozino, to write a review of the book he titled, "'Objective' History and Genocide Denialism."[16] The first paragraph sets its tone and content:

> *Writing the Nigeria-Biafra War*, edited by Toyin Falola and his doctoral student at the University of Texas, Austin, Ogechuwu Ezekwem (2016, Woodbridge, James Currey), is a highly anticipated volume about a country in which authoritarian dictators banned the teaching of history apparently out of fear that such an academic discipline would sooner or later excavate the atrocities that they engineered in a genocidal war for opportunistic selfish gains in the guise of national interest. The book is timely now as the *masses*

agitate for the actualization of Biafra, although the book is silent on the raging mass agitation and ongoing *extra judicial killings* and detentions of nonviolent protesters sometimes for waving the banned flag of Biafra which could have been permitted as a tourist attraction and as homage to the dead.

(p. 57) (emphasis added)

Thereafter, Agozino mentioned how impressed he was to see "the high caliber of intellectuals assembled in the book with essays from the eminent historian, Godwin Uzoigwe, and the Marxist literary theorist, Biodun Jeyifo, promising mouth-watering mussels of knowledge waiting to be carefully digested, etc." And his initial analysis of the essays led him to say, "Sadly, the intellectual cowardice that forced many into silence in the face of tyranny as condemned by Wole Soyinka in his detention memoir, *The Man Died*, was too evident in the book about a country where scholarship on the war was apparently censored and official archives were sanitized to erase much of the evidence while the prolific documentation of the war in novels, memoirs and biographies by Igbo survivors is relatively ignored in this book" (p. 61).

He divided the chapters into three groups: (1) those by Igbo intellectuals (Uzoigwe, for instance) painstakingly identified the avoidable causes of the war and the regrettable genocidal consequences; (2) those by Yoruba intellectuals, which "displayed intellectual dishonesty in an attempt to mitigate the course of the war"; and (3) those by non-Nigerian intellectuals, which are more sympathetic to the plight of the Igbo who managed to survive genocide in Biafra. He cited some statements made by the contributors, and concluded that

> The shortcoming of this promising book lies in the futile search for 'objectivity' when it has been established that 'committed objectivity' is the best that scholars can approximate either in their cowardly support of tyranny or in their heroic challenge to genocide wherever it may rear its ugly head. There is no such thing as a point-of-viewless history of genocide. Hence, he recommends that African intellectuals should renounce their shameless denial of the Igbo genocide and join courageous intellectuals like Soyinka in denouncing the evil that has been done to fellow Africans by greedy rulers of the neocolonial genocidal state, otherwise the culture of genocidal violence would continue to haunt the continent.

(p. 61)

Of all the chapters in *Writing the Nigeria-Biafra War*, only the one written by Biodun Jeyifo, titled "First, There Was a Country, Then There Wasn't: Reflections on Achebe's *There Was a Country*" (pp. 245–64), was devoted entirely to an analysis of Achebe's new book. The ethnic bias that Agozino identified in the Yoruba writers' chapters could not be clearer than in the one by Jeyifo:

> [Amazingly] even the self-professed Marxist, Jeyifo, condescended to use his verbose, self-opinionated, five-part serialized, newspaper book review of *There Was a Country* to describe that damning witness against genocide

by Achebe as the work of a "protagonist, media apparatchik, and ideological zealot" (p. 246). Biodun Jeyifo went on to unfairly abuse Achebe as an "Igbo supremacist" simply because Achebe reported the consensual fact that although the Igbo poor came relatively late to modern education, they quickly took the lead and have maintained that lead in the achievement of academic merit in Nigeria. Incredibly, Jeyifo neurotically attempted to deny the genocide against the Igbo masses by repeating 3.1 million times that the evidence only suggested "alleged attempted genocide." Lenin would have dismissed such a reactionary chauvinism as petty bourgeois "national defencism," since he called for the right to self-determination by oppressed nationalities with the right to secession inscribed in the constitution of the USSR. This allowed Finland to secede without firing a shot and allowing the USSR to dissolve peacefully when the people demanded it.

(p. 63)

While I cannot tell for sure that ethnic bias against the Igbo influenced Jeyifo's review of Achebe's book, his carping criticism against everything Achebe said in his discussion of issues, including the structure and genre of the book, makes me wonder if he was truly an ethnic bigot. For I have known many Yoruba people, especially our Nobel Laureate Wole Soyinka, who was detained by Nigerian military authorities for protesting the massacres of the Igbo during the Northern Nigeria riots. Since then, he has continued to fight for social justice and civil rights for all Nigerians even during the time General Obasanjo (a Yoruba) was the Nigerian head of state. And another Yoruba, Professor Falola, editor of *Writing the Nigeria-Biafra War* and other publications on African studies, has been using every editorial resource at his disposal to promote the works of Nigerian intellectuals here in America and in our country Nigeria. I have also talked about the unbreakable bond between the Igbo and the Yoruba in real time in my book, *The Nigerian Americans*,[17] in which I said:

Interethnic Marriage

One of the most significant but often underrated underlying factors in Nigerian national life is interethnic marriage. Before the civil war, some Igbo men in virtually all parts of Nigeria were interested in marrying women who lived near them. The result was the births of great Nigerians of interethnic marriages. For example, among such bi-ethnic children are General Ike Nwachukwu, whose father was Igbo and mother was Hausa, the Nigerian legal luminary and attorney-general of Imo State, Barrister Kalu Kalu Ogba, whose father was Igbo and mother was Efik, and the political leader of Action Group, Mazi S. G. Ikoku, whose father is Igbo and mother was Ibibio. Furthermore, the most revered and beloved Igbo leader and one-time president of the World Council of Churches, Ezeogo Akanu Ibiam, was married to a Yoruba woman, and the renowned Igbo novelist and one-time registrar of the West African Examination Council, Chukwuemeka Ike married a Yoruba woman.

(pp. 133–4)

And after I wrote the book, Chinua Achebe's second daughter, Nwando, I'm told, married a Yoruba man. That is why I would not attribute Jeyifo's attacks on Achebe solely to ethnic bigotry. But here are some examples of Jeyifo's utterances just within two pages of his review that smack of his ethnic bias:

> For me in particular, I have always regarded Achebe as one of the greatest realist writers in world literature in the last 150 years. The proof of these assertions is the fact that among all writers of the last half century, *and second only to Soyinka*, Achebe has been the writer to whose works I have returned again and again in the last three decades. . . .
>
> I can report that the Achebe I have personally encountered in this book is more or less the enormously powerful realist writer that I saw and greatly admired in nearly all his previous writings *minus his poetry.*
>
> (p. 245)

> In *There Was a Country*, Achebe operates under the presumption that regardless of how close and faithful he was to the Biafran leadership, his independence and autonomy as a writer and intellectual were intact. *But this is, at best, a genuine but mistaken assumption; at worst, it is more or less a self-serving delusion and mystification.*
>
> I intend to bring the "two Achebes" that we encounter in *There Was a Country* into a dialogical relationship with each other: on the one hand, the *superb realist writer and progressive intellectual*; on the other, *wartime propaganda and media warrior and ethnonational ideological zealot.* For those who might intuitively presuppose that I have in mind a hierarchy, a "higher" and "lower" *order of integrity between these two putative Achebes*, I hasten to say that this is not necessarily so. In other words, I will not hold one Achebe as a corrective, a benchmark for the other. Far from this, my central frame of reference simply is that against Achebe's own presuppositions we *must keep both in view: the writer and the ideologue.*
>
> (p. 247) (emphasis added)

These four randomly selected passages from Jeyifo's review of *There Was a Country* clearly reveal his intellectual chauvinism and rapaciousness. He claims that he has always regarded Achebe as one of the greatest realist writers in world literature in the last 150 years, whose works he enjoys reading minus his poetry. But there is no evidence or persuasive proof of his assertions that he read the works of the realist writers. In fact, Jeyifo's obsession with "Socialist Realism, a term used by Marxist critics for novels which they held to embody or 'reflect' characters and events that accord with the Marxist view that the struggle between economic classes is the essential dynamic of society,"[18] prevents him from differentiating Achebe's realistic novels from his nonfictional personal history of Biafra. That is also why he claims that Achebe is a realist writer only "second to Soyinka" and that there are two *Achebes*. Besides, to shoot down Achebe as an "Igbo supremacist" and arrogantly teach him how to write his own history unmask

Jeyifo's ethnic bigotry that seeps like blood all through the pages of his review; and its paper tiger quality diminishes the aspirational rhetoric of the book, which Chinua Achebe the patriot published to inspire scholars and general readers to work toward rebuilding the broken governmental systems in Nigeria.

Chinua Achebe published *There Was a Country: A Personal History of Biafra* in 2012 without being aware that it was his swan song, the last patriotic gift he would give to all Nigerians before his demise the following year. From the few reviews of the book that we have examined in this chapter, we can say that its contents are as controversial as Achebe knew they would be, for he once wrote in *Anthills of the Savannah*, "Writers don't give prescriptions," shouted Ikem. "They give headaches" (p. 161) That assertion turned out to be true, especially considering the issues he raised in his analysis of the unhealthy sociopolitical and economic conditions in Nigeria, beginning from the very time our country attained political independence, through the civil war period, to the postbellum era. The first part of the book entitled "There Was a Country," refers to the colonial period, when there was forced unity among Nigerians from all ethnic groups that began to unravel as soon as the colonial masters left the governance of the country in the hands of native rulers. And the second part of the title, "A Personal History of Biafra," expresses how Achebe personally saw the bloody events that took place in some parts of Northern and Western regions, during the 1966 military coup and countercoups, and how all of those events led to the 1967–1970 civil war and its aftermath. Considering the ethnic makeup of the country, it would be unrealistic to expect either Chinua Achebe or his reviewers to write emotionally detached analyses of the issues discussed in the book. However, what is expected of any readers is that they objectively judge Achebe according to his stated mission of recounting his personal history – his story, our story of Biafra. In other words, he did not write the book as fiction, for he clearly called it a personal history. Thus, it would be wrong for anyone to analyze and characterize it otherwise.

Nota bene: Apart from publishing this final book, Chinua Achebe did something else as part of his legacy before he passed on: He established the Chinua Achebe Annual Colloquium at Brown University, which serves as a platform from which African literary scholars and sociopolitical, economic, and scientific leaders here in America, and Africans in the Diaspora can discuss issues as they affect continental Africa. I attended one of these colloquiums in May 2014 at the invitation of President Christina Paxson of Brown University, Chinua Achebe's last place of employment. The paper I presented during the Colloquium is reproduced in the next chapter of this study.

Notes

1 Andrew Rosenbaum, "A Review of *There Was a Country: A Personal History of Biafra*," *New York Journal of Books*, October 11, 2012.

2 *Ibid.*

3 *Ibid.*

4 Rob Spillman, "A Review of 'a History of Person, Country in' *There Was a Country*," *Los Angeles Times*, November 9, 2012.

5   *Ibid.*
6   *Ibid.*
7   *Ibid.*
8   Ike Anya, "*There Was a Country*: A Review of Chinua Achebe's Biafran Memoir," *African Arguments*, October 10, 2012, https://africanarguments.org.
9   Ike Anya was reacting to a video review of Chimamanda Adichie's novel, *Half a Yellow Sun*. New York: Knof/Anchor Press, 2006.
10 *Ibid.*
11 Ernest N. Emenyonu, "A Critical Review of Chinua Achebe's *There Was a Country: A Personal History of Biafra*," *African Literature Today*, No. 30: Reflections and Retrospectives in African Literature (December 30, 2012): 187–98.
12 Achebe, *The Education of a British-Protected Child*, pp. 45–6.
13 Emenyonu, "A Critical Review of Chinua Achebe's *There Was a Country*," p. 189.
14 Ogbaa, *General Ojukwu*, p. 85.
15 Toyin Falola and Ogechukwu Ezekwem, eds., *Writing the Nigeria-Biafra War*. Suffolk, UK: James Currey, 2016.
16 Onwubiko Agozino, "'Objective' History and Genocide Denialism," in *Essays in Education and Popular Culture: Massliteracy*. Newcastle upon Tyne: Cambridge Scholars Press, 2019: 57–63.
17 Kalu Ogbaa, *The Nigerian Americans*. Westport, CT: Greenwood Press, 2003: 133–4.
18 See M. H. Abrams, *A Glossary of Literary Terms*, Sixth Edition. Orlando, FL: Holt, Rinehart and Winston, 1993: 176.

11 Chinua Achebe's *Arrow of God*

A Foretaste of Igbo Intra-Ethnic Democracy in the Present-Day Nigerian Geopolitical System*

Every society, whether ancient or modern, has an established system of governance through which it regulates the actions and lives of its inhabitants. Hence, when an individual or group in a given society attempts to impugn the authority of those in charge of the system, by threatening the security, harmony, and peaceful coexistence of its inhabitants, it becomes an unfailing duty of those in charge of its governance to take all necessary and adequate measures to prevent the threat and protect the people. In a literate society like the United States, the founding fathers established three branches of government and enshrined their respective roles in their constitution to ensure that the people enjoy their freedoms, happiness, and security of lives and property in their homes and communities. It is a democratic system that guarantees that everyone, including the President, is ruled by the same laws of the land. On the other hand, in non-literate, ancient African societies like those Chinua Achebe romanticized in his rural novels, *Things Fall Apart* and *Arrow of God*, readers can also find systems of governance established by Igbo religious, sociocultural, and political leaders, which were based on their traditional religion, cultural norms, and ethos to regulate the actions and lives of their people. Although those societies had oral traditions, their governing authorities unquestionably had positive aspirations to produce good and effective governance like those found in literate societies. In other words, the ancient Igbo systems, however imperfect they may appear to modern readers, ostensibly worked well for the people until the arrival of the British in their land. As a result, the encounter between the two peoples contributed profoundly to things falling apart for the Igbo religiously, culturally, politically, and economically. Hence, for Achebe, a candid exploration of the colonial and postcolonial conflicts between the British colonial powers and the Igbo native authorities on one hand, and those between the native authorities themselves on the other, became an overarching theme of his rural novels.

Writing under the topic "The novelist as teacher," Achebe explained why he was so driven to restoring, albeit fictionally, the sociocultural and political systems of his native Igbo when he said, "I would be quite satisfied if my novels (especially the ones I set in the past) did no more than teach my readers that their past – with all its imperfections – was not one long night of savagery from which the first Europeans acting on God's behalf delivered them."[1] Before that,

DOI: 10.4324/9781003184133-11

however, while discussing "The role of the writer in a new nation," Achebe said the following:

> For me, at any rate there is a clear need to make a statement. This is my answer to those who say that the writer should be writing about contemporary issues – about politics in 1964, about city life, about the last coup d'état. Of course, these are legitimate themes for the writer but as far as I am concerned the fundamental theme must first be disposed of. This theme – put quite simply – is that African peoples did not hear of culture for the first time from Europeans; that their societies were not mindless but frequently had a philosophy of great depth and value and beauty, that they had poetry and, above all, they had dignity. It is this dignity that many African people all but lost during the colonial period and it is this that they must now regain.[2]

The systems of governance that brought the Igbo people together, of which Achebe spoke, derived from their cosmological beliefs and a worldview which began "in the very distant past, when lizards were still few and far between the six villages – Umuachala, Umunneora, Umuagu, Umuezeani, Umuogwugwu and Umuisiuzo – lived as different peoples, and each worshipped its own deity,"[3] which I characterized as Igbo folkways in one of my books.[4] Some of these ways are folktales, proverbs, proper names, rituals, and festivals. Achebe beautifully expressed all of them poetically and metaphorically in virtually all of his five novels.

With the hindsight of over four decades of studying his novels, I must say that Achebe deserves all the acknowledgments and praises that literary critics from all over the world have been showering on him; for they attest to the tremendous impact of his arrival on the African literary landscape that began in 1958. Moreover, the crafting and publication of his first novel, *Things Fall Apart*, alongside his *magnum opus*, *Arrow of God*, persuaded some renowned critics to proclaim him the founder of the modern African novel, but that is not to say for sure that he is the founder of African literature, as other critics have also dubbed him. Nevertheless, it doesn't matter which of the two proclamations of Achebe's role as a literary ancestor a reader chooses to accept. What resonates with me, however, is that upon his graduation from the London University College at Ibadan, Nigeria, Achebe began his writing as a form of protest exercise, which challenged what he read from British novels on Africa – the notion that Africans had no respectable cultures and civilizations – and eventuated in sustained, thorough, and careful criticisms of the prejudiced colonizers' novels on Africa, such as Joseph Conrad's *Heart of Darkness* and Joyce Cary's *Mister Johnson*. Blessed with a vivid imagination for creative writing and a formal education in Western culture (especially comparative literature and religion), coupled with his informal education in Igbo storytelling that he received from his elder sister, Achebe positioned himself firmly in the role of the novelist as teacher – a self-imposed role that he distinctively played until his death in 2013.

In *Arrow of God*, the governing authorities in Umuaro clan are specifically Ezeulu the Chief Priest of Ulu, who serves as the clan's ritual and religious leader;

the priests of deities of the six villages that constitute the clan; the clan's titled and political elders (*ndichie*); and, the unseen but ubiquitous presence of the dead-living ancestors among living people. Achebe succinctly delineates the political failures of the clan, tracing their roots to the power struggle and political maneuverings of the rulers, who are purportedly backed by their various deities, and sees them as the main source of the divisions in their once-united clan. In other words, the ruling elders' impious and unethical struggle for power created hydra-headed conflicts in their society and, in the process, they committed *nso ala*, an abominable offense against Ala, also known as the Earth Goddess – an offense that necessitated a propitiatory sacrifice, albeit involuntarily, with the life of one of their own clansmen, Obika, the son of Ezeulu. Emmanuel Obiechina describes the complex conflicts in Umuaro as follows:

> The conflicts in *Arrow of God* develop around the person of the Chief Priest of Ulu, who is the ritual and religious leader in Umuaro. On the one hand, there is conflict between the local British administration represented by the old-fashioned administrator, Winterbottom, and the native authority repre- sented by the Chief Priest. On the other hand, there are the internal politics of Umuaro and the conflict between the supporters of the Chief Priest and those of his rival, Idemili. On yet another level belongs the conflict taking place within the Chief Priest himself, a conflict between personal power, the temptation to constitute himself into an "arrow" of God, and the exigencies of public responsibility. All these are handled in the main plot. A subsidiary plot deals with the domestic tensions and crises in Ezeulu's own house, the tensions and stresses between the father and his grown-up sons and between the children of different mothers in his polygamous household.[5]

The Umuaro internal conflicts, in the form of a sociocultural and political power struggle between ruling elders, could not have come at a worse time when Igboland and adjacent West African territories had just been amalgamated, colonized, and named Nigeria by Great Britain at the turn of the twentieth century. Ordinarily, one would expect such conflicts and power struggles in the novel between Umuaro clan elders to have been between Igbo political leaders and their counterparts from other Nigerian ethnic groups, or between the Umuaro clan and other Igbo clans. Unfortunately, however, the conflicts between members of the same clan of six villages aptly exemplify the pan-Igbo apothegm, "When two brothers fight a stranger reaps the harvest" (*Arrow of God*, p. 131). Contextually, the immediate beneficiaries of the clan's internal conflicts are the newly established European church and school, which the missionaries built under the leadership of Mr. Goodcountry, and the British political officials, who appointed Ezeulu a warrant chief, a role that he nevertheless rebuffed, saying: "Tell the white man that Ezeulu will not be anybody's chief, except Ulu" (p. 174).

This article discusses how Chinua Achebe's critical analysis of Igbo intra-ethnic conflicts between Umuaro elders in *Arrow of God*, which weakened their clan for easy colonization by the British, can be seen as a foretaste of Igbo people's

problems in the postwar Nigerian geopolitical system. More specifically, it discusses the inability of the Igbo political elite to speak with one voice in matters affecting the Igbo nation as an ethnic group. In addition, it highlights the
negative effects of some Igbo communities denying their prewar Igbo origin and
identity because mainland Igbo people, who fought as leaders on the Biafran
side of the Nigeria-Biafra War, were defeated. And it examines the unwholesome
changes in the Igbo value system and ethos since the end of that war and, currently, the inherent lack of a strong political will and leadership whenever Igbo
political representatives engage in fights with other Nigerian ethnic groups for
their fair share of "the national cake."

Even though some individual Igbo persons have been appointed every now
and then by non-Igbo political rulers to serve as leaders in various areas of Nigerian governance, we as an ethnic group seem to lack the prewar unity, courage,
and strategies that should have enabled us to produce a Nigerian president of
Igbo extraction as the other two dominant ethnic groups – the Hausa/Fulani and
the Yoruba – have been doing since the end of the civil war. Instead, we keep
lamenting our marginalization by other ethnic groups without doing much critical analysis of our plight, which could enable us to realize how and where "the
rain began to beat us" as a people. Hence, it is my hope that when we do sincere
soul-searching with a view to correcting our sociopolitical blunders, then we will
one day rise up to fight for our rightful position in our country so that other
ethnic groups cannot continue to see us as postwar exiles or aliens. Instead, they
would recognize us as the proud builders of Nigeria that we have always been.

In the novel, the narrator, who speaks on behalf of Achebe, on one hand
describes what evil things happened to the ancient Igbo clan of six villages when
they chose to live separately in disunity, and on the other hand describes the
good things they experienced when they decided to unite and find positive ways
of solving the problems their common enemy created for them:

> [The] six villages of Umuachala, Umunneora, Umuagu, Umuezeani, Umuog-
> wugwu and Umuisiuzo lived as different peoples, and each worshipped its
> own deity. Then the hired soldiers of Abam who used to strike in the dead of
> night, set fire to their houses and carry men, women and children into slav-
> ery. Things were so bad for the six villages that their leaders came together
> to save themselves. They hired a strong team of medicine-men to install a
> common deity for them. This deity which the fathers of the six villages made
> was called Ulu. Half of the medicine was buried at a place which became
> Nkwo market and the other half thrown into the stream which became Mili
> Ulu. The six villages then took the name of Umuaro, and the priest of Ulu
> became their Chief Priest. From that day they were never again beaten by
> an enemy.
>
> (pp. 14–15)

Anecdotally, Achebe drew inspiration for developing this part of the novel's
plot from an old Igbo adage, "Divided we fall but united we stand," which should

have inspired our present-day Igbo leaders in all walks of life to work for our ethnic unity in Nigeria and in the Diaspora. For adopting the adage in our daily lives would not only promote our collective progress, security, and development but also our social, political, and economic survival and wellbeing in any community where we live as a people. Unfortunately, however, that unity has persistently eluded us since the end of the civil war, and it even appears unreachable to many people, partly because of the evil deeds fellow Nigerians from other ethnic extractions continually do to us, and partly because of those evils that we inflict upon ourselves as a people. Hence, any candid discussions of both obstacles in our way to regaining our collective prewar unity and political leadership, which made us an enviable ethnic people in Nigeria, should help us to find our way out of our sociopolitical troubles quicker. When that happens, then no other ethnic groups can successfully thwart our unity, nor would that unity seem to us unachievable anymore.

The Nigerian civil war, also known as the Nigeria-Biafra War (1967–1970), brought unimaginable destruction upon the once lush and exquisitely idyllic Igboland as well as on the psyche of its proud and prosperous inhabitants. The people generally contributed enviable high-level educated personnel to the Nigerian labor force pool, which comprised civil service technocrats, teachers, and scientists, as well as millionaires, savvy politicians, and cultural icons. For that reason, Igbo talents were sought after like a beautiful bride by every administration of the Federal Government of Nigeria before the war. And because of their enterprising and entrepreneurial spirit, as well as their unflinching belief in Nigeria as one indivisible nation, the Igbo lived in all corners of the country, where they worked very hard to live in peace with others as neighbors. And yet, despite the patriotic sacrifices they made to develop the country right from the beginning, the Igbo were brutally attacked and slaughtered like animals, raped and treated like common criminals, and chased out of Northern Nigeria like aliens in their own country during the riots that followed Nigeria's first bloody coup on January 15, 1966.

Most unfortunately, the Igbo erroneously thought that the barbaric acts meted out to them during these Northern riots, which forced them and other Easterners to return to their native Eastern Nigeria, were just temporary incidents. Shortly thereafter, the federal military government realized that it could not find people to take over the irreplaceable Igbo services in the North. So they asked the charismatic military governor of their native Eastern Nigeria, Col. Chukwuemeka Odumegwu Ojukwu, for help by asking Igbo civil servants to go back to their stations in the North. As a military officer, the governor promptly obeyed the orders and made the appeal. Some of the workers blindly trusted and obeyed him, even as they privately counted their human and material losses with fortitude and rectitude. The turn of events made Ojukwu to regret for the rest of his life making that deadly appeal to his people.

Furthermore, following the example of the civil servants, the business class returned to the North, believing that the fractured nation could be healed soon. They also trusted that the federal military government's avowed promise would promptly quell the riots and guarantee them protection while they lived and worked there. Unfortunately, it was not until the onslaught of the second, third, and fourth bloody coups of May 29, July 29, and September 29, 1966, in which they were again systematically slaughtered in cold blood in the North and in some parts of Western Nigeria, that the Igbo belatedly realized that they were no longer welcomed in those regions of the country they had assiduously worked to develop. In the end, their gory experiences forced them back as refugees to Eastern Nigeria, where they were eagerly embraced by their kith and kin, and by an overwhelmed but empathetic, caring government that gave them both spiritual and material support. The Igbo adage, *"Onye aghala nwanne ya,"* [May no one leave their brother or sister behind], worked magically to save the Igbo nation in a time of need.

Finally, when all entreaties from the then Eastern Nigerian Government to the federal military government failed to bring the much desired peace and reconciliation between the two governments, the people of Eastern Nigeria were compelled by the events of those cruel months to declare themselves a separate country, the Republic of Biafra, under Governor Ojukwu, who later was promoted the *People's General*, as president. About a month after the declaration, Col. Yakubu Gowon, then head of the federal military government, declared war on the young republic in which, during 30 grueling months of strife, millions of Igbo people were killed, their grown-up girls and women raped, the pregnant ones disemboweled, and their young children and babies starved to death. So, to prevent further calamities, General Ojukwu flew out of the country "in search of peace with Nigeria" from some friendly African and European political leaders. In his absence, however, representatives of his military cabinet and civil political leaders surrendered Biafra to Nigeria to prevent the imminent annihilation of their people and destruction of their territory – a bold and courageous move that brought the war to an abrupt end on January 15, 1970. Although it was a relief to both sides, it marked the beginning of more agony for the ex-Biafrans who lost the war and were forced back to a country that had attempted to annihilate them all.

Like Ezeulu's polygamous family in *Arrow of God*, the Igbo ethnic group comprises men, women, and children who live in diverse clans and villages; they trace their origins to blood-related ancestors. Hence, their clan or village names begin with the prefix "Umu," which means *"children of"* as in the names of the six villages that comprise the Umuaro clan. Therefore, it behooves every clan member, no matter their particular village, to work for the growth, progress, stability, peace, and unity of the clan. If there is failure in any aspect of the clan's corporate life, all the clan members are held responsible for the failure and condemned for bringing disappointment and shame to their dead-living ancestors – a failure that portends the metaphoric death of their proud nation. The same philosophical and ethical beliefs regulate the actions and behaviors of Igbo people in general, no matter where they live and have their being. As it was in precolonial era, gods, oracles, and divination continue to play the important role of maintaining order and balance in Igbo clans and villages. They promote and foster peace and unity among the people, even though many of them now live in towns, cities, and foreign lands. So, whenever and wherever the people gather for meetings and ceremonies, they first have to break kola nuts and pour libation to their dead-living ancestors as a way of inviting them from *Ala mmuo* (spirit world) to accompany living human beings whose affairs they guide. After the kola-breaking and libation-pouring ritual, the oldest man calls the meeting to order by bellowing the phrase "Umuaro *kwenu!*" and the people answer "*Hem!*" in unison, which is the equivalent of "Amen" in Christianity or Judaism. For, it is a call-and-answer ritual that binds all those who utter it to the execution of whatever decisions they arrive at during their group deliberations. If after agreeing with others before men and the dead-living ancestors, a person flouts the decisions made at the meeting, they are punished by the omnipotent, omnipresent, and omniscient gods and goddesses for committing *nso ala*, an offense against the Earth Goddess Ala, who is in charge of the people's morality and ethos, as well as human, animal, and plant fertility. That is why all Igbo customs derive from, or are anchored on, a worldview known as *omenala*: that which is rooted on the ground. Therefore, for the Igbo, the whole Earth or ground, not just a specific portion of it, is sacred. Hence, right from their infancy, Igbo people are taught not to misuse or abuse the Earth or to take untrue oaths with sand or soil taken from the ground. Furthermore, they are not expected to tell the truth only when they are sworn to do so under oath, for they believe that the eyes of the dead-living ancestors are always upon them. Whenever they misbehave, even in private, the gods and goddesses must surely punish them in public.

In *Things Fall Apart*, whose events predated those of *Arrow of God*, the narrator laments the Igbo people's loss of their primordial piety, patriotism, and ability to fight a common enemy in defense of their clan. They attribute the loss to the presence of the British colonial master in their midst who is ignorant of the Igbo customary laws on land use. That is why when Okonkwo, who still embodies all of those great Igbo attributes now moribund, asks his friend Obierika, "Does the white man understand our custom about land?" Obierika replies in grief as follows:

> How can he when he does not even speak our tongue? But he says that our customs are bad; and our own brothers who have taken up his religion also say our customs are bad. How do you think we can fight when our own brothers have turned against us? The white man is very clever. He came quietly and peaceably with his religion. We were amused at his foolishness and allowed him to stay. Now he has won our brothers, and our clan can no longer act like one. He has put a knife on the things that held us together and we have fallen apart.
>
> (*Things Fall Apart*, p. 176)

Some of the factors that held the ancient Igbo people together were their customs and worldview, as well as their traditional religion, called *Igo mmuo*, which the white missionaries saw as heathen and fetish, hence condemnable.

For that reason, while some Igbo traditionalists held on to their traditional ways of life, the new Christian converts and Western-educated Igbo were bent on bringing some changes into old Igbo ways of life, and the changes resulted in dangerous divisions in their communities. And even though their ancestors fought hard to resist being colonized by the encroaching foreign powers, their colonizers ultimately succeeded in opening up the erstwhile closed Igbo societies to foreigners who brought in their religion, education, and employments to the native people. Consequently, such foreign elements became anathema to the internal weaknesses of ancient Igbo customary practices, such as the killing of twin babies and the banishment of their mothers to evil forests, as well as dedicating some free people to serve as priests of the gods and goddesses and branding them as *osu*, the untouchable people.

Furthermore, despite some obvious benefits of the British colonial system in Nigeria, many Igbo people continued to lament what the new dispensation did to their societies: that colonialism seriously affected their ability to speak with one voice as they used to in precolonial eras, this being part of its effort to destroy all their traditional ways, including those that promoted peace and unity among the people. Nevertheless, although Igbo culture was not built on granite, it was not so fragile that the British agents could destroy it completely. That is why, in contemporary Nigeria, the indigenous Igbo culture is able to coexist with the foreign ones, such as the British and the American.

The ability of the Igbo culture to coexist with other cultures was due to a stoic and resilient spirit. Once Great Britain found an irremovable foothold in Nigeria, the Igbo ethnic group quickly devised some clever ways to hold on to their customs and traditions in spite of the serious threats the colonial authorities posed. Politically, they exploited the British parliamentary system of governance in Nigeria, which had three strong regional governments and a central government that was not so strong in Lagos, then the capital of Nigeria. For the British allowed each of the regional governments (with capitals in Enugu for Eastern Nigeria, Ibadan for Western Nigeria, and Kaduna for Northern Nigeria) to maintain their individual and unique paces of development. In their sociopolitical practices, the Igbo-dominated Eastern Region, in Southern Nigeria, was a model region in terms of governance, education, and management of its natural and human resources; so was the Yoruba government of Western Region, also in Southern Nigeria. But the Hausa/Fulani-dominated Northern Region, in Northern Nigeria, was behind those of the two southern regions. I believe that the disparity between the northern and southern regions, in terms of their internal developments, was largely due to the differences in their respective precolonial histories, including their divergent religious, educational, and cultural backgrounds, as well as their political viewpoints, all of which are discussed in detail in Obaro Ikime's edited book, *Groundwork of Nigerian History*.[6]

At the end of the civil war, some Igbo communities outside the Igbo heartland were enticed to renounce their Igbo heritage for political and financial advantage. For example, the Igbo people who lived before the war in Port Harcourt Province of Eastern Nigeria became part of a new state, named Rivers State, which the federal military government carved out of the erstwhile Eastern Nigeria on May 27, 1967. Thereafter, in the mid-1970s, the state government hired Kay Williamson, a British linguist who specialized in the study of African languages, to develop linguistic studies of the languages of the Niger Delta, especially Ijaw, which she offered as a course at the University of Port Harcourt. While doing her studies, she changed the names of the Igbo communities in the state to sound Ijaw. For instance, the original Igbo community of Umumasi became Rumumasi, and Umuodumaya became Rumuodumaya. As a reaction to the changes, many mainland Igbo scholars argued that the Igbo inhabitants of those areas supported the state government's move to enable them to dissociate themselves from the political "sins" that the "secessionist" Igbo people committed against Nigeria when they led the Biafran cause of the civil war. From then onwards, some of the politicians of Igbo descent in Rivers State changed their attitude toward mainland Igbo people to the extent that they even colluded with their government to confiscate Igbo landed properties whose owners had left behind when they fled the state at the onset of the war.

However, the more devastating effect of the change in the attitudes of some Rivers State politicians was the disunity it brought into the global Igbo ethnic nation. For example, the governor of that state, Chibuike Amaechi (2007–2015), who rode on the political coattails of another Rivers State governor of Igbo descent, Hon. Peter Odili, categorically disavowed his Igbo descent and heritage when he came to New Jersey to receive "The 2013 Quintessence Award" given by an Igbo book publisher, Dr. Ugorji O. Ugorji. In his acceptance remarks before some Nigerian Americans – I was one of them on the occasion – Governor Amaechi opined that unlike other ethnic groups (including his own Ikwerre group) the Igbo were naïve in the way they were playing politics in contemporary Nigeria. Like a drunken masquerade, he went around Nigeria fighting President Goodluck Jonathan, a fellow People's Democratic Party (PDP) politician from the same South-South geopolitical zone. As he viciously attacked the president politically with reckless abandon, he fell out of favor with many of his political associates, including members of his cabinet such as Chief Nyesom Ezenwo Wike who fought back and won the May 2015 gubernatorial election, thus becoming governor of Rivers State on the platform of the PDP, instead of that of All Progressives Congress (APC), Amaechi's new political party.

Savvy Nigerian political observers and media gurus, who followed Amaechi's political activities, opined that he not only decamped from PDP, which made him a state governor but also took with him many members of the party to the APC party so he could become a running mate to Maj-Gen. Muhammadu Buhari, who quickly made him head of his presidential election campaign organization. And even though Amaechi acknowledged on several occasions that he was not Igbo, yet in the dying days of the campaigns he brought Buhari to the Igbo Enyimba City of Aba to campaign for him, hypocritically claiming there and then in public that he was after all an Igboman. He also thought that the Igbo people would easily forget his condemnation of President Jonathan for helping Igbo people develop some parts of the South East geopolitical zone. He urged other Nigerians not to support the president's bid for reelection because, according to him, the president's development effort was tantamount to rehabilitation of the former Biafran enclave: "The Governor Amaechi in an interview with AIT television said that President Jonathan has developed Abia and Imo but he has refused to develop Rivers. Are we Biafrans?"[7] In the end, however, Governor Amaechi failed woefully in his attempt to become the vice president of Nigeria; neither did he win his state's electoral votes for the APC.

In contrast to Amaechi's negative effort, all the five South East states voted for President Jonathan because of what he did politically for their development. Although he did not win the presidency, the grateful Igbo nation did not regret casting their votes for a man who helped to make their sociopolitical lives a little better than they were before his tenure. In essence, Amaechi's political fights with President Jonathan and members of the PDP brought so much destruction to the human and natural resources of Rivers State that his political mentor, the former Governor Odili, publicly expressed his regret for having worked hard to make Amaechi his successor in office. Nevertheless, while the political struggle between Amaechi and Wike continues, politicians of non-Igbo descent in the state have been watching both of them in utter disdain and disbelief. Their fight once again reminds people of the Igbo adage, "When two brothers fight, a stranger reaps the benefits." Every Igbo person is anxiously waiting for the time when the two Igbo political gladiators' quarrels would end in Rivers State and its environs.

The devastating political wrangle and disunity that Nigerians are currently witnessing among politicians of Igbo descent in Rivers State are a child's play when compared to what has been happening in all five mainland Igbo states since the end of military administrations in Nigeria. In Anambra State, for example, after Governor Chinwoke Mbadinuju (May 29, 1999 to May 29, 2003) finished his tenure in office under PDP, Chris Ngige of PDP and Peter Obi of All Progressives Grand Alliance (APGA) competed to succeed him. Although Peter Obi won the election, Chris Ngige and his party managed to deprive him of victory, an act that led to Ngige becoming governor from May 23, 2003 to March 17, 2006. However, through the concerted effort of APGA and the indefatigable General Ojukwu, Peter Obi regained the stolen mandate. That was after three years of brutal court battles. He became the state governor from March 17, 2006 through November 3, 2006; but the state legislature impeached him for alleged gross misconduct. In his place, the deputy governor, Dame Virginia Etiaba, was appointed to serve as governor on November 3, 2006. Three months later, she transferred her powers back to Peter Obi on February 9, 2007. In the interim, a PDP candidate, Emmanuel Nnamdi Uba (Andy Uba), was elected and sworn in as governor of the state on May 27, 2007, but he was removed by a Supreme Court decision on June 18, 2007. That means he illegally governed the state for only 22 days. On the other hand, Governor Peter Obi served as the duly elected governor from February 9, 2007 to March 17, 2014. He was reportedly the first modern Nigerian governor to leave office with a surplus in the state's coffers. Thereafter, he was succeeded in office by another APGA candidate, Willie Obiano, who won the election and began serving as governor of the state from March 17, 2014 up to now. He is said to have since completed most of the projects Governor Obi left uncompleted and then some. So far, most Anambra people love and respect him for the work he is doing in all parts of the state.

From the foregoing, one can see that there was a lot of political dysfunction in the state, which produced six governors in 11 years – a period of time that should have been the constitutional tenure of only three governors. It was a period marked by political godfatherism, blatant rigging of elections by PDP, politically motivated kidnappings of people, wanton destruction of people's lives and property, as well as many incidents of arson. Regrettably, during the dark period, Anambra State, which had boasted politicians of "timber and caliber" such as Dr. Nnamdi Azikiwe, Dr. Nwafor Orizu, Dr. Kingsley Ozumba Mbadiwe, Dr. Alex Ekwueme, and General Chukwuemeka Odumegwu Ojukwu, became the most politically violent state in the post-era of military administrations in Nigeria. And there were no effective political interventions by some of its clear-headed sociopolitical and religious leaders.

As a politically conscious Igboman, what bothered me most about the situation is that a revered politician like Dr. Alex Ekwueme from Anambra State could not make the warring politicians in his home state see reason in what they were doing as he did whenever there was political turmoil at the national scene. He served meritoriously as vice president of Nigeria during the postwar civilian administration of Alhaji Shehu Shagari (1979–1983), was a founding member of the PDP in 1998, introduced and canvassed the concept of geopolitical zones in the country, served as a PDP presidential candidate in 1999 and as chair of PDP Board of Trustees for a considerable period of time. In addition, in consideration of his negotiation skills, President Olusegun Obasanjo sent him all over the country to troubleshoot political problems in the PDP constituencies. And he did so with great success that earned him the respect and admiration of the political class from all ethnic and political spectrums. The question then arises, "Why didn't he succeed in quelling the internal political quagmire in his native Anambra State?" Or, as the Igbo would ask proverbially, "How could an old man sit idly by and watch his tethered goat suffer the pains of parturition without giving her any assistance?" Although many political observers think that that was what he did, no one could tell with certainty the extent to which he tried privately to make peace among his people but in the end failed. The curious thing though is that although he was aware of the criticisms, as a very private person, Dr. Alex Ekwueme refused to stoop and quibble with his critics, whether informed or uninformed.

While the political dysfunction went on in Anambra State, another Igbo state, Abia State, seemed to enjoy initial stability in its governance under Governor Orji Uzor Kalu of the Progressive Peoples Alliance (PPA). It was a mini party he formed for the South East geopolitical region to checkmate such other regional parties as All Peoples Party (APP) – primarily for Northerners, and Alliance for Democracy (AD) – primarily for the South West. Governor Kalu was so successful in controlling his government functionaries as the party's leader that he completed two terms in office (May 29, 1999 to May 2007). Thereafter, he was also successful in handing over power to his chief of staff and protégé, Chief Theodore A. Orji, whom he helped to win the gubernatorial election on a PPA platform from prison under some dubious circumstances. But while in office, Governor Orji defected to PDP and allegedly ruled the state like a tyrant for two terms (May 29, 2007 to May 29, 2015). Ultimately, he and Governor Kalu clashed and became mortal enemies. As a consequence, Governor Kalu's political appointees whom Governor Orji retained in his administration found themselves dispensable and ultimately relieved of their positions.

Furthermore, unlike Governor Kalu, his political mentor and predecessor who brought visible developments in the commercial city of Aba, rebuilt some state roads and paid state workers' salaries regularly most of the time, Governor Orji did more to help himself and members of his immediate family than he did for the people of the state. Many of them allege that he converted some public facilities into his personal businesses, especially those sited at Umuahia, the state capital and his birthplace. There were also some published and privately asserted incidents of the governor bulldozing the landed properties of his neighbors, especially those he disagreed with politically before and during his tenure as governor. Reportedly, his son, Chinedum Orji, fired at will some state commissioners he did not like and replaced them with those who were willing to become his stooges. His doting father accepted his recommendations enthusiastically. Also, Chinedum so intimidated many other state workers that they lost their freedom of speech for fear of being removed from office, physically manhandled, or even killed. Finally, on leaving office, Governor Orji created a strong niche for Chinedum in the Abia State House of Assembly where he now serves as a member.

But the most despicable political decision Governor Theodore A. Orji made, which momentarily brought a visible crack in the unity of the Igbo nation, was firing all workers from other Igbo states who had lived and worked in Abia State even long before he became the governor. And yet, Abia State indigenes working in other Igbo states were retained and treated as brothers by their respective governors. It took the effort of the apex Igbo sociocultural organization, Ohanaeze Ndigbo, to dissuade the governors from retaliating in the national interest of Igbo ethnic unity.

Against the backdrop of these allegations of corruption against the former governor, a voluntary association of concerned Abia citizens, "Save Abia Initiative for Change (SAIC)" has petitioned the Economic and Financial Crimes Commission (EFCC) "detailing how the erstwhile governor, Chief Theodor Orji, his wife, Mercy Odochi, their son, Chinedum (a. k. a. Ikuku) and a few of their cronies allegedly squandered N474 billion of Abia State funds between 2011 and this year."[8]

In contrast to the disappointing roles that some Igbo politicians in both Igbo mainland and elsewhere played that brought disunity in the Igbo nation, other politicians of Igbo descent outside the mainland have played roles that demonstrate in practical terms the adage that where people have the will, there can be unity in spite of the great odds against them. For example, the Igbo sociopolitical leaders in the old Bendel State, now Delta State, have done things in present Nigerian geopolitics that have not only showcased their love of country, but also the love and defense of Igbo ethnic nationalism to the admiration of all fair-minded Igbo people both in Nigeria and in the Diaspora. This they did in spite of the slaughter of the Niger Igbo in Asaba during the war because they supported the Biafran cause and were being exterminated by the Nigerian armed forces. Anyone who reads the gory experience of the Niger Igbo in Emma Okocha's book, *Blood on the Niger,*[9] cannot but marvel why their love of the Igbo nation is so great and unshakable.

One of those Igbo personalities from Delta State who helped to foster Igbo ethnic unity and nationalism is Col. J. O. G. Achuzia. Those of us who were old enough to experience the Nigeria-Biafra War are familiar with the story of how he gallantly fought the war in defense of "Biafra as an experiment of the black man's ability to survive in the face of an impossible living history," which earned him the monikers "Hannibal" and "Air Raid." Although Biafra collapsed, it continued to exist as a noble idealistic struggle in the hearts and souls of patriotic Igbo people now dubbed ex-Biafrans. Achuzia's roles in that war and what Biafra meant – and continues to mean – to many an Igbo man is brilliantly discussed in his book, *Requiem Biafra: The True Story of Nigeria's Civil War.*[10] Furthermore, since after the war, Achuzia has been fighting with the same soldierly zeal in the major Igbo sociocultural organization, Ohanaeze Ndigbo, to ensure that the marginalization of the Igbo people in the Nigerian nation state becomes a thing of the past. Hence, some Igbo people like me applaud him for his unalloyed Igbo ethnic patriotism and nationalism. May he live long for the benefit of our people!

Another great personality of Igbo descent from Delta State is Ralph Uwechue, who was a former Nigerian career diplomat. In 1966, he opened Nigeria's embassy in France. However, "strongly disagreeing with the federal government's handling of the situation produced by the massacres of September 1966, he decided to quit the federal service to help present the case of the Igbo to the French world. This he did with remarkable effect in his capacity as Biafra's representative." But he resigned that appointment in December 1968 "in protest against the Biafran leadership's attitude towards absolute sovereignty." Most of his thoughts on the Nigerian civil war can be found in his book, *Reflections on the Nigerian Civil War: Facing the Future.*[11] Although many ex-Biafrans were disappointed in what he did then, they are currently happy with what he did since after the war. He became a great advocate for the unity and survival of the Igbo nation inside Nigeria and in the Diaspora. Specifically, he worked assiduously to unite the Igbo people in Rivers and Delta States. One easily admires how politically savvy and well-informed he was by reading his published analysis of the Igbo situation in present Nigerian geopolitics as revealed in the interview he granted to *The Sun News Publishing,* titled "How Zik Stopped Nigeria from Breaking up in 1957" (See *The Sun News online,* Wednesday, March 10, 2010). He also served as one in the leadership cadre of Ohanaeze Ndigbo and later became its president before he died in 2014. His political sagacity is missed by patriotic Igbo persons today.

Among the people Ambassador Uwechue lionized in the interview is his fellow Delta Igbo, Prof. Patrick O. Utomi. Many Igbo people (especially me) consider him as their personal hero because he epitomizes all the attributes one finds in a phenomenal Igbo person: acquisition of higher education, professional excellence, civil rights advocacy and rule of law, uncommon political leadership, and endless committed service to one's community. Professor Utomi is a native of Igbuzo in the Oshimili North Local Government Area of Delta State. After attending high school and the University of Nigeria, Nsukka, where he earned a bachelor's degree in Mass Communication, he came to the USA for graduate studies, where he earned his Ph.D, MPA, and MA at Indiana University in Bloomington. He also became a scholar-in-residence at Harvard Business School and the American University in Washington, DC. Thus, academically and professionally equipped, Utomi returned to Nigeria to serve both the Nigerian nation and his people, including his Igbuzo community and the Igbo people at home and in the Diaspora. He helped to reenergize Ohanaeze Ndigbo and raised the political profile of the Igbo nation when he ran as a candidate for the office of the Nigerian presidency in 2007 and 2011. Although he did not win, he became a powerful force that no Nigerian politician or political party can ignore. Hence, he has served some Nigerian presidents, especially President Jonathan, as an official or private advisor. Furthermore, he successfully co-founded a political party ADC as well as some banks and businesses that have created numerous employment opportunities for many Nigerians. He is the author of several management and public policy books that professional organizations and universities have adopted in Nigeria and abroad. If I were to speculate on this quintessential Igbo son's greatest achievement, I would say it is his service to his people as the traditional ruler of Asaba, an ideal, if exemplary, Igbo community, and his indefatigable effort to restore the dignity of the postwar Igbo nation in Nigeria. I personally pray than he runs again for the Nigerian presidency in future.

Another major cause of Igbo marginalization in present-day Nigerian geopolitics is the unwholesome changes that have occurred in the postwar Igbo value system and ethos. As an enterprising ethnic group, the Igbo people have always pursued every legal and ethical means of acquiring wealth for the common good of the community. For example, in the ancient clan of Arochukwu, the people's entrepreneurial and frontier spirit drove them to various places in precolonial Eastern Nigeria where they founded plantations that they called *uno ubi* – an act that earned them the moniker "Aro Okigbo," which means "Aro the great Igbo people." They live in the present-day Arochukwu Local Government Area in Abia State. In those primordial years, they developed their own peculiar governance, a code language, *Insibiri*, and commercial systems, which the British missionaries and government functionaries waged battles to destroy. But their failure to win the cultural battles caused the British to respect and work with the Aro people – a bold act that elevated their status as a strong clan in Igboland and Nigeria as a whole.

In the same manner, the people of Abiriba developed commercial, trade, and blacksmithing businesses, collectively called *ikpu ozu*, which took them everywhere in Eastern Nigeria. In their trade and commercial industry, they specialized in smuggling illicit goods from foreign countries, especially secondhand clothes, stock fish, tobacco, and hot drinks into Nigeria. Through such enterprises, the men and their young apprentices made a lot of money and became rich, not just for the benefit of their immediate families but also for the entire community. In fact, the Abiriba business class and artisans were so successful in what they did that they built secondary schools and hospitals for the clan without any government assistance that made Abiriba one of the most developed clans in Igboland. People in Old Bende used to refer to the clan as "Small London." In addition, they gave massive university scholarship awards to their young men and women to study in local and foreign universities. And during the civil war, Abiriba businesspeople purchased and smuggled food, medicine, and small arms into Biafra to feed and protect all the people in their clan and its environs, regardless of their socioeconomic class and gender.

Some of these altruistic endeavors, enviable community development efforts, and time-tested commonweal aspirations found in Arochukwu and Abiriba clans could be found also in other Igbo communities, though not in the same scope or amplitude. If you were a rich farmer, you could take titles involving the slaughter of cows to feast a whole village with yam foo-foo and drinks. That way, you became *Ogbuefi* – killer of cows. From time to time though, the villagers would offer free labor on your farms in appreciation of how well you have been supporting and caring for them as a rich *brother*. As a village elder, you would take care of orphans and widows and always find a way to make peace between warring neighbors without the involvement of police and the courts. Above all, the seasonal rituals and ceremonies were staged in the village to promote the unity and comradeship of the people who are descendants of a common ancestor and should not wage wars against each other. For the security of the people, men sent their able-bodied sons to serve in the village vigilante outfit. And finally, because of the sense of unity inculcated in the people to defend all aspects of their communal life, there was peace in those rural communities most of the time. Nevertheless, all this could not happen if there were no established mechanisms to maintain law and order in the villages, which no villager, however rich or powerful, could impugn without incurring severe sanctions and punishment from their gods and goddesses and human authorities.

Unfortunately, however, such neighborly attitudes of the villagers changed after the war. People began to pursue the acquisition of wealth for the benefit of their nuclear families only. The moral and ethical standards that used to guide their behavior drastically changed, ostensibly because people now lived outside their villages and clans most of the time. Anyone who is able to defraud or steal from other people and thereby become rich overnight is applauded by some fellow villagers without qualms. And for too long, the broad day thievery has been happening to the extent that the village, which used to be the conscience of the people, is now deserted by the thieves and criminals who now make the towns, cities, and foreign countries their permanent abode. In the face of these reprehensible activities of some of our people, we the Igbo people need to go back to our spiritual past and pick up our abandoned prewar moral compass to enable us to live better lives morally and ethically.

Before the war, those who gave the Igbo nation visibility and recognition in Nigeria and Africa were the political class because of their selfless contributions to the country and the continent. Who could ever forget some of such great nationalists as Dr. Nnandi Azikiwe the great Zik of Africa, Dr. Nwafor Orizu, Dr. Michael Okpara, Dr. Kingsley Mbadiwe, Dr. Francis Akanu Ibiam, Dr. Alvan Ikoku, Mazi Mbonu Ojike (of the "boycott the boycottable" fame), Chief Dennis Chukudebe Osadebey, Dr. Okechukwu Ikejiani, Chief Jaja Wachuku, Chief Nathan Ejiogu, Chief Raymond Amanze Njoku, Chief Sam Ikoku, Chief Sam Mbakwe, and Mrs. Margaret Ekpo?

How many mansions and edifices did they build for themselves except when leading the war of independence against the British colonial powers that resulted in Nigeria attaining self-rule in 1957 and independence in 1960; building the first Nigerian indigenous bank, African Continental Bank, Enugu, in 1954; founding the first indigenous Nigerian university, the University of Nigeria, Nsukka, in 1955; founding the first indigenous Nigerian college of education, Alvan Ikoku College of Education, Owerri, in 1974; and, founding the first indigenous Nigerian state university, the Imo State University, Etiti, in 1981 for other Nigerian states to emulate? As one can clearly see, the Igbo elder statesmen were concerned only with contributing peace, unity, and progress to the Igbo nation in Nigeria and not with increasing their personal wealth or fame. The heroes' achievements speak eloquently for them after their deaths.

Now the question arises: Can anyone of us favorably compare what our current Igbo political class or leaders are doing with what our renowned past leaders did before? I personally do not think so. In fact, as a result of the creation of many states in Nigeria and the way the federal government has been sharing petro money to each state every month, many of the politicians – especially state governors, senators, and members of the House of Assembly and State Legislatures – have ample opportunities and the wherewithal to develop Igboland faster and better than their counterparts in the past and to promote peace, unity, and economic wellbeing for people in the South East geopolitical area if they if they wanted to. Unfortunately, however, because of their greediness, selfishness, mediocrity, political ineptitude, indiscipline, and what Achebe once called "crude showiness,"[12] the politicians are unable to forge any strong political bonds and leadership as well as the willpower that would enable them to fight for a fair share of the metaphoric Nigerian national cake. No, they could not even unite to recommend one additional Igbo state when it was rumored that the federal government might create one in the South East geopolitical zone to bring the number to six, the same number as in the five other geopolitical zones of the country. Instead, Ukwa and Ngwa clans in Abia State, Orlu and Uguta clans in Imo State, Nsukka and Awgu clans in Enugu State, and Afikpo and Edda clans in Ebonyi State, each want the one additional state to be created in their backyard, as it were. Thus, the other ethnic groups who have always been opposed to creating an additional state for the Igbo nation (for the sake of equity and balance) were happy about the Igbo political leaders' disunity and disagreement on the issue. What a shame and ethnic disgrace!

Even when they are given the opportunity by politicians from other ethnic groups to serve, the Igbo leaders squander their political capital very easily. We saw that happen during President Olusegun Obasanjo's two-term administration. Senator Evan Enwere was elected Senate President on June 3, 1999 but was sacked on November 18, 1999, following his impeachment; Senator (Dr.) Chuba Okadigbo served as Senate President from 1999 to 2000, and was also impeached; Senator Pius Anyim Pius served honorably as Senate President from 2000 to 2003; Senator Adolphus Wabara served as Senate President from 2003 to 2005 and resigned because of charges of corruption; and Senator Ken Nnamani served as Senate President as well from 2005 to 2007. In other words, within a period of eight years five Igbo senators served as presidents of the red chamber. One can see how disappointing their collective service and reputation (even though not all of them were bad) can be viewed by other Nigerian ethnic peoples, especially when compared to the tenure of the immediate past Senate President, Senator (General) David Mark from Benue State, who served from 2007 to 2015, which is eight consecutive years. And they sarcastically ask, "If the Igbo senators could not complete their senate presidency tenures meritoriously, how could anybody trust that they would do so if they were elected President of the Federal Republic of Nigeria?" What those Igbo senate presidents did can be seen proverbially as a case of one finger that collects dirty oil and smears other fingers with it. Hence, in our Igbo intra-ethnic democracy, all our smeared fingers must be washed clean.

Now that we have examined where the trouble with our Igbo ethnic people lies, the question becomes "What can we do to extricate ourselves from it?" First of all, we must decide that our collective problems are not unsurmountable, for other ethnic groups have had their own peculiar sociopolitical problems in the past and took care of them. The Yoruba and the Hausa/Fulani had their own share of problems in the 1960s, but after fighting each other for a while, they came together in unity and dealt with the problems. Who could forget the Yoruba division between the Awolowo and Akintola factions that partially caused the army to stage the first Nigerian bloody coup of January 15, 1966? For us Igbo people, our present task is to let the Igbo nation be Igbo again. Doing so involves harnessing our ethnic consciousness, all the brainpower, foresight, soul force, and determination that guided our past heroes to make the Igbo a great ethnic people in Nigeria. Even though my analysis of our situation has been focused on the sociopolitical class in Nigeria, we must also emphasize what we the Igbo people in the Diaspora can do to help our people in Nigeria solve the Igbo problems at home, because we have the higher education, more experience, and the wherewithal to deal with such problems without the fear of being thrown out of jobs or assassinated politically by the powers that be in Nigeria.

As a matter of fact, the rescue operation has already begun in Nigeria and in some foreign countries, including the United States, Brazil, the United Kingdom, Canada, and France. For example, while Professor Austine S. O. Okwu and I were brooding over the situation of our Igbo people in current Nigerian geopolitics following the 2015 Nigerian national elections, an Igbo blues song came to my mind: "Where are the young suckers that would replace the old banana trees after they die?" Both of us were saddened by the sorry situation of our people in general. Anybody who knows Professor Okwu would not be surprised that I had this type of conversation with him, for he has done a lot of things toward achieving the unity, survival, and progress of the Igbo more than most of the people I know about here in the United States. To know about this quintessential Igboman necessitates a review of some of his services to the Igbo nation in particular and Nigeria in general. As a diplomat, Okwu began his professional journey in the Nigerian Foreign Affairs Ministry from 1961 to 1967 during which period he served in Ghana, Tanganyika (now Tanzania), Britain, and the United States. In Tanganyika, Okwu negotiated with that government's officials to fill vacant positions in their judiciary with Nigerian lawyers as magistrates and judges. In 1967, before the Nigeria-Biafra War broke out, Colonel Ojukwu sent Ambassador Okwu to go open the Biafran Foreign Office in London, from where he could plead the Biafran cause before the outside world. Later on, he was redeployed to serve as an ambassador to East Africa, where he won for Biafra the first two diplomatic recognitions from Tanzania and Zambia. The two other countries that recognized Biafra diplomatically, Gabon and the Ivory Coast, and then Haiti in the Western hemisphere, took their cues from those countries that Ambassador Okwu first persuaded to recognize Biafra as a country. He continued his ambassadorial services in East Africa up to the end of the civil war.

Thereafter, Ambassador Okwu and his family emigrated to the United States where he attended Columbia University, New York, and earned a Ph.D. in history. After that, he taught in some American colleges, serving as a dean in some of them. What is most admirable in this great Igbo son is the life of service he has led up to his early 90s. He spearheaded the founding of an Igbo sociocultural organization, "Igbozue," alongside his wife Dr. Beatrice Okwu, who herself spearheaded the founding of the "Igbo Women Association of Connecticut." Both organizations in Connecticut State serve as platforms from where they taught Igbo people through personal experiences how to unite and uphold their cultural norms and traditions. Above all, since his retirement, Professor Okwu has been busy visiting Igbo organizations in other states in the United States as well as in Nigeria to ensure that our culture never dies.

Acting as a bridge between the old generation of sociopolitical leaders (some of whom he worked with) and the new class of leaders (some of whom seem ignorant of what sincere public service means to our people), Professor Okwu has been making presentations in some Igbo academic institutions like Abia State University, Okigwe. In March 2014, he attended and contributed a paper to a conference, titled "The First International Colloquium on The Igbo Question in Nigeria: Before, During, and After Biafra," which was organized by the Alaigbo Development Foundation of which he is a founding member. The papers delivered at the Colloquium eventuated in the publication of a monumental two-volume book, *Igbo Nation: History & Challenges of Rebirth and Development*,[13] whose contents teach and exemplify what the Igbo people must do to overcome their challenges in order to achieve the kind of rebirth, unity, and development that empower their geopolitical situation in Nigeria. Most of these sociopolitical and ambassadorial roles that Ambassador (Professor) Augustine S. O. Okwu has played for more than five decades can be found in his memoir, *In Truth for Justice and Honor: A Memoir of a Nigerian-Biafran Ambassador*.[14]

Another Igbo scholar who is working tirelessly to unite the Igbo in thought and reason in Nigeria and in the Diaspora is Professor Herbert Ekwe-Ekwe, who currently lives in and writes from Brazil. His forward-looking blog, *Rethinking Africa*, is dedicated to the exchange of innovative thinking on issues affecting the advancement of African peoples wherever they are. He provides rigorous and insightful analyses on the issues affecting Africans and their vision of the world.[15] In 2014, I attended a conference in which I observed Ekwe-Ekwe make incisive, erudite, and thought-provoking arguments in defense of the African cause in the world. Also, his book, *The Biafra-Nigeria War and the Aftermath*, is one of the best reads on the Nigerian civil war.[16] The more I read his blog entries, the better I appreciate the Igbo nation and the Black World. His article "Does *Arrow of God* Anticipate the Igbo Genocide?" contains a complex argument that the novel presents a highly imaginative and anticipatory insight to the turbulent trajectory of post-(European) conquest African history and politics. This insight anticipates the catastrophe of the Igbo genocide[17] Of course, the anticipated genocide in the novel Ekwe-Ekwe referring to in the article is the massacre of the Igbo that began during the 1966 northern riots and ended in the civil war.

In the end, after this metaphoric journey through the Igbo geopolitical terrain in which we have seen some examples of the activities of our fellow Igbo people at home and abroad, what is there to be said about Igbo intra-ethnic democracy in present-day Nigerian geopolitics? One can say that issues have been raised and observations made on the performances of the Igbo sociopolitical class in Nigeria. So an attempt has been made to draw attention to how, when, and where the rain started to beat us as a people. If we now become more conscious of the causes of our downfall, even our marginalization, and thereby decide to do something positive as Umuaro clan did in *Arrow of God*, then we will have started to reenergize and reinvent ourselves without lamenting the noble effort we made to build experimentation on the building of a new nation – Biafra, our New Jerusalem. And if we realize that Nigeria is the only native country that our Igbo nation has in the world, then we must always fight with every means available to us without retreat to ensure our survival in it politically, socially, economically, and emotionally.

> *Igbo ndi oma m, anyi ga adi ooo!* [My awesome Igbo people, we shall surely live!]

Notes

* Presented at Brown University's Annual Colloquium, May 2–3, 2014, under the topic "*Arrow of God*: New Insights into Achebe's Magnum Opus.," and published in *Rethinking Africa Blog Spot*, July 24, 2015, http://re-thinkingAfrica.blogspot.co.uk/2015/07/by-kalu-ogbaa-every-society-wether.html.

1   Achebe, "The Novelist as Teacher," p. 59.
2   Achebe, "The Role of the Writer in a New Nation," pp. 157–8.
3   Chinua Achebe, *Arrow of God*. London: Heinemann, 1964: 14.
4   Ogbaa, *Gods, Oracles and Divination*.
5   Emmanuel Obiechina, "The Human Dimension of History in *Arrow of God*," in C. L. Innes and Bernth Lindfors, eds. *Critical Perspectives on Chinua Achebe*. Washington, DC: Three Continents Press, 1978: 170.
6   Obaro Ikime, ed., *Groundwork of Nigerian History*. Ibadan, Nigeria: Heinemann Educational Books (Nigeria) Ltd, 1980.
7   See www.universalreporters247.com/2014/01/rivers-group-scolds-amaechi-over-his. html 9/26/2014.
8   See http://sunnewsonline.com/new/group-reports-orji-wife-son-to-efcc Accessed 7/20/2015.
9   Emma Okocha, *Blood on the Niger, First Black on Black Genocide: The Untold Story of the Asaba Massacre during the Nigeria-Biafra War*. New York: Triatlantic Books, 2006.
10 Joe O. G. Achuzia, *Requiem Biafra: The True Story of Nigeria's Civil War*. Asaba, Nigeria: Steel Equip Nigeria Ltd., 2002.
11 Ralph Uwechue, *Reflections on the Nigerian Civil War: Facing the Future*. Paris: Jeune Afrique, 1970.
12 Achebe, *The Trouble with Nigeria*, p. 46.
13 T. Uzodinma Nwala, Nath Aniekwu, and Chinyere Ohiri-Aniche, eds., *Igbo Nation: History & Challenges of Rebirth and Development*, Vols. One and Two. Ibadan, Nigeria: Kraft Books, Ltd., 2015.
14 Austine S. O. Okwu, *In Truth for Justice and Honor: A Memoir of a Nigerian-Biafran Ambassador*. Princeton, NJ: Sungai Books, 2011.
15 See http://re-thinkingafrica.blogspot.co.uk/2015/07/federal-ministry-of-education-has. html. Accessed 7/7/2015.
16 Herbert Ekwe-Ekwe, *The Biafra-Nigeria War and the Aftermath*. Lewiston, NY: E. Mellen, 1990.
17 Herbert Ekwe-Ekwe, "Does *Arrow of God* Anticipate the Igbo Genocide?" http://pombazuka.org/en/category/books/93141,2014-10-16, Issue 698. Accessed 10/16/2014.

12 Remembering Achebe the Man, His Creative Mission, and His Achievements

What I can say is that it was clear to many of us that an indigenous African literary renaissance was overdue. A major objective was to challenge stereotypes, myths, and the image of ourselves and our continent, and to recast them through stories – prose, poetry, essays, and books for children. That was my overall goal.

– Chinua Achebe[1]

In his poem, "Among School Children," the Irish poet William Butler Yeats famously asked, "How can we know the dancer from the dance?" The multilayered poem is a meditation by an aging man on life, love, and creativity. As we wind down our exploration of the life, creativity, and times of Chinua Achebe, the Nigerian writer and nationalist, we wonder if he, like his fellow writer and Irish nationalist Yeats, ever asked a similar question about himself and his creativity. We also wonder whether his worldwide readers, particularly his fellow Nigerian citizens, truly understand the life and patriotic mission of this renowned Igbo-Nigerian-African writer through his lifetime works and services. I personally believe that Achebe, like other great nationalist writers, was conscious of the work his personal God – *Chi-na-Eke ya* – ordained him to do among his people. Still, he must have had some moments when he wondered whether people fully understood him and his mission through the creative, social, and political works he was doing. To me, his reflection would have been like that of Yeats who had a similar mission for his Irish people. As an avid reader of Irish literature, Achebe was familiar with the life and mission of Yeats and why he would ask the question in the poem "Among School Children," which was obviously meditative in nature. For in it, Yeats wanted to know if the readers of his nationalistic poems (especially those he wrote in protest of British colonization of Ireland) understood him, the metaphoric dancer in context, through his poetry, the metaphoric dance. He asked the question toward the end of his mission because he was worried about his legacy. From his writings, we know that Achebe also wrote some of his critical essays and last book, *There Was a Country: A Personal History of Biafra*, toward the end of his writing career and life, to ensure that people did not misunderstand his mission and the legacy he was leaving behind as an author. To underscore that fact, we ask at this point, what then is Achebe's mission, and the means through which he attempted to achieve it?

DOI: 10.4324/9781003184133-12

It seems appropriate to open the discussion of this chapter with the epigraph above, which contains Achebe's mission statement on reclaiming the good image of his people and continent that was tarnished by Europe, and the means of achieving it. It was important for him to articulate his mission lest readers and critics forget to judge him by his stated goal. Ironically, however, even when he clearly stated it in his last book, some reviewers still mischaracterized his arguments, his goal, and the genre of the book. For example, Biodun Jeyifo, whose review we analyzed earlier, represents those who wrote unfair reviews of the book just to serve their personal purposes. Nonetheless, despite some critics' occasional misunderstandings of him and his works, Achebe was unfazed by them and stoically committed to achieving his stated goal throughout his publications – a goal he began to actualize practically with the publication of his momentous first novel *Things Fall Apart*, in which he famously mounted a challenge to the British colonial activities in Nigeria. He adopted a verse from William Butler Yeats's poem, "The Second Coming," as a befitting epigraph of the novel, which reads as follows:

> Turning and turning in the widening gyre
> The falcon cannot hear the falconer;
> Things fall apart; the center cannot hold;
> Mere anarchy is loosed upon the world.

Achebe began his discussion of that anarchy, which the British colonial system "loosed" upon the world of the Nigerians, especially in his native Igboland, where he first witnessed the effects of the white men's presence and his people's struggles to overcome them. Thereafter, he turned his attention to other parts of Nigeria and Africa. In his effort to reclaim the realistic image of the Igbo people, he created characters who possessed both human virtues and vices (like other human beings elsewhere in the world), and who were guided by important Igbo folkways[2] that constituted their viable traditional culture and civilization. His description was unlike the stereotypes, myths, and false images of Africa and Africans that Europeans created in their African novels, such as Joseph Conrad's *Heart of Darkness*, and Joyce Cary's *Mister Johnson*. Moreover, Achebe continued the exploration of the same themes in *No Longer at Ease* and *Arrow of God*. In 1988, he published the three novels in one volume, which he titled *The African Trilogy*.

In his initial discussions of African issues, Achebe focused his attention on the effects of British colonial activities on the Igbo people in *Things Fall Apart* and *Arrow of God* – his rural novels. Thereafter, he discussed similar issues as they affected other Nigerian peoples living outside of Igboland in *No Longer at Ease* and *A Man of People* – his urban novels. In them, he laid emphasis on the fundamental theme of public office holders' corruption that was corroding the moral compass of the country. He began in *No Longer at Ease* with an Igbo character, Obi Okonkwo the grandson of Okonkwo of Umuofia village, who lives in Lagos without the moral control of his Igbo village. After that, Achebe focused his discussion on the corruption of another Igbo character, Chief M. A. Nanga, in *A Man of the People*, who also embraced the culture of corruption that most postcolonial Nigerian office holders practiced, which Igbo villagers abhorred. Ostensibly, Achebe's goal was to expose such corrupt practices and then suggest ways of correcting them. He implied that if the characters had been living under moral authority of the precolonial Igbo villages, they could not have been so morally bankrupt, and their crimes would have been dealt with in their traditional way. Unfortunately, however, because the British rulers had urbanized the villages and usurped the governing authorities of the village elders, *ndichie*, things fell apart for the people and the center of their sovereignty could no longer hold, as it were.

After establishing his fame solidly as a world-class author with these hybrid novels, Achebe continued his mission by writing critical essays through which he taught other African writers to see African literature as restoring a celebration of Africa's dignified past culture and history:

> that African peoples did not hear of culture for the first time from Europeans; that their societies were not mindless but frequently had a philosophy of great depth and value and beauty, that they had poetry and above all, they had dignity. It is this dignity that many African peoples all but lost in the colonial period, and it is this that they must now regain. The worst thing that can happen to any people is the loss of their dignity and self-respect. The writer's duty is to help them regain it by showing them in human terms what happened to them, what they lost. There is a saying in Ibo that a man who can't tell where the rain began to beat him cannot know where he dried his body. The writer can tell the people where the rain began to beat them.[3]

Achebe sounded the clarion call early in his long writing career for African writers to embrace the duty of rendering patriotic services to their individual fatherlands and the continent. Obviously, what he said in that 1964 lecture was an eloquent testimony of his own patriotism, which began in Igboland and spread from Nigeria to other African countries. It was this call that he would repeat from time to time throughout his writing career. Therefore, it should not surprise any reader to find him restating it in his final book, *There Was a Country*.

In his review of *A Man of the People*, Bernth Lindfors explains why Achebe ended the novel with a coup that mirrored the actual bloody coup that the Nigerian Army staged on January 15, 1966:

> I believe Achebe ended the novel with a military coup in order to enlarge the picture to include Nigeria's neighbors, several of which had experienced coups. By universalizing the story in this way Achebe could suggest to his countrymen that what had happened in other unstable independent African countries might easily have happened in Nigeria too. The coup was meant as an African parable, not a Nigerian prophecy.[4]

Lindfors was responding to some readers' suspicion that Achebe could not have accurately predicted the coup in the novel where he wrote "But the Army obliged us by staging a coup at that point locking up every member of the Government"[5] without getting prior information from the coup planners. Actually, Achebe's novel came off the press in London on January 24, 1966, which is nine days after the army staged the first bloody coup in Nigeria on January 15, 1966 in real life, which rebuts the suspicion that Achebe had prior information about the coup that enabled him to predict it prophetically. Instead, the truth is that Achebe was living in Lagos while working in the NBC, which created ample opportunities for him to observe closely the social and political events in Nigeria and enabled him to fictionalize the events accurately in the novel. Nonetheless, the 30-month civil war that followed those coups in 1966 did not create a conducive environment for Achebe to write another novel until 21 years later. Besides, he was busy rendering important services to the Republic of Biafra as its Ambassador Extraordinaire as he went to many places in the world pleading the Biafran cause. Still, he managed to write a few shorter literary pieces, such as poems, short stories, and books for children[6] to keep his writing career alive.

When the war ended, and the federal military regime lifted the ban on political activities in the country, Achebe patriotically yearned to help build a united postwar Nigeria. So he decided to join the PRP, a political party whose leadership and general membership were predominantly Northerners. That decision was seen by some politicians as a rejection of the NPP, a party formed by the Igbo people. When I asked him about it, he told me that he did so with a view to bridging the deep divide between the North and the South. And in the same patriotic spirit, he published *The Trouble with Nigeria*, in which he carefully analyzed the causes of the problem that was breeding disunity and hate among the citizens; his conclusion was that the problem emanated from leadership failures at all levels of the Nigerian government. As we saw in an earlier discussion of the book, Achebe fearlessly blamed political leaders, such as Chief Obafemi Awolowo (from the West) and Dr. Nnamdi Azikiwe (from the East), for introducing the tribalism, nepotism, and corruption that had been ravaging the whole nation. He then offered readers concrete ways of dealing with the problem, including showcasing the exemplary leadership role of a Northern politician, Mallam Aminu Kano, who was sincerely trying to unite the country politically before his sudden death.

Furthermore, Achebe wrote many critical essays in such books as *Hopes and Impediments* (1989), *Home and Exile* (2001), and *The Education of a British-Protected Child* (2009). Some of these essays had been published earlier in another book, *Morning Yet on Creation Day* (1975). Reading them, one may find their contents repetitive because they are about the same evil effects of European colonialism and imperialism, which continued to afflict every African country. That is why he insisted that African writers help their leaders to solve their problems. Achebe wrote critical essays to inspire them to perform more effectively. We can see examples of him doing so in such essays as "What is Nigeria to Me?", "Africa's Tarnished Name", "African Literature as Restoration of Celebration", and "Martin Luther King and Africa," all of which are collected in *The Education of a British-Protected Child*.

The contents of some of these latter books of essays are reminiscent of the articles he published earlier in *Nigeria Magazine* in the 1960s, which were about

Nigerian national issues and pan-African sociopolitical and economic issues. Achebe published his last novel, *Anthills of the Savannah*, in 1987, in which he recorded the corroding effects of warfare and military regimes in Africa, especially in his native Nigeria. He gave as an example the ruthless dictatorship of His Excellency (HE), a corrupt ruler of Kangan. The references Achebe makes to other African dictators like Idi Amin of Uganda underscored his deep empathetic feelings for the masses who suffered under such cruel leaders in a fictional West African country. Until the end of his career, Achebe never stopped writing to encourage the efforts of literary writers and politicians to reform their nations that he saw as a moral obligation without prescribing to them how they should write:

> At the same time it is important to state that words have the power to hurt, even to denigrate and oppress others. But before I am accused of prescribing a way in which a writer should write, let me say that I do think that decency and civilization insist that the writer take sides with the powerless. Clearly there is no moral obligation to write in any particular way. But there is a moral obligation, I think, not to ally oneself with power against the powerless. I think an artist, in my definition of that word, would not be someone who takes sides with the emperor against his powerless subjects.[7]

Achebe's writings on the subject of the liberation of African countries from the clutches of European colonialism, imperialism, and neocolonialism seem to have been understood and copied by some African writers, who adopted his works as templates to produce patriotic works. He even inspired renowned freedom fighters to persevere in their struggles. For example, the most celebrated African freedom fighter, Nelson Mandela, who was imprisoned for 27 years by white South African government authorities, came out of prison and campaigned to become president of his country. He won the election in a landslide and thus became the first black president of that country. Acknowledging how reading Achebe's works helped him to endure the pain of his life in jail, President Mandela said that Achebe was "a freedom fighter in whose company the prison walls fell down."[8] Similar praises were showered on Achebe by his fellow Nigerian writers, as well as by scholars and critics from other parts of the world.

As our exploration of the life, creativity, and times of Chinua Achebe has so far shown in this study, Chinua Achebe was a man who grew up during the colonial and postcolonial periods in Nigeria and spent virtually 20 of his final years on Earth in the United. The experiences he acquired in all those years and from the many places in which he lived or visited enabled him to lead a life of purpose. His education at all levels prepared him to embrace and write about concepts of otherness and multiculturalism that are found in every human community, from villages, through towns and cities, to various countries and continents. Once, while delivering a distinguished lecture at Harvard University, Achebe made a statement that explains the Igbo people's multicultural orientation, which informs their sociopolitical behavior and the strong republican streak in their institutions:

a   Igbo people are not primitive; if we were I would not be offering this distin-
    guished lecture, or would I?

b   Igbo people are not linked by blood ties, although they may share many cul-
    tural traits;

c   Igbo people do not speak one dialect; they may speak one language that has
    scores of major and minor dialects;

d   and as for having one recognized leader, Igbo people would regard the absence
    of such a recognized leader as the very defining principle of their social and
    political identity.[9]

It was also Achebe's belief in the concepts of duality, pluralism, and otherness, especially in the realm of Igbo religious and cosmological beliefs, which led him to make the following statement that some of his critics found controversial, thereby doubting that he was truly a Christian believer:

> It is important to stress what I said earlier: the central place in Igbo thought of the notion of duality. Wherever Something stands, Something Else stands beside it. Nothing is absolute. *I am the truth, the way, and the life* would be called blasphemous or simply absurd, for is it not well known that a man may worship Ogwugwu to perfection and yet be killed by Udo? The world in which we live has its double and counterpart in the realm of spirits. A man lives here and his chi there. Indeed the human being is only one half (and weaker half at that) of a person. There is a complementary spirit being, chi.[10]

Furthermore, until the advent of European missionaries in precolonial Igbo territory, the numerous villages and clans that became Igboland was a closed society whose sovereignty was never seriously challenged by the outside world. In Ogidi, for example,

> What mattered to them on a daily basis was the sovereign authority they enjoyed in practical matters in their eight hundred or so villages. As was their habit, they made a proverb to sanctify their political attitude: *nku di na mba na-eghelu mba nni*, every community has enough firewood in its own forest for all the cooking it needs to do.[11]

In other words, the people were contented with their life as they knew and led it, before the Europeans came and challenged their indigenous authority. Even though the war of resistance the Igbo mounted against the intruding British colonizers, which ended in 1902, was traumatic to them, it helped them to learn new ways of life, some good and some bad. The Igbo realized then that the proverbial firewood in their forests was not enough for all the cooking they needed to do. That is why Achebe created a wise village elder, Ezeulu, in *Arrow of God*, who understood the coming changes in their erstwhile closed community, which white missionaries and British officials forcefully opened up. So he sent his son to "be my eye" in the new school the missionaries built in Umuru, saying to those who challenged his decision, "The world is like a Mask dancing. If you want to see it well you do not stand in one place" (p. 55). In the end, the price Ezeulu paid in the struggle between Umuaro and the British officials resulted in a compromise between them: the British officials established a strong foothold in the clan, and their children got the opportunity to attend school, where they were exposed to Western education and culture.

Achebe depicted in *The African Trilogy* the Igbo people's acquisition of Western education and culture in three stages: Christian Sunday school education in *Things Fall Apart*, primary school education in *Arrow of God*, and high school/university college education abroad in *No Longer at Ease*. The same three-tier educational system in those novels mirrored the real educational system in the colonial Nigeria, which Achebe went through. We discussed in Chapter 2 of this study how his education became a template for other Nigerian children and their parents/guardians, and teacher to follow. Without the Western education, complemented with informal Nigerian cultural education, Nigerians could not have been enabled to fight European colonialism and imperialism in Africa, which they blindly fought initially. In the end, the multicultural education Achebe acquired both at home and in academic institutions enabled him to understand the educational, literary, social, and political systems of the world, which empowered him as a writer to serve the Igbo, Nigerian, African, and other peoples of the world. At long last, he became recognized as one of the most influential authors of the twentieth century.

Figure 12.1 Chinua Achebe and President Nelson Mandela of South Africa

Source: Getty Images

Finally, as the Igbo people say, "The most important days in a man's life are the day he was born and the day he died." That is because they are interested in knowing where and when the man was born, his family background, and his upbringing. Such information enables people, especially those from his village, to predict or speculate the kind of man he would become when he grows up. In other words, from his birth to death their eyes are upon him to observe and evaluate his achievements and failures critically. And because of the Igbo age grade system – people born within a three-year bracket – every man's achievements or failures are weighed against those of his agemates. For that reason, the Igbo live a very competitive life wherever they live and have their being, be it in Igboland or outside of it. It is out of his thorough knowledge of the Igbo cultural norm and work ethic that Achebe created Igbo characters like Okonkwo Unoka in *Things Fall Apart* and his grandson Obi Okonkwo in *No Longer at Ease*. Both characters are hard-working high achievers and heroes who were brought low by their character flaws combined with the roles that the gods played in their lives. Judged by such metrics, we have already established that Achebe was undoubtedly a world-renowned author and scholar of the twentieth century. Needless to say, people are interested in knowing who Achebe was as a person beyond his creative work and official engagements from the time he was born in Ogidi, through his years of education to the years of his long exceptional career until the day he died. Because it is not easy to obtain this kind of information, we have to rely on the testimonies of people who had intimate knowledge of his private life. They include his immediate family members, blood relatives, and friends. For these are the people who were privileged to observe his private behavior when he thought no one was watching him perform privately his duties to his family, Ogidi, Igboland, and his country Nigeria.

My appreciation of Chinua Achebe the man begins with my own experiences with him that began in 1972, when I went as President of the English Association at the University of Nigeria at Nsukka to have a conversation with him in his office where he was serving as Director and Senior Research Fellow of the Institute of African Studies. My purpose was to discover why he was not hired to teach as a professor in English Department where we could learn a lot from him about the art of fiction writing. Although I have narrated how the meeting went earlier in this study, I am reiterating the incident here to emphasize the man's humility and humanity, his vision for Igbo studies and concern for his people's wellbeing, and the fatherly care I saw in him during our first meeting. Before he ushered me in to see his boss, the secretary told me that my time slot for the meeting was 15 minutes, but because of our mutual interest in the issue I raised, Achebe and I ended up spending 45 minutes. I came out of the meeting so highly impressed by the kind treatment and time he gave me, that I decided there and then to pursue his fiction as an area of concentration in my prospective graduate studies.

Another important incident between me and Achebe happened eight years later while I was working on my doctoral dissertation on his novels at the University of Texas at Austin. He and I met again at the University at Florida at Gainesville, where both of us were attending the 1980 annual conference of the ALA.

My professor and director of my dissertation, Bernth Lindfors, arranged privately for me to interview Achebe, who kindly obliged. He still remembered our 1972 encounter in his office at Nsukka, so he spared me the trouble of reintroducing myself to him, saying that he knew who I was, and said jokingly that I should go ahead to ask him as many questions as I had for him. He said this even though he knew that other people were waiting to interview him as well. All through the interview, Achebe showed me the same grace, love, and kindness I had witnessed in 1972. When the interview was over, he took more time to advise me to work hard for the completion of my dissertation. In addition, he asked me to feel free to call him whenever I had any questions about his novels. In the end, the interview was published as the first article in the special volume of *Research in African Literatures* devoted to him and his publications in January 1981, which I have reproduced as Chapter 5 of this study. Moreover, this second meeting was an opportunity for me to forge strong ties with him as my Igbo literary ancestor and mentor.

The third incident, which opened my eyes to see clearly the man behind the literary icon, happened about three years after Achebe took up residence at Bard College, New York. Around 11:00 am on that fateful day, I called him on the phone, but a young lady, who I later learned was his second daughter Nwando, picked up the phone and asked, "Who is calling, please?" And I told her my name and that I wanted to speak with Nna anyi Achebe. "Oh, he is in the bathroom; can I take a message for him?" she asked. At that moment, Achebe heard my name and voice and asked her to tell me to wait for him. When he came out and picked up the phone, he apologized for keeping me waiting. In response, I told him how sincerely sorry I was, thinking that I offended him by hurrying him out of the bathroom, and because I was mindful of his disability. He listened carefully to the issue I was calling to discuss with him and gave me very constructive ideas. I found that he handled the whole incident with his usual grace and candor. And I also surmised that he responded to the situation the way he did in fulfillment of the promise he made me in 1980 at Gainesville, Florida. Overall, observing his considerate behavior and amiable personality during the three occasions I was fortunate to meet him personally over three decades, I continued to regard Achebe as a man of great wisdom, integrity, compassion, and complex simplicity!

While his wisdom can easily be found in his writings, his other personal qualities that I have identified may not be so easily apprehended by those who are not intimate with him. So for corroboration of them, I now turn to testimonies of some of those who knew him intimately: his relatives, close friends, and public officials who worked with him closely. Some of these testimonies were obtained through the interviews Phanuel Akubueze Egejuru conducted for her book, *Chinua Achebe Pure and Simple: An Oral Biography*,[12] and I rely on them because they can be authenticated by the people she interviewed, people who understood and appreciated the human side of Achebe:

> This present study specifically focuses on the human as opposed to the artistic side of Chinua. Although Chinua frowns on this arbitrary separation of

the man from the artist, he recognizes its validity. Thus, what we have here is an oral biography compiled from information obtained during face-to-face interviews with Achebe himself, his blood relatives and other people who have intimate knowledge of him from infancy through adolescence to adulthood (the blurb).

Talking about Achebe's integrity and trustworthiness, she says:

> There is no better or higher testimony to Chinua's integrity than his appointment as Goodwill Ambassador for the United Nations, in January 1999. It is because of his uprightness that the United Nations, whose gestures are constantly viewed with skepticism, chose Chinua to speak for them. Whatever the qualifications are, integrity and respectability must be there. As shown by the words of interviewees, Chinua has a certain *gravitas* about him. Many compare his ideas and opinions to those of wise men of earlier times. People crave for and respect his opinion. Simply put, Chinua inspires trust, and any messages coming through him would resonate with trustworthiness.
>
> (p. 150)

I agree that it was the same attributes of integrity and trustworthiness that the Biafran government saw in Achebe that led them to appoint him Ambassador Extraordinaire during the Nigeria-Biafra War. While performing this ambassadorial role, Achebe shunned the vices of corruption and nepotism that many Nigerian public officials are known for. His brother Augustine said, "Chinua is not one you can attract with money. Once something is right, he will continue to stick with it. You can't sway him with money. He is a man of the old" (p. 150). However, another relative, Tochukwu Okocha, wanted Achebe to commit acts of nepotism like other corrupt Nigerians in order to help his relatives live easier lives, which was an idea Achebe vehemently rejected. The dejected relative confessed:

> We would like him to use his position to help us so we can come out like him. We thought that we his relatives would have things smoother and easier. But he wants each man to make himself. *He treats his children the same way.* This is the problem we have. We think he should serve our interest with his position.
>
> (pp. 151–2) (emphasis added)

That is the kind of pressure that the relatives of Obi Okonkwo put on him in *No Longer at Ease*, to which he succumbed and went to jail. Achebe practiced what he wrote in his fiction, insisting that an artist must practice decency in both the human and creative sides of his life.

If you hadn't met Achebe in person before going to see him, you might have expected to see a man exhibiting elitist behavior: speaking in highfalutin English language, wearing a three-piece suit in hot and humid Nigerian weather, and

Figure 12.2 J's Theatre: Remembering Chinua Achebe at the United Nations

Source: Photograph taken by "John Keene."

dismissive of whatever ideas you express. All that could make you anxious and nervous. So, when eventually you saw him face-to-face, you might be surprised. This was my experience when I met him the first time but it was also the experience of another person who went to see him for the first time. Egejuru reported how Chinua's sister Grace told a similar story of a young Yoruba man who was doing his national youth service in the Ogidi area. He was very anxious to meet Chinua in person. Mrs. Okocha promised to let him know when her brother would be in town.

On the appointed day, the young man appeared in his best suit and waited nervously. Eventually, Chinua appeared. The young man mistook him for one of the people waiting to see him. Then Mrs. Okocha came in and said to the young man, "That's Chinua." The young man exclaimed, "Is this the person?" "He was expecting to see a man dressed to kill, but he only saw a simple fellow," commented Mrs. Okocha. She gave more instances to show how Chinua has remained constant in his simple ways despite his fame:

> His relationship with those he has known from childhood remains the same. People still come to ask about him as they are used to, and they would say, "tell Albert I asked of him," and when Albert returns, he tours the village on foot, greeting people as he used to do in the old days.
>
> (p. 128)

Egejuru adds that another family member impressed by Chinua's unassuming nature is his sister-in-law, Lucy, who said:

> What impresses me the most about Chinua is, with all his greatness, he doesn't know that he is a great man at all. Any time he comes, we still converse with him and talk the same way as of old. He does nothing to draw attention to himself. God created him to be different and important, but he does not brag about it nor is he arrogant about it.

(p. 128)

Once again, we emphasize that Achebe was never interested in the kind of pomposity and flamboyant attire that some Nigerians associate with greatness, either in real life situations or in writing. Readers of his novel *No Longer at Ease* will recall that the greatest mistake Obi Okonkwo made upon arrival in Lagos from London was to dress in simple short-sleeved shirt instead of wearing a three-piece suit like the British colonial officers. Moreover, he spoke in simple English, almost colloquial, language. The Umuofia Progressive Union who came receive him at the Lagos Airport were disappointed, just as some Ogidi and Igbo people were with Achebe who appeared in simple clothes and exhibited his usual simplicity, even during the Eagle on Iroko Celebrations of his 60th birthday in 1990. I never saw him wearing a suit during conferences or when he organized seminars or granted interviews to people.

To gain more information about this world-renowned author, people should read what his family members and a number of world leaders wrote as tributes to him in *Celebrating the Life of Chinua Achebe: A Life of Purpose, November 16, 1930 – March 21, 2013*, and *Chinua Achebe, 1930–2013: A Book of Tributes*.[13] These two books contain snapshots of everything worth knowing about the life and art of Chinua Achebe.

In the final analysis, we find it necessary to underscore the rich legacy that Chinua Achebe left for his Igbo people and the world at large. We begin to do so by first acknowledging that he was a sophisticated master storyteller and savvy political analyst, who used a combination of his Igbo storytelling habits and acquired Western fiction writing skills to tell memorable stories about his native Igbo people and other Nigerians, Achebe's obsessive commitment to challenging warped European views of Africa and Africans was germinated while he was at the University College, Ibadan. It was there that he began to understand that "there is such a thing as absolute power over narrative. Those who secure this privilege for themselves can arrange stories about others pretty much where, and, as they like. Just as in corrupt, totalitarian regimes, those who exercise power over others can do anything."[14] The statement is a truism shared by all colonized and oppressed peoples in Africa and other places in the world. Hence, the first feature of Achebe's legacy is his ability to tell true stories about Africans in order to help them reclaim their past histories and cultures. Thus, his literary teaching became a catalyst that facilitated African writers' sociopolitical revolutionary actions in the 1960s. To begin writing his fiction from a historical perspective was highly

Figure 12.3 Achebe's Nigerian flag draped casket being received for burial by his people

Source: Getty Images

significant because, as he explained proverbially, the people must first learn where the rain began to beat them before they can know their destination. So he published his novels as analyses of the monumental historical and sociopolitical events that took place particularly in Nigeria and generally in more African countries.

Achebe's legacy can be seen as well in his writing style that many African writers have been adopting as templates for their own novels. This has made him founder of modern African fiction. The qualities of Africanness, such as proverbs, local figures of speech, realistic African settings, and other indigenous elements have brought African literature to international attention and made it a viable addition to world literature today. His books are now a part of curricular offerings in major African and world universities.

Finally, Chinua Achebe's artistic work and personal qualities have identified him as an intellectual. But with his usual humility he had said, "To me, being an intellectual doesn't mean knowing about intellectual issues; it means taking pleasure in them."[15] He has lived by the precepts he preached, which have made him a man of his people and a moral exemplar, whose works will continue to inspire others. Yes, Professor Chinualumogu Achebe left the world on March 21, 2013, but the bright light of his humanity continues to burn eternally. So, in the tradition of my Igbo people, I end this study in the life and times of Chinua Achebe with a parting dirge:

Figure 12.4 Achebe's memorial service in his hometown in Nigeria

Source: Ainehi Edoro, Brittle Paper.

"A Wreath for the Iroko"[16]

Oh, come, all you lovers of the Iroko
Come let us behold the face of a giant taking a final bow
Please, come without tears, only joy and gratitude to the Creator
In your hearts as we celebrate the passing of a hero
For casting off his shroud of dust
In a necessary ritual that liberates an encaged immortal Soul
Now taking a second flight to Heavensgate
Oh, how the door opens and closes gently as he goes into Eternity!

I

The car crash that once sent Chinua Achebe spiraling down
Milken Hill cliff into a shadowy abyss caused a passerby to lament:

> *Ewu-oo C.A. is dead, C.A. is dead*
> *Call on his Chi; call for his urgent help*
> *Please, God, don't let him die!*

While his battered body lay still his transcendent Soul flew out
Like an Eagle off an Iroko tree
And perched at Heavensgate on his way to Eternity
But blinded by perpetual light he groped for the door that failed to open
Alas, a voice once familiar to him screamed

> *Go back, go back home*
> *Your work is not yet fully done*
> *Neither is your night yet come!*

He turned toward the direction of the voice and asked:
Is that you my friend Christopher Okigbo? Why shouldn't I come in now to
    be with you?
Was your poetic work fully done when you left us at noonday?

Yes, my work was done, for I was just a town-crier
But you are the God-ordained Olu Igbo, Voice of the Igbo Nation
One who still has a lot to accomplish for all of us before the night comes
For now, look behind you to see who is waiting!

As he turned to look, his Soul flew back into his paralyzed body below
He blinked his hazy eyes and vaguely beheld the Love of his life
Tears coursing down her tender face; her tremulous lips moved; no voice nor
  words!
Though deeply touched, C.A. could not exclaim what he felt within:

Oh my dear wife, the Rock of my life . . .
Where have you been?
Were you riding with me to Glory?

He looked sympathetically at her, but no sound came out of his barely open
  dry mouth
And wondered, "Is that how Soul and Body will meet on Resurrection
  Morning?"

II

Oh you sympathizers! That was the right time to weep: but not in mourning
  of his death
Indeed, the world wept for joy, because a life of creativity was unleashed
  again on Earth
Still, some questioned in wonder: "Would he write again?"
Yes, he made it! The benevolent Gods of the Igbo, Nigeria, Africa, and the World
Blessed and allowed him to resume his spirituality
For him, it was morning yet on Creation Day!
Providence decreed that C.A. live at Bard College in America where he
  became the Bard of
Africa, creating shorter pieces like poems, essays, and keynote addresses,
Which reveal the *inner workings of his human conscience through the predica-*
  ment of Africa
And his own intellectual life; hence, Henry Gates concludes that *Home and*
  Exile is a story of
The triumph of the mind, told in the words of one of this century's most gifted writers.
We all witnessed that neither physical disability nor limitations in time and
  space deterred
C.A. from fighting to give voice to the sociopolitical and economic justice
  of the weak and
Down-trodden in his native Nigeria; neither political appointments nor
  highest national honors
From two Nigerian presidents – all of which he rejected – could sway him to
  change his mission

To bring positive changes to a country he loved, now on the brink of collapse as one nation

Neither criticism nor vilification of his great character could break the back of the great Iroko!

III

Twenty-two years after the car crash, the Soul of the Iroko takes another flight to Heavensgate

Nevertheless, not until the master storyteller has performed the last act of his play on Earth:

C.A. told his personal story of Biafra in *There Was a Country*, which Nadine Gordimer saw as

A mediation on the condition of freedom; a revolutionary entry into the intimate character of the

Writer's mind. To many a reader, C.A. stirred the hornet's nest, and yet

The master storyteller and noble warrior lived up to his reputation: a serious writer gives his

Readers headaches, not prescriptions. Indeed, the book compelled Nigerians to look themselves

In the mirror, no matter what side of the national debate they took

Oh, how the ugliness they saw kept them talking . . .

Nevertheless, the master storyteller kept smiling with the achievement of his desire!

Oh, final flight to Heavensgate! Were you prompted by Nature's design or mortal accident?

Could it be that your *Chi-na-Eke*, who allowed you to survive the first flight, blocked your

Entrance into the Great Beyond so you might work harder and further to give your beloved Igbo People greater relevance to Nigerian, African, and World literatures, culture, and civilization?

Is your Soul passing through to Eternity for rest fifty-four years after *Things Fall Apart*?

As we say our goodbyes to this great Son of Africa, Lover of his native Nigeria and humanity.

And the Odoziobodo na Olu Igbo, I can hear some commotion coming from Heavensgate

As Okigbo, Ekwensi, Mbabuike, and Obiechina are planning to introduce him to Olaudah

Equiano who first hewed the wood for the Iroko and others to carve; Nwoga and Ezenwa-Ohaeto

Are standing by and listening intently. How joyful their final meeting will be!

Dim! Dim! Dim! Dim! Dim! Dim! the cannons sound. Twenty-one gun-salute for the Biafran

Ambassador Extraordinaire arranged by General Aguiyi-Ironsi, General Ojukwu, and Major

Nzeogwu. Great rejoicing among thousands of Biafran troops, and women and children starved To death while on Earth: casualties of Nigeria's use of starvation as legitimate weapon of war.

> *Oh, we heard about your recounting of our stories in your last book. Daalu ooo! We can't wait to take you to your lovely parents anxiously awaiting your arrival!*

Could such preparations take place beyond Heavensgate? I wondered in my mind.

Oh, yes! As it is on Earth so it will be in Eternity, the Scriptures say.

Here's a wreath for you my literary mentor and ancestor. In your own words, I humbly say:

Nna anyi, Chinua Achebe: *If you had been poor in your last life, I would have asked you to be rich when you come again. But you were rich. If you had been a coward, I would have asked you to bring courage. But you were a restless warrior. If you died young, I would have asked you to get life. But you lived long. So I shall ask you to come again the way you came before. If your death was the death of nature, go in peace. But if a man caused it, do not allow him a moment's rest.*

Go in peace, Great Warrior of my people; I hope we will meet again in Glory at the right time!

Notes

1 Chinua Achebe, *There Was a Country: A Personal History of Biafra*. New York: Penguin, 2012: 53.
2 Kalu Ogbaa, *Gods, Oracles and Divination: Folkways in Chinua Achebe's Novels*. Trenton, NJ: Greenwood Press, 1992.
3 Achebe, "The Role of the Writer in a New Nation," 157.
4 Bernth Lindfors, *Early Achebe*. Trenton, NJ: Africa World Press, 2009: 136–7.
5 Achebe, *A Man of the People*, pp. 147–8.
6 For the titles and dates of these books, see "Publications by Chinua Achebe."
7 Achebe, *There Was a Country*, pp. 58–9.
8 Quoted on the blurb of *Celebrating the Life of Chinua Achebe: A Life of Purpose, November 16, 1930–March 21, 2013*. Compiled and printed by Doubleday/Anchor Press, for the funeral celebrations of Chinua Achebe in March 2013.
9 Achebe, *Home and Exile*, pp. 4–5.
10 Achebe, *Morning Yet on Creation Day*, p. 133.
11 Achebe, *Home and Exile*, p. 7.
12 Phanuel Akubueze Egejuru, *Chinua Achebe: Pure and Simple*.
13 Both books were compiled by the Achebe family for the funeral celebrations of Chinua Achebe in March 2013.
14 Achebe, *Home and Exile*, p. 24.
15 Quoted in the front cover of *Celebrating the Life of Chinua Achebe*. Published in *Chinua Achebe 1830–2013: A Book of Tributes*, pp. 88–91.
16 I read the poem during the burial ceremony of Chinua Achebe at Brown University, Providence, Rhode Island.

Bibliography

I Publications by Chinua Achebe

Novels

Anthills of the Savannah. London: Heinemann, 1987.
Arrow of God. London: Heinemann, 1964.
A Man of the People. London: Heinemann, 1966.
No Longer at Ease. London: Heinemann, 1960.
Things Fall Apart. London: Heinemann, 1958.

Historical biography

There Was a Country: A Personal History of Biafra. New York: Penguin, 2012.

Short stories

African Short Stories (ed. with C.L. Innes). London: Heinemann, 1985.
Girls at War and Other Stories. London: Heinemann, 1972.
The Heinemann Book of Contemporary African Short Stories (ed. with C.L. Innes). London: Heinemann, 1992.
The Sacrificial Egg and Other Stories. Onitsha, Nigeria: Etudo, 1962.

Children's books

Chike and the River. Cambridge, UK: Cambridge UP, 1966.
The Drum. Enugu, Nigeria: Fourth Dimension, 1977.
The Flute. Enugu, Nigeria: Fourth Dimension, 1977.
How the Leopard Got His Claws (ed. with John Iroaganachi). Enugu, Nigeria: Nwamife, 1972.

Poetry

Aka Weta: An Anthology of Igbo Poems (ed. with Obiora Udechukwu). Nsukka, Nigeria: Okike Magazine, 1982.
Another Africa (ed. with Robert Lyons). New York: Doubleday/Anchor, 1998.
Beware Soul Brother and Other Poems. London; Heinemann, 1972.
Collected Poems. New York: Penguin, 2004.

Don't Let Him Die: An Anthology of Memorial Poems for Christopher Okigbo (ed. with Dubem Okafor). Enugu, Nigeria: Fourth Dimension, 1978.

Criticism/essays

The Education of a British-Protected Child. New York: Knopf, 2009.
Home and Exile. New York: Oxford UP, 2000.
Hopes and Impediments. London: Heinemann, 1988.
Morning Yet on Creation Day. London. Heinemann, 1975.
The Trouble with Nigeria. Enugu: Fourth Dimension, 1983.

II Secondary sources

Abrams, M.H., *A Glossary of Literary Terms*, Sixth Edition. Orlando, FL: Holt, Rinehart and Winston, 1993.
Achuzia, Joe O.G., *Requiem Biafra: The True Story of Nigeria's Civil War*. Asaba, Nigeria: Steel Equip, 2002.
Adichie, Chimamanda, *Half a Yellow Sun*. New York: Knof/Anchor, 2006.
Agozino, Biko, "Objective' History and Genocide Dualism," in Onwubiko Agozino, ed. *Essays in Education and Popular Culture: Massliteracy*. Newcastle upon Tyne: Cambridge Scholars, 2019: 57–63.
Amuta, Chidi, "Eagle on Iroko," *Daily Times*, 12 February 1990.
Ankomah, Baffour, "Awo: Achebe Puts the Knife in," *New African*, August 1987, pp. 38–9.
Anwuna, Patrick A., *The Nigeria-Biafra War (1967–1970): My Memoirs*. Ibadan: Spectrum, 2007.
Anya, Ike, "There Was a Country: A Review of Chinua Achebe's Biafran Memoir," *African Arguments*, 10 October 2012. https://africanarguments.org.
Arinze, Francis A., *Sacrifice in Ibo Religion*. Ibadan: Ibadan UP, 1978.
Ashley, Leonard R.N., "Names Into Words, and Other Examples of the Possibilities of Extending the Boundaries of Literary Onomastics," *Literary Onomastics Studies* 7 (1980): 1–24.
Awoonor, Kofi, *The Breast of the Earth*. Garden City, NY: Anchor/ Doubleday, 1976.
Awoyinfa, Michael, "Chinua Achebe, *Things Fall Apart* Was Nearly Stolen from Me," *Sunday Concord Magazine*, 6 November 1983, pp. i, v, and xi.
———, "Dogs Eat Dogs: Professors Attack Professor Achebe," *Sunday Concord Magazine*, 3 February 1986, p. 1.
Basden, G.T., *Among the Ibo of Nigeria*. New York: Barnes and Noble, 1966.
Bonneau, Danniell, "Approaches to Achebe's Language in *Arrow of God*," *Echos du Commonwealth* 5 (1979–80): 68–88.
Brown, Lloyd, "Cultural Norms and Modes of Perception in Chinua Achebe's Fiction," in Bernth Lindfors, ed. *Critical Perspectives on Nigerian Literatures*. Washington, DC: Three Continents, 1976.
Bulfinch, Thomas, *Bulfinch's Mythology*. New York: Avenel Books, 1978.
Carroll, David, *Chinua Achebe*. New York: Twayne, 1970.
———, *Chinua Achebe: Novelist, Poet, Critic*. Basingstoke and London: Macmillan, 1990.
Chinweizu, *Decolonizing the African Mind*. Lagos: Pero, 1987.
———, *The West and the Rest of Us: White Predators, Black Slavers and the African Elite*. New York: Random House, 1975.
Chukwukere, B.I., "The Problem of Language in African Creative Writing," *African Literature Today* 3 (1969): 15–26.

Collis, Robert, *Nigeria in Conflict*. London: Secker and Warburg, 1970.

Dudley, William J., *Party and Politics in Northern Nigeria*. London: Frank Cass, 1969.

Dundes, Alan, *The Study of Folklore*. Englewood Cliffs, NJ: Prentice-Hall, 1965.

Echeruo, Michael, "Chinua Achebe and His Critics," in Bruce King and Kolawole Ogung-besan, eds. *A Celebration of Black and African Writing*. Zaria and Ibadan: Ahmadu Bello UP and Oxford UP, 1975: 150–63.

———, *The Conditioned Imagination: From Shakespeare to Conrad*. London: Macmillan, 1978.

———, "The Dramatic Limits of Igbo Rituals," in Bernth Lindfors, ed. *Critical Perspectives on Nigerian Literatures*. Washington, DC: Three Continents Press, 1976: 75–85.

Egejuru, Phanuel Akubueze, *Chinua Achebe Pure and Simple: An Oral Biography*. Ikeja: Malthouse, 2001.

Ehling, Holger, ed., *Critical Approaches to Anthill of the Savannah*. Amsterdam: Rodopi, 1990.

Ekechi, Felix K., *Tradition and Transformation in Eastern Nigeria*. Kent: The Kent UP, 1989.

Ekwe-Ekwe, Herbert, *The Biafra-Nigeria War and the Aftermath*. Lewiston, NY: E. Mellen, 1990.

———, "Does *Arrow of God* Anticipate the Igbo Genocide?," http://pombazuka.org/en/category/books/93141.2014-10-16. Issue 698. Accessed 10/16/2014.

Emenyonu, Ernest N., "African Literature: What Does It Take to Be Its Critics?," *African Literature Today* 5 (1971): 1–11.

———, ed., *Emerging Perspectives on Chinua Achebe, Volume 1: Omenka the Master Artist: Critical Perspectives on Achebe's Fiction*. Trenton, NJ: Africa World, 2004.

———, "Ezeulu: The Night Mask Caught Abroad by Day," *Pan-African Journal* 4, 4 (1971): 407–19.

———, *The Rise of the Igbo Novel*. Ibadan: Heinemann, 1978.

Emenyonu, Ernest N. and Pat Emenyonu, "Achebe: Accountable to Our Society," *Africa Report* 7, 5 (1972): 26–7.

Emenyonu, Ernest N. and Iniobong I. Uko, eds., *Emerging Perspectives on Chinua Achebe, Volume 2: ISINKA, the Artistic Purpose: Chinua Achebe and the Theory of African Literature*. Trenton, NJ: Africa World, 2004.

Ezenwa-Ohaeto, *Chinua Achebe: A Biography*. Oxford, UK and Bloomington, IN: James Currey and Indiana UP, 1997.

———, "A Literary Celebration of the Achebes," *ALA Bulletin* 15, 2 (1989): 16–18.

Falola, Toyin and Ogechukwu Ezekwem, eds., *Writing the Nigeria-Biafra War*. Oxford, UK: James Currey, 2016.

Fanon, Frantz, *The Wretched of the Earth*. New York: Grove, 1968.

Finnegan, Ruth, *Oral Literature in Africa*. Nairobi, Kenya: Oxford UP, 1976.

Firor, Ruth A., *Folkways in Thomas Hardy*. Philadelphia: U of Pennsylvania P, 1931.

Forsyth, Frederick, *The Biafra Story*. London: Penguin, 1969.

Fraser, Robert, "A Note on Okonkwo's Suicide," *Kunapipi* 1, 1 (1979): 108–13.

Furguson, Paul F., "By Their Names You Shall Know Them: Flanner O'Connor's Onomastic Strategies," *Literary Onomastics Studies* 7 (1980): 87–105.

Gbulie, Ben, *Nigeria's Five Majors: Coup D'état of 16th January, 1966*. Onitsha: Africana Educational, 1981.

Griffiths, Gareth, "Language and Action in the Novels of Chinua Achebe," *African Literature Today* 5 (1971): 88–105.

Gutteridge, W.F., *The Military in African Politics*. London: Methuen, 1969.

Hall, Tony, "I Had to Write on the Chaos I Saw," *Sunday Nation*, 15 January 1967, pp. 15–16.

Hill, Alan, "Chinua Achebe: A Personal View," in Edith Ihekweazu, ed. *Eagle on Iroko: Selected Papers from the Chinua Achebe International Symposium 1990*. Ibadan: Heinemann, 1996: 548–51.

———, *In Pursuit of Publishing*. London: John Murray, 1988.

Ihekweazu, Edith, ed., *Eagle on Iroko: Selected Papers from the Chinua Achebe International Symposium 1990*. Ibadan: Heinemann, 1996.

Ikime, Obaro, ed., *Groundwork of Nigerian History*. Ibadan, Nigeria: Heinemann, 1980.

Innes, C.L., "A Source for *Arrow of God*: A Response," *Research in African Literatures* 9, 1 (Spring 1978): 16–18.

Innes, C.L. and Bernth Lindfors, eds., *Critical Perspectives on Chinua Achebe*. Washington, DC: Three Continents, 1978.

Irele, Abiola, "Creative Pacesetter," *West Africa*, 10–16 December 1990, p. 2992.

Jackson, Angela, "Interview with Chinua Achebe," *Black Books Bulletin* 8 (1991): 53–8.

Jahn, Janheinz, *Muntu: The New African Culture*. New York: Grove, 1961.

Jeyifo, Biodun, "The Author's Art and Role," *West Africa*, 5 November 1984, pp. 2211–3.

———, "First, There Was a Country, Then There Wasn't: Reflections on Achebe's *There Was a Country*," in Toyin Falola and Ogechukwu Ezekwem, eds. *Writing the Nigeria-Biafra War*. Oxford, UK: James Currey, 2016: 245–64.

———, "Literature and Conscientization: An Interview with Chinua Achebe," in Biodun Jeyifo, ed. *Contemporary Nigerian Literature: A Retrospective and Prospective Exploration*. Lagos, Nigeria: Nigeria Magazine, 1985: 19.

Johnson, John W., "Folklore in Achebe's Novels," *New Letters* 40, 3 (1974): 95–107.

Jones, Eldred, "Language and Theme in *Things Fall Apart*," *Review of English Literature* 4, 4 (1984): 39–43.

Killam, G.D., *The Novels of Chinua Achebe*. London: Heinemann, 1971.

King, Bruce, ed., *Introduction to Nigerian Literature*. Lagos, Nigeria: U of Lagos and Evans Brothers, 1971.

King, Bruce and Kolawole Ogungbesan, eds., *A Celebration of Black and African Writing*. Zaria, Nigeria: Ahmadu Bello UP, 1978.

Lindfors, Bernth, "Achebe's African Parable," *Presence Africaine* 66 (1968): 130–6.

———, "The Blind Men and the Elephant," *African Literature Today* 7 (1975): 53–64.

———, ed., *Conversations with Chinua Achebe*. Jackson, MS: UP of Mississippi, 1997.

———, *Critical Perspectives on Nigerian Literatures*. Washington, DC: Three Continents, 1976.

———, *Early Achebe*. Trenton, NJ: Africa World, 2003.

———, *Folklore in Nigerian Literature*. New York: Africana, 1973.

———, "Popular Literature for an African Elite," *Journal of Modern African Studies* 12 (1974): 471–86.

Madiebo, Alexander A., *The Nigerian Revolution and the Biafran War*. Enugu: Fourth Foundation, 1980.

Mahood, M.M., "Idols of the Den: Achebe's *Arrow of God*," in C.L. Innes and Bernth Lindfors, eds. *Critical Perspectives on Chinua Achebe*. Washington, DC: Three Continents, 1978: 180–206.

Mbiti, John S., *African Religions and Philosophy*. New York: Praeger, 1969.

Michaels, Marguerite, "The Power of Silence," *Time Magazine*, 28 August 1993, p. 25.

Moore, Gerald, "Achebe's New Novel: *Arrow of God*," *Transition* 14 (1964): 52.

Munonye, John, "As We Saw Him," in Edith Ihekweazu, ed. *Eagle on Iroko: Selected Papers from the Chinua Achebe International Symposium 1990*. Ibadan, Nigeria: Heinemann, 1996: 543–7.

Muoneke, Romanus Okey, *Art, Rebellion and Redemption: A Reading of Chinua Achebe*. New York: Peter Lang, 1994.

Njoku, Benedict Chiaka, *The Four Novels of Chinua Achebe: A Critical Study*. New York: Peter Lang, 1984.

Nkosi, Lewis, *Home and Exile*. London: Longman, 1983.

———, *Tasks and Masks: Themes and Styles of African Literature*. Essex, UK: Longman, 1981.

Nnolim, Charles E., "A Source for *Arrow of God*," *Research in African Literatures* 8 (Spring 1977): 1–26.

Nwagbara, Chinyere, "'A Woman Is Something': A Re-Reading of Achebe's *Anthills of the Savannah*," in Ernest N. Emenyeonu, ed. *Emerging Perspectives on Chinua Achebe, Volume 1: Omenka the Master Artist: Critical Perspectives on Chinua Achebe's Fiction*. Trenton, NJ: Africa World, 2004: 343–61.

Nwala, T. Uzodinma, Nath Aniekwu, and Chinyere Ohiri-Aniche, eds., *Igbo Nation: History & Challenges of Rebirth and Development*, Volumes One and Two. Ibadan, Nigeria: Kraft Books, 2015.

Nwankwo, Arthur and Samuel Ifejika, *The Making of a Nation: Biafra*. London: C. Hurst, 1969.

Nwoga, Donatus I., "Achebe's Vision in a New Africa," in Edith Ihekweazu, ed. *Eagle on Iroko: Selected Papers from the Chinua Achhebe International Symposium 1990*. Ibadan, Nigeria: Heinemann, 1996: 152–63.

———, "The Chi Offended," *Transition* 15 (1964): 5.

———, "From Dialectal Dichotomy to Igbo Standard Development," in Kalu Ogbaa, ed. *The Gong and the Flute: African Literary Development and Celebration*. Westport, CT: Greenwood, 1994: 103–17.

Nzimiro, Ikrona, *The Nigerian Civil War: A Study in Class Conflict*. Enugu: Frontline, 1982.

Obiechina, Emmanuel, *Culture, Tradition and Society in the West African Novel*. Cambridge: Cambridge UP, 1975.

———, "The Human Dimension of History in Arrow of God," in C.L. Innes and Bernth Lindfors, eds. *Critical Perspectives on Chinua Achebe*. Washington, DC: Three Continent, 1978.

———, *Language and Theme: Essays on African Literature*. Washington, DC: Howard UP, 1990.

———, "In Praise of The Teacher," in Edith Ihekweazu, ed. *Eagle on Iroko: Selected Papers from the Chinua Achebe International Symposium 1990*. Ibadan: Heinemann, 1996: 22–41.

———, *The Story, Memory, and the Continuity of Igbo Culture* (An Ahiajoku Lecture). Owerri: Imo State Government, 1994.

Ogbaa, Kalu, *Blood and Bravery: Voices of Biafran Veterans of the Nigeria-Biafra War*. Princeton, NJ: Sungai, 2010.

———, *A Century of Nigerian Literature: A Select Bibliography*. Trenton, NJ: Africa World, 2003.

———, "Chinua Achebe's *Arrow of God*: A Foretaste of Igbo Intra-Ethnic Democracy in the Present-Day Nigerian Geopolitical System," in Herbert Ekwe-Ekwe, *Rethinking Africa Blog Spot*, 24 July 2015. http://re-thinkingAfrica.blogspot.co.uk/2015/07/by-kalu-ogbaa-every-society-wether.html.

———, *General Ojukwu: The Legend of Biafra*. New York: Triatlantic, 2007.

———, *Gods, Oracles and Divination: Folkways in Chinua Achebe's Novels*. Trenton, NJ: Africa World, 1992.

———, ed., *The Gong and the Flute: African Literary Development and Celebration*. Westport, CT: Greenwood, 1994.

————, "An Interview with Chinua Achebe," *Research in African Literatures* 12, 1 (1981): 1–13.

————, *The Nigerian Americans*. Westport, CT: Greenwood, 2003.

————, *Understanding Things Fall Apart: A Student Casebook to Issues, and Historical Documents*. Westport, CT: Greenwood, 1999.

Ojinmah, Umelo, *Chinua Achebe: New Perspectives*. Ibadan: Spectrum, 1991.

Ojukwu, Chukwwuemeka Odumegwu, *Biafra Volume 1: Selected Speeches and Random Thoughts of C. Odumegwu Ojukwu with Diaries of Events*. New York: Harper & Row, 1969.

————, *Biafra Volume 2: Random Thoughts of C. Odumegwu Ojukwu, General of the People's Army*. New York: Harper & Row, 1969.

————, *Because I Am Involved*. Ibadan: Spectrum, 1989.

————, *Principles of the Biafran Revolution as Enunciated by General C. Odumegwu Ojukwu*. Cambridge, MA: Biafra Review, 1969.

————, *The Wisdom Words of a Great Man*. Enugu: Ojukwu Presidential Campaign Information Center, 2003.

Okafor, Dubem, *The Dance of Death: Nigerian History and Christopher Okigbo's Poetry*. Trenton, NJ: Africa World, 1998.

Okafor, Kez, "The Quest for Social Change: Reformation or Revolution?," in Edith Ihekweazu, ed. *Eagle on Iroko: Selected Papers from the Achebe International Symposium 1990*. Ibadan: Heinemann, 1996: 224–33.

Okocha, Emma, *Blood on the Niger, First Black on Black Genocide: The Untold Story of the Asaba Massacre during the Nigeria-Biafra War*. New York: Triatlantic, 2006.

Okpewho, Isidore, *The Last Duty*. London: Longman, 1976.

Okwu, Augustine S.O., *Igbo Culture and the Christian Mission 1857–1957: Conversion in Theory and Practice*. Lanham, MD: The UP of America, 2010.

————, *In Truth for Justice and Honor: A Memoir of a Nigerian-Biafran Ambassador*. Princeton, NJ: Sungai Books, 2011.

Rosenbaum, Andrew, "A Review of *There Was A Country: A Personal History of Biafra*," *New York Journal of Books*, 11 October 2012.

Sallah, Tijan M. and Ngozi-Okonjo-Iweala, eds., *Chinua Achebe: Teacher of Light*. Trenton, NJ: Africa World, 2003.

Segun, Mabel, "Achebe's Character-Building Books for Children," in Edith Ihekweazu, ed. *Eagle on Iroko: Selected Papers from the Chinua Achebe International Symposium 1990*. Ibadan: Heinemann, 1996: 205–44.

Seitel, Peter, "Proverbs: A Social Use of Metaphor," *Genre* 2 (1969): 143–61.

Shelton, Austin J., "The Offended Chi in Achebe's Novels," *Transition* 13 (1964): 36–7.

Soyinka, Wole, *Art, Dialogue, and Outrage: Essays on Literature and Culture*. Ibadan: New Horn, 1988.

————, *The Man Died*. New York: Harper & Row, 1972.

————, *This Past Must Address Its Present*. New York: Anson Phelps Stokes Institute, 1988.

Spillman, Rob, "A Review of 'a History of Person, Country in' *There Was a Country*," *Los Angeles Times*, 9 November 2012.

Taylor, Archer, *The Proverb*. Cambridge, MA: Harvard UP, 1931.

Thiong'o, Ngugi wa, "Chinua Achebe: A Man of the People," in C.L. Innes and Bernth Lindfors, eds. *Critical Perspectives on Chinua Achebe*. Washington, DC: Three Continents, 1978: 279–82.

Uchendu, Victor C., *The Igbo of Southeast Nigeria*. New York: Holt, Rinehart and Winston, 1965.

Ugah, Ada, *In the Beginning . . . Chinua Achebe at Work*. Ibadan: Heinemann, 1990.

Uwechue, Ralph, *Reflections on the Nigerian Civil War: Facing the Future*. Paris: Jeune Afrique, 1970.

Wali, Obi, "The Dead-End of African Literature," *Transition* 10 (September 1963): 13–15.

Wilkinson, Jane, "Chinua Achebe," in *Talking with African Writers*. London: James Currey, 1992: 55–6.

Wren, Robert M., *Achebe's World: The Historical and Cultural Context of the Novels*. Washington, DC: Three Continents, 1980.

———, *Those Magical Years: The Making of Nigerian Literature at Ibadan: 1948–1966*. Boulder, CO: Lynne Rienner, 1990.

Index

Note: Page numbers in *italics* indicate a figure on the corresponding page. Page numbers followed by "n" indicate a note.